The School Counselor as Consultant

The School Counselor as Consultant

Expanding Impact from Intervention to Prevention

Karen Dickinson

& Richard Parsons

cognella® | ACADEMIC PUBLISHING

Bassim Hamadeh, CEO and Publisher
Amy Smith, Project Editor
Alia Bales, Production Editor
Emely Villavicencio, Senior Graphic Designer
Sara Schennum, Licensing Associate
Natalie Piccotti, Director of Marketing
Kassie Graves, Vice President of Editorial
Jamie Giganti, Director of Academic Publishing

Cover: Copyright © 2015 iStockphoto LP/Chaofann.
Cover: Copyright © 2017 iStockphoto LP/Stillfx.

Printed in the United States of America.

ISBN: 978-1-5165-4668-8 (pbk) / 978-1-5165-4669-5 (br)

cognella® | ACADEMIC PUBLISHING

To counselors and all those who,
by nature of who they are and what they do,
care and advocate for those whom they serve.

Brief Contents

Detailed Contents

Preface

To suggest that school counselors face incredible demands is perhaps stating the obvious. Every school, every counselor, has experienced the challenge of addressing not only students performing below their academic potential but also those who are engaged in bullying, substance abuse, self-harm, and other destructive behaviors. Today's school counselor is expected to support students, parents, and teachers and provide interventions for a variety of needs, such as mental health issues, disabilities, and more.

This situation of asking too much of too few is not new to school counselors. However, what is different about this situation is that the very quantity and severity of the issues presented has grown exponentially. The changing needs of those served by school counselors, including the students, their parents, the faculty, and the entire school community, demands that school counselors employ an alternative method of service delivery, one that not only remediates but impacts in such a way so as to prevent. The integrated model of school-based consultation presented within this text will assist school counselors in their efforts to intervene when necessary and to promote growth and prevention when possible.

About the Format of This Book

You will notice that each chapter opens with a reflection of a school counselor. These opening vignettes are used to set the stage for the content that follows. It is suggested that you return to these opening vignettes after you have read the chapter and apply what you have learned to that scenario. In addition, each chapter will provide case illustrations and guided exercises designed to make the concepts discussed come alive. Finally, in Section IV of this text you are guided in the application of all that you have learned. These last chapters are developed in the form of a culminating case. The reflections provided within these chapters along with the questions posed will help you to step into the role of counselor-as-consultant and apply all that you have learned.

While we hope that this text will help you in the development of new skills and knowledge, the real desire is that it stimulates your valuing of a new perspective on service delivery. It is in embracing the consultation model described that you will not only be able to serve as an effective interventionist but that you will also become an agent of change in service of prevention.

KLD/RDP 2019

Acknowledgments

The credit for the work that goes into the creation of a book is far reaching. We particularly would like to acknowledge the guidance of those who initially reviewed the material. Special thanks to Melissa A. Bray, University of Connecticut; J. P. Oehrtman, Pickerington LSC, Ohio State University; and Esther C. Bubb, St. Joseph's University. Their insightful feedback enhanced this text, increasing its relevancy.

We would like to acknowledge the outstanding support provided by the people at Cognella. Kassie Graves continues to be a guiding light for our work. We are equally grateful for the professional expertise of Julia Black, Jamie Giganti, Amy Smith, Alia Bales, and Theresa Winchell.

Additionally, we express our heartfelt thanks to Clara Morgan, our graduate assistant, who reviewed each chapter and provided excellent feedback as a professional counselor entering the field.

Cognella, Incorporated, gratefully acknowledges the following reviewers:

- Melissa A. Bray, PhD, Professor and Director, School Psychology Program, University of Connecticut
- J.P. Oehrtman, PhD, LPSC, Pickerington LSC, The Ohio State University
- Anonymous
- Esther C. Bubb, EdD, BCBA, LBS, St. Joseph's University

Section I

The Changing Needs of Our Consumers

CHAPTER 1

The School Counselor Addressing Increasing Need for Services

——————————— ○ ———————————

EAT LUNCH!!!

These two words, posted on a middle school counselor's computer screen, are more than a reminder, or even a plea. The message in all its simplicity is a very succinct statement of the life of a school counselor in the 21st century. What started at the turn of the 20th century to address the vocational needs of students and assist in transitions into the workforce (Herr & Erford, 2011) has, in today's vernacular, come a long way.

Today's school counselors face impossible demands for service, so much so that the simple directive to "eat lunch" often goes unheeded. From the moment the counselor walks through the door, her professional calendar jumps to attention with overcrowded planned activities that are then overlaid by the unexpected, and often multiple, crises. The reflection shared by the following middle school counselor is not unique to her. It is more the rule than the exception, one that is highlighting the ever-increasing demand for school counselor services (see Case Illustration 1.1).

Case Illustration 1.1
A "Typical" Day

The following is a reflection of one day in the life of a suburban middle school counselor.

So, I had to laugh when one of my neighbors, a financial planner, said to me it must be nice to be able to spend your day merely chatting with young people. Well, to be honest, it wasn't that I had to laugh; it was that I was restraining myself from being inappropriate in my response. Really? "Chatting with young people?"

Now don't get me wrong, there are times when I am having a delightful conversation with my middle school students. They are, or can be, a real hoot at times. But it would be an injustice to them to paint the picture that their lives are all sweet and innocent. Just this past week we had to deal with an unexpected death of a student's mother, followed by that student's own attempt to take his life.

My students are not insulated in some quaint, cute, covering of preadolescence, and my job is not simply to be the adult who chats.

Look at yesterday. It was a typical day.

Time	Scheduled	Nonscheduled	Observation/Reminder
7:15	Check phone and email messages		*Need to follow up with Mr. L. regarding Andrew's participation in class
7:30	Meet with J.P. (Principal)		Work on Back to School Night presentation for next Thursday night
7:45			
8:00	Angelina M. (eat today?)		
8:15	IEP meeting— remember to discuss new social group		Need to contact Mrs. Z. to follow up on today
8:30			
8:45			
9:00	Rob and Michael... why the conflict?		Follow up on cooperation plan. Consult with Mr. Y regarding the 'fight.' Reschedule R & M
9:15	(Cancel) Simone -reschedule	Meet with Aaron – Walked out of Class –vulgarity to Ms. L.?	Need to have Mr. and Mrs. J. come in to discuss Aaron... some issues and maybe referral required
9:30			
9:45	Observe Robbie— Collect behavior data in English		Talked to Robbie...no longer taking his medication Connect with Mr. P. to see why?
10:00			
10:15	Return phone calls		

		Tomasina– Mr. B's math class (sent down) Deshane—drop in (wanted to show his A on his project... very proud)	Schedule to see Jon D's parents—begin process for 504 Get back to Mr. B. (about today's visit from Tomasina)
10:45	7th gr. Lunch Bunch		Focus on Carlos engagement with group
11:00			
11:15	(Cancel second lunch bunch because of issue in lunch room)	Intervene with lunchroom fight between Liz, Eileen, Simone	Inform all parents; this needs to be stopped—social media shaming
11:30			
11:45	Eat .... Cancelled ...	No lunch...needed to meet with Mrs. C (regarding EL transfer student)	Need to discuss/have administration look at policies and procedures for collecting data on transfers
12:00			
12:15			
12:30	Classroom guidance –lesson 3		
12:45			Schedule Tonya to follow up on comment made during lesson
1:00	Office	Phone call Mr. P New living arrangement for the twins	Let Elliot know about the transportation issue with the twins
1:15	Office		
1:30	Meet with 7th-grade team	Called out –respond to Mrs. L who is in the office re: 'R being bullied.'	Need to invite the 7th gr girls to discuss this tomorrow during lunch bunch
1:45			
2:00			
2:15	Meet with 6th-grade team		Discuss Jon D again, schedule with parents regarding 504 meeting
2:30			

2:45		Check in with Liz, Eileen, Simone Re: incident today	
3:00	Hall watch—look for Tomasina/ ask her to stop in before homeroom		
3:15			
3:30	Office		
3:45	Return Phone calls and reply to emails		Talk to Elliot regarding request by Mr. and Mrs. R. regarding having Robbie tested
4:00	Write notes regarding sessions today –		
4:15		Follow up memo to Elliot about Mr. & Mrs. R. and Robbie testing	
4:30	Check Lesson for to-morrow's period eight lesson on conflict - copy handouts		
4:45	Home	Unexpected meeting with Elliot—working on Robbie's testing and new issue with new teacher Requested consult	Need to watch union issues Meet with Elliot tomorrow 7:30 regarding Robbie testing Check with K.C. about a possible observation in his 4th period?
5:15	Leave...		

There is much demanded of our school counselors, a point that becomes even clearer when we consider the number of students with whom they are entrusted. According to the American School Counselor Association (ASCA) (2015a), the average school counselor-to-student ratio for the United States is 1:482, almost twice the recommended ratio of 1:250. Some schools have lost school counseling positions while student numbers remained the same, and in the entire country, only three states have maintained a ratio lower than 1:250 (ASCA, 2017).

While these numbers are staggering, they become almost mindboggling when one considers that for services to be truly effective they need to address not only the needs of the students but also those of their parents and the faculty who teach them. Given this context, the reminder, the request, the plea to eat lunch takes on a whole new meaning.

The current chapter introduces the reader to the changing and expanding need for counselor service as well as the requirement that counselors adopt a model for service delivery that not only provides intervention but also, through collaboratively engaging and consulting with the significant players within the system, delivers prevention services. After completing this chapter, the reader should be able to

1. describe the nature of the increased demands being experienced by the school counselor in the 21st century;
2. identify the specific limitations to a direct service approach to these demands; and
3. describe the need and value for a new collaborative, preventive approach to counseling services.

Expanding the Role and Service of School Counselors

Perhaps the image of what was once referred to as the "guidance counselor" pictured as sitting in the office, drinking coffee, and simply handing out college applications, or comforting the elementary-aged child who lost her lunch, or perhaps addressing the antics of the class clown was never really an accurate portrayal of a school counselor's life. It is certainly not anything that reflects the professional life of the 21st-century school counselor, one that is a far stretch from the "guidance counselor."

As Arne Duncan, former U.S. Secretary of Education, stated, "School counselors are pivotal in helping students manage their academic programs as well as the inevitable life events that may threaten students' ability to succeed in school" (Duncan, 2014). School counselors are called upon to develop school guidance curriculum, provide individual and group counseling, and engage in consultations and referrals while offering psychoeducation programs for parents and faculty (ASCA, 2012a). While school counselors serve as advocates for all students, there is a heightened awareness and greater emphasis for school counselors to advocate and support students so that they may have "equal right and access to free, appropriate public education...in which students are not stigmatized or isolated based on their housing status, disability, foster care, special education status, mental health or any other exceptionality or special need" (ASCA, 2016a; see A.10.f).

School counselors work to create an environment that encourages all students to feel comfortable to come forward with problems, and remain current to the ever-changing and complex world of students' culture in order to support students and staff (ASCA, 2012b). Exceedingly more students have diverse and special needs that call for the school counselor to provide increased direct and indirect services, including

- providing school counseling curriculum lessons, and individual and group counseling to students with special needs (ASCA, 2016b);

- practicing culturally sensitive advising and counseling (ASCA, 2015b);
- consulting and collaborating with staff and families to understand the special needs of a student and understanding the adaptations and modifications needed to assist the student (ASCA 2016b), and with stakeholders to create a school climate that welcomes and appreciates the gifts of culturally diverse students (ASCA 2015b); and
- collaborating with other related student support professionals (e.g., school psychologists, physical therapists, occupational therapists, special education staff, speech and language pathologists) in the delivery of services (ASCA, 2016b).

To suggest that the role and functions of the school counselor are demanding is indeed an understatement. The demand for school counselors' expertise and engagement is stretching the limits of their time and energy, and making a simple directive such as "eat lunch" more and more difficult to fulfill.

Not Just More—More Complex and Demanding

Not only has the need for school counselor involvement increased but so has the nature of the issues presented (DeKruyf, Auger, & Trice-Black, 2013). A Currier and Ives portrayal of the rural schoolhouse with children innocently playing at recess, engaging in the arts and music, and being challenged in the basics of reading, writing, and arithmetic are regularly assailed by news reports of students being victimized and bullied, coping with debilitating anxiety and depression, and engaging in self-harm behaviors. Our society is in crisis, and our students are under attack. To the growing statistics on divorce rates, poverty, sexism, racism, violence within and outside of our families and institutions, drug and alcohol abuse, sexual abuse, joblessness, and homelessness, we now add the threat of terrorism and school invasion. The times and the needs have changed.

The issues presented to the 21st-century school counselor have increased in severity and complexity, whereas there was a time when a student's failure to do homework was caused by disinterest or failure to bring home the appropriate materials. Given the reports of over 1.26 million homeless youth (2014–2015), of which 95,032 were unaccompanied (U.S. Department of Education, 2015), the issue of failure to complete homework or even attend school may be the tip of more significant concerns. Student complaints about being teased may have been formerly addressed by the counselor in direct service by providing a caring, supportive ear or perhaps assistance with the development of social skills but may now reflect realistic fears for the student's safety of greater magnitude and stresses the need to provide a safe school environment (ASCA, 2016a), calling for intervention and prevention strategies at many levels.

Student issues today are more complex and more severe, and if the school fails to address these issues and support students in their social-emotional needs, academic achievement becomes difficult if not impossible. For example, one study (Mojtabai, Olfson, & Han, 2016) stated that the prevalence of teens who reported a major depressive episode in the previous 12 months jumped from 8.7% in 2005 to 11.5% in 2014. The following case illustration highlights the complexity of the issues confronting our students (Case Illustration 1.2).

Case Illustration 1.2
Tina—Problems with Homework?

Carol W., the school counselor, was asked to meet with Tina, a fifth-grade student who was reported to be failing all her subjects, primarily due to her failure to complete home assignments. Tina by all accounts is a sweet, very cooperative and bright young lady. While she has struggled to complete assignments in the past, it has never been as bad as it is currently.

Tina's family was not unknown to the school or social service agencies. Sadly, her 17-year-old brother died of a drug overdose, and her mother has been arrested on multiple occasions for disorderly conduct. While neither the counselor nor the school nurse has been able to identify any physical signs of abuse, there is a suspicion that the children may be experiencing some form of abuse at the hands of the mother's current boyfriend. It is clear in talking with Tina that she has taken on the duties of maintaining the house and caring for her younger siblings. She noted that her mother stays away days at a time and sometimes they are all alone with Ramon, the mother's boyfriend. The absences of the mother and the anxiety that Tina exhibits when talking about her mother's boyfriend are enough for the counselor, the nurse, and the principal to reach out to children and youth services. Somehow, given these conditions, completing her fifth-grade assignments are not a priority.

While it would be a relief if Tina's story was rare, and perhaps the specifics are, the truth is that the core elements of her experience are shared by many students. It is not uncommon for school counselors to find themselves at one point assisting a student with a scheduling issue or college choice, only to engage with the next student around matters of familial violence, drug abuse, suicidal ideation, or panic attacks.

Too many of our students are struggling in school as a result of attempting to adapt to a home life and a world in which there are real physical, social, and psychological threats. There are many of our students who are attempting to balance the challenges of their development, the demands of school, and the demands of their life, and are realizing that such a balance is not possible. The conditions experienced by many of our students are not only interfering with their education but are wreaking havoc on their emotional well-being. Table 1.1 provides a small sampling of the statistics reflecting increasing significant issues and challenges facing our students and requiring the attention of our school counselors.

The data presented in Table 1.1 reflect a period prior to 2010. And while it would be affirming to believe that things have changed for the better, data from the Substance Abuse and Mental Health Service Administration would suggest that is not the case. Data from 2015 reveal that more than 40% of youth ages 13–17 have experienced a behavioral health problem by the time they reach seventh grade. Further, 11.4% of youth ages 12–17 had a major depressive episode, up from the 8.1% reported

TABLE 1.1 **Expanding Need for School Counseling Service**

- In 2009, an estimated 3.1 million persons aged 12 or older used an illicit drug for the first time within the past 12 months.

- In 2009, an estimated 22.5 million persons (8.9% of the population aged 12 or older) were classified with substance dependence or abuse in the past year based on criteria specified in the *Diagnostic and Statistical Manual of Mental Disorders*, 4th edition (DSM-IV).

- Suicide is the third leading cause of death among Americans aged 15–24 and the second leading cause of death among those aged 25–34. Among college students, suicide is the third leading cause of death.

- In 2009, 23.5 million persons aged 12 or older needed treatment for an illicit drug or alcohol use problem (9.3% of persons aged 12 or older). In 2006, 5% of children aged 4–17 were reported by a parent to have severe difficulties with emotions, concentration, behavior, or being able to get along with other people. In any given year, about 5% to 9% of children have a severe emotional disturbance. These figures mean that millions of children are disabled by mental illnesses every year.

- Each year, more than one million youth come in contact with the juvenile justice system, and more than 100,000 youths are placed in some correctional facility. An astounding 80% of children entering the juvenile justice system have mental disorders. Many juvenile detention facilities are not equipped to treat them.

- In 2009, there were two million youths (8.1% of the population aged 12–17) who had a major depressive episode (MDE) during the past year. An estimated 1.4 million youths aged 12–17 (5.8%) had an MDE with severe impairment in one or more role domains (i.e., chores at home, school or work, close relationships with family, or social life) in 2009.

Source: **The American Counseling Association, " The Effectiveness and Need for Professional Counseling Services." Copyright © 2011 by American Counseling Association.**

for 2009, and suicide was found to be the third leading cause of death among youth ages 15–24 after accidents and homicide (Substance Abuse and Mental Health Service Administration, 2015).

This assault on our students' well-being does not stop at the school door nor do the devastating effects remain outside of the classroom. In fact, according to Ringeisen, Henderson, and Hoagwood (2003), schools, and the school counselor in particular, now serve as major players in the effort to provide mental health services to those students in need. The need for school counseling services appears to be particularly important given the fact that an estimated 75% of children with emotional and behavioral disorders do not receive specialty mental health services (Huang et al., 2005).

School counselors are becoming increasingly aware that what at first may appear to be a minor social or academic problem can, and with increasing frequency does, unfold to test the limits of a counselor's ability, time constraints, and position as a school counselor. While the experience of Carol W., the counselor, working with Tina (see Case Illustration 1.2) may be somewhat unique, most school counselors can identify with the experience of approaching what appeared to be a manageable issue only to have it rapidly unfold and reveal a more serious concern. It is not unusual to find that the failure to complete homework is compounded and exacerbated by many other factors in the child's life (e.g., learning disability, negligent or absent parents, family alcoholism). Exercise 1.1 is provided to assist you in gaining first-hand knowledge of the realities of school-based counseling in your area.

There was a time when the most significant concerns facing a school counselor were how to assist a new, anxious student in adjusting to the school environment or how to help a student develop some time management and organizational study skills. While these needs continue to exist, the nature of student concerns and issues has extended well beyond adjustment anxiety and study skills acquisition. The current exercise invites you to become familiar with the changing needs of today's students and the impact that has on the role and function of today's school counselor.

Directions: Visit three school counselors: an elementary, middle, and high school counselor. Find counselors who have been working as a school counselor for at least five years. Ask them each of the following questions, and fill out an answer sheet for each school counselor:

1. How long have you been working as a school counselor?
2. In the early years of your career, what were the problems or student concerns you most typically experienced?
3. In the last few years (or year), have you noticed a change in the type of concerns and problems students now present? If so, in what way have these changed?
4. Please identify the degree or extent to which you encountered each of the following, first during the early years of your career and next, most currently.

(Code response as: none, very few, some, quite a few, a lot).

Student Problem/Concern	Early Part of Career	Most Recent Part of Career
Eating disorders (e.g., anorexia, bulimia)		
Special learning needs (e.g., learning disabilities, attention deficit, medical conditions)		
Mood disorders (e.g., major depression, bipolar disorders)		
Anxiety disorders (e.g., specific phobias, obsessive-compulsive disorders, generalized anxiety)		
Drug and alcohol dependency/ addictions		
Sexual orientation issues		
Explosive/hostile behavior		
Bullying/targets of bullying		
Homelessness		
Family-related concerns (e.g., separation, divorce, domestic violence)		
Social/peer group problems		
Other: (indicate)		

Exercise 1.1 Student Concerns—Then and Now

Not only have student concerns and problems increased in depth and complexity, the school counselor is now asked to serve in a variety of support roles, such as those listed (planning specialist, crisis interventionist, violence prevention programmer, etc.). These multiple demands and job requirements take the counselor out of the office and away from one-on-one student contact. It will be the extent to which counselors not only balance these multiple demands but also find ways to integrate each demand as part of a comprehensive counseling program that will determine their level of effectiveness.

Directions: While you can, and most likely have, read accounts of the various roles and functions school counselors perform, the lived experience can prove much more insightful. Your task is as follows:

1. Ask a counselor if he would keep a diary or a professional calendar (or share if he already does) marking the various activities throughout a one-week period. Review the journal with the counselor, assessing the degree to which this reflects a typical week.
2. Ask that counselor if you could "shadow" him for a single day. Keep a journal of all of the planned and unplanned services and activities in which that counselor was asked to engage. Record your reflections as you go through the day.
3. Based on these two tasks, write a summary of what you learned about the role and function of the school counselor.
4. What have you identified as the knowledge, skills, and attitude you will need to be effective in this professional role?
5. In a class discussion surrounding these findings, share what reflections you have regarding different levels of service (elementary, middle, high school) and other factors such as population, socioeconomic status, geographics, and private or public school.

Exercise 1.2 One Week in the Life of...

New Demands and the Need for a New Approach

The nature and extent of the demands placed on today's school counselor have changed, and as a result, a traditional approach to service delivery such as seeing each student one-on-one, in direct service, is simply inadequate (see Exercise 1.2).

There is a need for new strategies and resources to meet the needs of all students (Hughey, 2011). The high workloads, large numbers of diverse students, and extent to which many students experience significant educational challenges and emotional and mental health issues challenges the effectiveness of the traditional direct service, one-on-one approach to counseling services. Further, school counselors have been called to move beyond assisting those who may be experiencing difficulty and "provide effective, responsive interventions to address student needs" (ASCA, 2016a; see A.1.g). As such, school counselors must now employ methods that foster healthy development, resiliency, and academic success *for all students*, while at the same time identify and remove factors that place students' academic achievement at risk. Such a model is one that approaches student issues from a systemic, ecological perspective and engages all stakeholders by way of coordination, collaboration, and consultation.

Summary

- According to ASCA (2015), the average school counselor-to-student ratio for the United States is 1:482, and this is the average with some schools having but one counselor for a population of over 1,000.
- Counselors are called upon to develop school guidance curriculum, provide individual and group counseling, and engage in consultations and referrals while offering psycho-education programs for parents and faculty (ASCA, 2012a).
- School counselors serve as advocates for students with special needs, providing these students with both direct and indirect services.
- Data from 2015 reveal that more than 40% of youth aged 13–17 have experienced a behavioral health problem by the time they reach seventh grade (Substance Abuse and Mental Health Service Administration, 2015).
- The nature and extent of the demands placed on today's school counselor have changed, and as a result, a traditional approach to service delivery such as seeing each child one-on-one in direct service is inadequate.

Additional Resources

Print

American School Counselor Association (ASCA). (2012). *The ASCA national model: A framework for school counseling programs* (3rd ed.). Alexandria, VA: Author.

Erford, B. (2014). *Transforming the school counseling profession* (4th ed). New York, NY: Merrill Counseling.

Forman, S. G. (2015). *Implementation of mental health programs in schools: A change agent's guide*. Washington, DC: American Psychological Association.

Web-Based

American Counseling Association (ACA). http://www.counseling.org

American School Counselor Association (ASCA). http://www.schoolcounselor.org

American School Counselor Association (ASCA). (2012). *School counselor competencies*. https://www.schoolcounselor.org/asca/media/asca/home/SCCompetencies.pdf

References

American School Counseling Association (ASCA). (2017). *State-by-state student-to-counselor ratio report*. Retrieved from https://www.schoolcounselor.org/school-counselors-members/publications.aspx

American School Counselor Association (ASCA). (2016a). *ASCA ethical standards for school counselors*. Retrieved from https://www.schoolcounselor.org/asca/media/asca/Ethics/EthicalStandards2016.pdf

American School Counselor Association (ASCA). (2016b). *The school counselor and students with disabilities*. Retrieved from https://www.schoolcounselor.org/asca/media/asca/PositionStatements/PS_Disabilities.pdf

American School Counseling Association (ASCA). (2015a). *Student-to-school-counselor ratio 2014-2015*. Retrieved from https://www.schoolcounselor.org/asca/media/asca/home/Ratios14-15.pdf

American School Counselor Association (ASCA). (2015b). *The school counselor and cultural diversity*. Retrieved from https://www.schoolcounselor.org/asca/media/asca/PositionStatements/PS_CulturalDiversity.pdf

American School Counselor Association (ASCA). (2014). *Role of the school counselor*. Retrieved from https://www.schoolcounselor.org/administrators/role-of-the-school-counselor

American School Counselor Association (ASCA). (2012a). *The ASCA national model: A framework for school counseling programs (3rd ed.)*. Alexandria, VA: Author.

American School Counselor Association (ASCA). (2012b). *The school counselor and equity for all students*. Retrieved from https://www.schoolcounselor.org/asca/media/asca/PositionStatements/PS_Equity.pdf

American School Counselor Association (ASCA). (2011). *Student to school counselor ratios 2010-2011*. Retrieved from https://www.counseling.org/PublicPolicy/PDF/2010-2011_Student_to_Counselor_Ratio.pdf

DeKruyf, L., Auger, R., & Trice-Black, S. (2013). The role of school counselors in meeting students' mental health needs: Examining issues of professional identity. *Professional School Counseling, 16*(5), 271–282.

Duncan, A. (2014). *Key policy letters from the Education Secretary and Deputy Secretary*. Washington, DC: U.S. Department of Education. Retrieved from http://www2.ed.gov/policy/elsec/guid/secletter/140630.html

Herr, E. L., & Erford, B. T. (2011). Historical roots and future issues. In B. T. Erford (Ed.), *Transforming the school counseling profession* (3rd ed., pp.19–43). Columbus, OH: Pearson Merrill Prentice Hall.

Huang, L., Stroul, B., Friedman, R., Mrazek, P., Friesen, B., Pires, S., & Mayberg, S. (2005). Transforming mental health care for children and their families. *American Psychologist, 60*(6), 615–627.

Hughey, J. (2011). Meeting the needs of diverse students: Enhancing school counselors' experiences. *Educational Considerations, 38*(2), 20–27.

Mojtabai, R., Olfson, M., & Han B. (2016). National trends in the prevalence and treatment of depression in adolescents and young adults. *Pediatrics*. Retrieved from http://pediatrics.aappublications.org/content/pediatrics/early/2016/11/10/peds.2016-1878.full.pdf

Ringeisen, H., Henderson, K., & Hoagwood, K. (2003). Context matters: Schools and the "research to practice gap" in children's mental health. *School Psychology Review, 32*(2), 153–168.

Substance Abuse and Mental Health Services Administration (SAMHSA). (2015). *National survey on drug use and health (NSDUH)*. Washington, DC: SAMHSA, Department of Health and Human Services. Retrieved from https://www.samhsa.gov/specific-populations/age-gender-based

U.S. Department of Education. (2015). *Education for homeless children and youths (EHCY) program*. Retrieved from https://www2.ed.gov/programs/homeless/ehcyprogramprofile.pdf

CHAPTER 2

An Expanded Perspective

It seems like I see the same children over and over. We make progress and then either something in the classroom or at home starts them up again. Jasmine responds well when I work with her in my office, and the next thing I know a group of students are in here complaining about her rudeness.

——————————— ○ ———————————

The reflection with which we open this chapter is shared by many school counselors who understand that for real, permanent change to occur, it is not enough to help the student adjust to current conditions. Rather, the circumstances and the system need to change. Given this reality and the call to address the needs *of all* students and not just those in crisis (Paisley & McMahon, 2001), the more traditional view of the counselor as a direct service provider to those students presenting with a definite need of assistance is no longer adequate. Counselors in this new reality will need to expand their perspective on both those elements, which serve as barriers to our students' fulfillment of their educational potential, and the need and value of counselors engaging all stakeholders in the removal of these obstacles.

To be successful at this task, school counselors need to embrace a more ecological, systemic view of student achievement and engage in their use of collaboration, coordination, and consultation (ASCA, 2012).

After reading the chapter, the reader should be able to:

1. describe what it means to have an ecological perspective;
2. explain the need for a systemic approach to school counseling; and
3. describe the value of an ecological, systemic approach to school counseling.

An Ecological, Systemic View of Need and Service

The Education Trust (2009) invited school counselors to expand their perspective to include one that was more systemic, more ecological. "School counseling is a profession that focuses on the relations and interactions between students and their school environment to reduce the effects of environmental and institutional barriers that impede student academic success" (Education Trust, 2009, para. 3). This observation reflects an ecological perspective (Conyne & Cook, 2004) and is one which holds that for real, permanent change to occur, the system in which one operates must be changed. While such an ecological perspective has been employed by school psychologists (Sheridan & Gutkin, 2000), social workers (Unger, 2002), and professional counselors (Conyne & Cook, 2004), it has only recently become a paradigm guiding the work of school counselors (McMahon, Mason, Daluga-Guenther, & Ruiz, 2014).

One model of such an ecological perspective defines counseling as "contextualized help-giving that is dependent on the meaning clients derive from their environmental interactions" (Conyne & Cook, 2004, p. 6). Any efforts at intervening with a student who is failing as a result of skipping class and refusal to complete assignments without an appreciation of the influence of the environment this student inhabits, a situation in which education is devalued, will most likely prove ineffective or at best short lived. It is essential to view the behavior from an ecological perspective, one that highlights the role and influence of that student's physical, social, and institutional realities.

The school counselor operating from an ecological perspective appreciates that any one child's behavior is a reflection of the interaction of that child's developmental status, attitudes, and motivations with the teacher's attitudes and behavior in a setting that has physical, social, and cognitive elements all influencing that behavior.

Bronfenbrenner's Ecological Framework

Urie Bronfenbrenner (1979) presented an ecological framework that is helpful in understanding the various systems in which a student operates and how these interact to impact that student's behavior and achievement. For Bronfenbrenner (1979), the smallest and most immediate of the systems in which a child operates is the **microsystem**(s). These are the daily interactions occurring at home and school, within the community, and with peers, and most often involve personal relationships with family members, classmates, and teachers. The interactions are reciprocal. For example, how a teacher interacts with the child will influence that child's reaction that in turn will affect that teacher's future interactions. Thus, it is possible that for one teacher, the student is the "problem child" performing well below expectations, whereas for another teacher, the interactions are such as to result in heightened performance and a more favorable view of the experience for both teacher and student.

The next level is what is termed the **mesosystem**. The mesosystem is the composite of interactions among the various microsystems. Thus, a child's engagement in school may be the outcome of the interaction not only of the microsystem of the classroom (e.g., teacher-student interactions) but also of how these interact with the microsystems of peer involvement or home life. Consider the potential impact of a teacher praising of a student (microsystem) is met by taunts and jeers of "teacher's pet" delivered by that student's peer group in the playground. Is it possible such an interaction would suppress the students desire to perform in class? Or how about the differential impact on one's ability to achieve academically if living in a safe, comfortable, suburban home versus existing homeless or living in a shelter.

When a student's microsystems are in conflict and place the student in a state of emotional and behavioral upset, it is insufficient to counsel the student in the absence of addressing the microsystem conflict. One of the authors (Parsons) taught in the inner city where he had a student who, while being very motivated to go to college, was also engaged with peers who not only devalued education but also would punish those who aspired to achieve academically. The two microsystems were not supportive of one another, and as a result, the student found himself in disequilibrium and conflict. One strategy that helped the student navigate these two conflicting microsystems was to provide him two sets of books. One set of books he left at home, and the other was available in his locker at school. Such a simple strategy helped him avoid potential confrontation about carrying books through his neighborhood while at the same time allowing him to complete his assignments at home. The school counselor often finds himself working with situations that occur in the mesosystem, such as interactions between the teacher and the parent of a particular student.

The next level of system to influence our students is the **exosystem**. The exosystem refers to the broader social system. The student is not a direct participant in their exosystem but is impacted by the structures in this system as they interact with some structure in the student's microsystem (Berk, 2000). For example, an advocacy group within a student's community may interact with the school in which the child attends, which causes the school to adjust and adapt its curriculum. As a result, this one student begins to receive additional support services, and the classroom teacher modifies his approach to instruction in a way that benefits that student. While the student was not directly involved in the creation of the changes, she did experience the positive impact of the interaction of these mesosystems. Another example could be the negative impact should a school board decide to cut funding for art and music in a school, which in turn reduced one student's ability to experience these creative outlets and as a result negatively impacted that student's view of school and his motivation to engage in class.

The layer considered by Bronfenbrenner (1979) as the outermost layers of the child's environment is the **macrosystem**. This is not a specific framework but instead comprises the students' culture (values, beliefs, patterns, customs) as well as the political, legal, and economic systems in which they live. The effects of larger principles defined by the macrosystem influence the interactions of all the other layers and filter down to impact the student. For example, consider the situation where a student's culture promotes and values working in the family business and providing lifelong support for aging parents. How might these familial values potentially limit a student's view of post–high school career and educational options? Or, consider the impact on a student's aspirations if her macrosystem is one that actively promotes the value and view of a female as that of mother and wife to the exclusion of roles such as professional or entrepreneur. The counselor who is working with a student who excels in math or science might find it difficult to understand her lack of interest and her actual resistance to considering college as a postgraduation option unless that counselor had a full appreciation of the student's macrosystem and its impact.

Lastly, Bronfenbrenner (1979) explains a fifth system, the **chronosystem**. The chronosystem includes transitions and significant events that occur over a student's lifespan. An example would be the experience of divorce as a major transition, affecting not only the parents but also their children. The impact of this event can clearly manifest within the school. But beyond such familial experience, other sociohistorical events such as war, major economic recession, social movements such as the civil rights movement, and more recently the violent gun assaults on our schools can continue to have effect over time. One can only imagine the ongoing impact of the students experiencing the events of the Sandy Hook shootings or the more recent shootings at Marjory Stonemason Douglas High School in Parkland, Florida. Clearly, these singular events will have a lifelong impact on the students who encountered them, and that impact may help explain any current difficulty these students are experiencing in their academic pursuits. Factors in all five systems may play an important role in the thoughts and behavior of a student.

School Counselor with a Contextual View

The school counselor who engages from a contextual framework is not employing unique procedures or techniques. The use of a contextual framework, or a systems-ecological orientation, is merely that, an orientation or perspective. With a more systemic and ecological perspective, school counselors will recognize that most clinical and nonclinical concerns reflect the context (i.e., extrapersonal) within which the student is attempting to function. The counselor engaging such an ecological perspective will employ multilevel assessments and incorporate multilevel interventions to impact the various systems in which the student is performing (McMahon et al., 2014).

For example, a counselor employing such a systems-ecological perspective would consider the degree to which one student's difficulty in academic performance reflects a mismatch of instructional environment or teacher pedagogical style with the student's learning style and developmental readiness. As such, in addition to working with the student, the counselor may invite the teacher to consider such variables as the pace of instruction, the use of visual or audio aides, the degree to which group or individual activities are employed, et cetera, all with the intent of improving that student's achievement. With an ecological systems perspective, the school counselor engaging in a wide variety of multilevel assessment and interventions may resemble the information in Table 2.1, adapted from McMahon et al. (2014), showing an ecological model of school counseling and providing some assessments and interventions of such a multilevel approach.

Approaching our students with the perspective that all behavior is contextual enables the school counselor to view each presenting concern as an invitation to consider much broader system issues. These issues, once addressed, not only will assist the student at hand but will reach all students and serve a preventive function. Consider the case of absenteeism reflected in Case Illustration 2.1.

TABLE 2.1 **Ecological School Counseling Skills and Practices**

ECOLOGICAL LEVEL	ASSESSMENT	INTERVENTION
Individual	Testing (nondiagnostic), career assessment, suicide assessment, psychosocial counseling, clinical interview	Individual counseling, student planning, goal setting, crisis intervention, behavioral management, teaching self-advocacy
Interpersonal/group	Collecting and examining perception data (focus groups, student/faculty surveys) Outcome data (school achievement, achievement gap)	Small group responsive services, core counseling curriculum, Closing the Gap projects, advocacy
Institutional	Reviewing school improvement plans, program assessment; examining the process, school counselor competencies assessment; investigating school process data (opportunity gaps)	Committee, building, district, or organizational leadership; advocating for policy change on behalf of students, families, or staff; providing professional development
Community	Advisory boards, collecting and analyzing community perception data (focus groups, surveys), completing needs assessments, examining census data	Collaboration with school staff, families, and community; community social justice activism, political activism

Source: H. George McMahon, et al., "An Ecological Model of School Counseling," *Journal of Counseling and Development*, vol. 92, no. 4, pp. 462.
Copyright © 2014 by John Wiley & Sons, Inc.

Case Illustration 2.1
Devaluing Education?

The increase in the number of students from the 10th grade, referred because of repeated absenteeism, was indeed a wake-up call. Initially, both the principal and counselor questioned whether it was evidence of a sophomore slump or the fact that the individuals referred were not valuing their education. The counselor, Mr. Roberts, took the opportunity to interview many students, both those demonstrating problems with attendance and those whose attendance was good. In the process of gathering data, he found that almost all of the students expressed a desire to do well in school. Thus, it did not appear to be an issue of motivation. However, he also found that of the eight students identified with chronic attendance problems, six were the oldest in the family and each was required to prepare younger sibling for school. Further, in three of the six cases, they were expected to walk their younger siblings to school. These caretaking duties resulted in their missing their bus, accounting for either their lateness or absenteeism. And as one student explained, it was easier to not go to school when late then have to stay for detention, which would interfere with her ability to get home in time to meet her younger sibling.

In this case, the recognized problem, one of increased absenteeism, was not the result of the student's lack of motivation or a devaluing of education. Instead, what became clear when viewed through an ecological, systemic lens was that this behavior was a result of the conflict of multiple demands and a system that punished tardiness more than absenteeism. With this as the focus, numerous points of intervention and systemic change become apparent. Targets once addressed would not only remedy the current situation but would result in prevention of future occurrence. Perhaps it would be possible to modify bus schedules or to offer multiple pick up times. Perhaps providing after-school activities for the younger students would remove the pressures on the older siblings. Another intervention could be to simply change policies that reduced the negative consequence to tardiness when such was the result of responding to different social responsibilities. In shifting attention from individual students to the system factors operating to impede their performance is not only more effective as an intervention to those currently manifesting this problem but would undoubtedly serve a preventive value for similar students who are soon to follow.

Embracing an ecological approach does not require the counselor to stop doing what they currently do. It merely invites the school counselor to view presenting concerns as possible announcements that something else, within the system, is going on. Seeing referrals through an ecological lens positions the counselor to look for contributing factors as well as solutions, within the student and the context in which the student is functioning. With this perspective and the identification of contextual factors contributing to the situation, the counselor will be able to identify multiple points of intervention and opportunities for prevention. Case Illustration 2.2 considers the case of Alfred, a sixth grade "bully."

Case Illustration 2.2
Alfred—A Sixth Grade "Bully"

It was not the first time that Alfred appeared in the school counselor's office. Alfred, according to his counselor, was indeed an adorable, bright, and funny child. Sadly, Alfred was having some real difficulty in his first-period class.

It appears that Alfred has been making some very sarcastic comments about some of his classmates' style of dress, physical characteristics, and even speech patterns. While Ms. Cramer, his teacher, noted that none of these were malicious, they were very sarcastic and often hurtful. She stated that she had "tried everything" and yet it seems to continue. With a little investigative work, Mrs. Morton discovered the following:

  a. First period was the only period this problem seemed to occur.
  b. When confronted by Ms. Cramer, Alfred was apologetic and typically stopped the behavior for the balance of the period.

c. Alfred was driven to school each morning by his two older brothers, both attending the adjacent high school (11th and 12th grade).

d. According to Alfred, the ride in was often marked by a lot of "cutting up," "teasing," and "getting on each other's cases about hair, girlfriends, and stuff like that."

With these as data points, Mrs. Morton hypothesized that it wasn't that Alfred was attempting to be hurtful. Further, it was clear that he was acutely aware that it was not appropriate school behavior. It seemed, however, that he was merely having difficulty transitioning from the context of the car to the context of the first period. She shared her observations with Ms. Cramer, and in the discussion, Ms. Cramer decided to modify her class procedures. She shared with her class her desire to start each day in a way that would help them "have a great school day," and to that end she had them help create a morning "salutation." The salutation, created by the class, was one that included a morning greeting to one another and then the saying of a pledge to "work hard, do our best, and help each other so that we would be the STARS of R. J. Pickers Middle School."

In follow-up, Ms. Cramer reported that not only had Alfred significantly reduced his inappropriate comments, but that three other students who were having difficulty getting focused and on task once the bell rang were now following the morning salutation and jumping right in.

When effective changes to the system can be implemented, as illustrated in the case of Alfred, they quite often not only provide remediation of the initial presenting concern but also result in positive change for others within that system.

While the student who is presenting at the counselor office door—in this case, Alfred—does require attention, seeing this student in isolation of an understanding of the systemic reality in which the student is operating would be a mistake. School counselors need to engage a paradigm that allows them to see all referrals collectively. Not only will such a consideration help counselors identify issues that may warrant group, classroom, or school-wide programs, but it will also help the counselor determine all of the significant players (e.g., teachers, support staff, administrators, parents) who can and should be engaged. Seeing each referral through a prism of the school as a system invites the school counselor to consider strategies that have an impact well beyond this one referral and may, in fact, be of a preventive value. As another example, consider the reflections of one counselor in response to the recurring presentation of anxiety among third-grade students (Case Illustration 2.3).

Case Illustration 2.3
Rampant Test Anxiety

It started with one parent phone call. Allison, one of my third graders, was apparently showing signs of anxiety regarding the upcoming standardized testing. This is certainly not something with which I was unfamiliar. There are always a couple of students who get worked up around taking tests, especially something like the "big" one we are taking this Friday. So, I intended to meet with her and help her develop a few self-soothing, relaxing strategies. This was my intent, at least until I received a flood of referrals from the school nurse about third-grade students coming to her office with upset stomachs, crying, and even having some difficulty breathing. The very fact that we jumped from one concerned parent to now eight students from the same third grade experiencing signs of anxiety suggested this was more than Allison's problem and reflected that something was going on in the third grade and perhaps the school.

I met with Fran S., the third-grade teacher. She is in her second year and is well liked and respected by the students and their parents, and her colleagues. Meeting with her over coffee made it clear that she is a wreck about the pressure she is feeling regarding the upcoming performance of her students on Friday's test. She is herself exhibiting signs of anxiety and verbalizes a concern that should they not perform optimally, it may impact her tenure.

The climate in the school regarding this test is indeed stressful and ultimately will prove detrimental to our students' optimal performance. I was able to meet with Dr. R., and together we spoke to Fran and allayed her fears about tenure. I was also able to convince Dr. R. to institute a "Mindful Minute" twice a day in every classroom, and have a school rally day on Thursdays where we will do some fun activities and help reframe the perspective on the testing as something useful and not a life or death situation. It would help if we could look at this situation, learn from it, and do something different for the teachers, parents, and students before the next round.

Engagement of Others: Collaboration, Coordination, and Consultation

Approaching the delivery of school counseling service from an ecological perspective will require school counselors to engage with the other significant players in the school and community to improve student functioning and achievement (Bryan & Holcomb-McCoy, 2010; Epstein & Van Voorhis, 2010). Operating within an ecological framework will require the counselor to embrace skills of consultation and collaboration in addition to those already employed with their direct service to students. While the American School Counseling Association (ASCA, 2016) notes that this is a task to be done in coordination and collaboration with others, we would argue that it is a task that can only be done through collaboration, coordination, and consultation with all of the significant players affecting our students.

The idea of coordinating services, sharing expertise, and consulting is far from a new or novel approach. In the early 1960s, consultation was highlighted as an essential element of the school counselor's role and function (Wrenn, 1962). However, when embracing an ecological, systemic perspective, school counselors will see consultation not simply as an added form of service delivery or a technique but rather as a paradigm guiding the delivery of all of their services. The value of employing consultation as the umbrella beneath which to modify and deliver numerous forms of intervention, prevention, and postvention services is that it allows for a systemic approach and the engagement of the expertise of all involved in the academic, social, and career development of our students. This point is more fully developed in Chapter 4.

The call to see consultation as the primary mode of school counseling service delivery may be difficult for some to embrace for fear of losing their ability to engage in direct, one-to-one service. As will be discussed, even with a more ecological perspective and a role of school counselor as consultant, direct service to our students will remain our mainstay. It just will be done in a way that provides remediation and a level of prevention. Exercise 2.1 invites you to identify today's counselor's view of consultation.

Consultation, as will be presented throughout this text, is considered a mode of service delivery from which to implement all the tasks counselors are called to perform. However, many counselors have viewed consultation not as an umbrella for all service delivery but as an added technique, a technique which they may not have time nor energy to employ.

Directions: Interview three school counselors, across grade levels (i.e., elementary, middle, and high school). Ask each of them the following questions:

1. Do you employ consultation in your role as a school counselor?
2. If not, why not? (List all the reasons.)
3. If yes,
   a. Would you tell me what consultation is to you?
   b. When and where do you employ a consultative approach?
   c. What, if any, are the benefits of using consultation as a method of service delivery?
   d. What, if any, are the drawbacks or costs of using consultation as a method of service delivery?

Finally, review your data, looking for reasons that may explain the limited or lack of use of consultation as a mode of service delivery. Keep this list handy, and as you read through this text, begin to identify the knowledge, the skill, and the attitude you will need to develop to employ consultation in a way that maximizes the impact of your services while reducing your costs (in terms of time and energy).

Exercise 2.1 The Counselor's View of Consultation

Expanding Impact: Intervention and Moving to Prevention

As noted above, embracing an expanded, more ecological perspective on the needs to be addressed and the services to be provided does not mean that direct service, one-on-one counseling will no longer be a mainstay of a counselor's day. It does mean, however, that even when engaged in such direct service, counselors will have an eye on the identification of those systemic, ecological factors that may be impacting this one student and thus have the potential to impact others. With this ecological perspective, the counselor is positioned to conceptualize services that extend beyond interventions that are directed to one student and to develop and deliver those services that will facilitate development and wellness of all students and insulate them from the potentially damaging effects of systemic factors affecting this one student. It is in this process of moving beyond the singular student to consider the systemic elements impeding that student's progress that the school counselor will begin to formulate and implement preventive measures and thus expand the impact of his service. We invite you to explore this idea a bit more in Exercise 2.2.

Directions: Consider the case of rampant anxiety described in Case Illustration 2.3. Review the description using Bronfenbrenner's system model as your ecological lens. With this as your perspective, develop working hypotheses and interventions, reflecting on each system's impact. Some examples have been given to get you started. You may find it helpful to work on this exercise with a classmate or colleague.

Issue: Student has test anxiety

	Microsystem	Mesosystem	Exosystem	Macrosystem	Chronosystem
Sample Questions/ Hypotheses	Does the student have learning difficulties? Is English the student's first language?	Do the parents and teachers deliver the same message regarding the importance of tests? What messages are being conveyed?	Is the math curriculum appropriate? Does the school reinforce quantity over quality?	Is it the norm to be competitive and high achieving? Has the state or government set standards that are developmentally appropriate?	Have the students had extended absences? Or has there been a school merger or some other community event that has caused them to miss key instruction?
Sample Interventions	Schedule assessment and engage learning-support personnel.	Hold informational meeting for teachers and parents to diffuse misconceptions.	Meet with math department and central office math supervisor to strategically review data and trends over the past three years.	Invite administration to discuss goals and objectives for both the math curriculum and the testing protocol.	Check profile of students impacted, targeting possibility of significant personal and/or communal events.
Your Questions/ Hypotheses					
Your Interventions					

Exercise 2.2 Taking an Ecological Perspective

Summary

- Given the demands placed on school counselors, a traditional view of the counselor as a direct service provider to those students presenting with a definite need for assistance is no longer adequate.
- Approaching our students from an ecological perspective that all behavior is contextual enables school counselors to increase their impact and levels of effectiveness.
- With an ecological focus, school counselors will engage in strategies that target change in those conditions that challenge healthy development.
- With a more systemic and ecological perspective, school counselors will move the more traditional one-on-one direct form of service delivery to one that recognizes that most clinical and nonclinical concerns reflect the context within which students are attempting to function.
- Operating within an ecological framework will require the counselor to embrace skills of consultation and collaboration.
- With this ecological perspective, the counselor will be positioned to conceptualize services that extend beyond interventions that are directed to one student, and develop and deliver those services that will facilitate development and wellness of all students.

Additional Resources

Print

Cooke, E. (2012). *Understanding people in context: The ecological perspective in counseling.* Alexandria, VA: American Counseling Association.

Hatch, T. (2014). *The use of data in school counseling.* Thousand Oaks, CA: Corwin/Sage Publications.

Web-Based

American School Counseling Association. *ASCA National Model.* Retrieved from: https://www.schoolcounselor. org/school-counselors-members/asca-national-model

References

American School Counselor Association. (2012). *The ASCA National Model: A framework for school counseling programs* (3rd ed.). Alexandria, VA: Author.

American School Counselor Association. (2016). *ASCA ethical standards for school counselors.* Alexandria, VA: Author.

Berk, L. E. (2000). *Child development* (5th ed.). Boston, MA: Allyn and Bacon.

Bronfenbrenner, U. (1979). *The ecology of human development: Experiments by nature and design.* Cambridge, MA: Harvard University Press.

Bryan, J., & Holcomb-McCoy, C. (2010). Collaboration and partnerships with families and communities. *Professional School Counseling, 14,* ii–v.

Conyne, R. K., & Cook, E. P. (2004). Understanding persons within environments: An introduction to ecological counseling. In R. K. Conyne & E. P. Cook (Eds.), *Ecological counseling: An innovative approach to conceptualizing person-environment interaction* (pp. 3–36). Alexandria, VA: American Counseling Association.

Education Trust. (2009). *The new vision for school counseling.* Retrieved from https://edtrust.org/resource/ the-new-vision-for-school-counselors-scope-of-the-work/

Epstein, J. L., & Van Voorhis, F. L. (2010). School counselors' roles in developing partnerships with families and communities for student success. *Professional School Counseling, 14*, 1–14.

McMahon G. H., Mason, E. C.M., Daluga-Guenther, N., & Ruiz, A. (2014). An ecological model for school counseling. *Journal of Counseling and Development, 92*, 459–471.

Paisley, P. O., & McMahon, H. G. (2001). School counseling for the 21st century: Challenges and opportunities. *Professional School Counseling, 5*, 106–116.

Sheridan, S. M., & Gutkin, T. B. (2000). The ecology of school psychology: Examining and changing our paradigm for the 21st century. *School Psychology Review, 29*, 485–502.

Unger, M. (2002). A deeper, more social ecological social work practice. *Social Service Review, 76*, 480–497.

Wrenn, C. G. (1962). *The counselor in a changing world.* Washington, DC: American Personnel and Guidance Association.

CHAPTER 3

Beyond Intervention to Prevention

Unbelievable! Just finished my first lesson on conflict resolution with Jasmine's fifth-grade class and I cannot believe how well it went. Mrs. Lane is so excited, and she and I are going to gather data to see how it may impact how well her students work together in groups and if there is a decrease in the amount of behavior complaints during lunch and recess.

———————————— ○ ————————————

While counselors are trained in and possess the skills necessary to intervene with those experiencing emotional and behavioral difficulties, they are by the nature of their professional identity called to value the provision of preventive care over mere remediation. The "excited" counselor who was sharing her experience in regards to her classroom guidance lesson is giving voice to this valuing of preventive service.

Unlike other professions that serve the mental health needs of their clients, school counselors are called to move beyond intervention and remediation, and attend to the fostering of the healthy development of all whom they serve. The American School Counselor Association (ASCA) has on more than one occasion and through more than one medium noted that school counselors should design and deliver services that are comprehensive in scope, preventive in design, and developmental in nature (ASCA, 2016; ASCA, 2017). As noted by Witmer & Granello (2005), unique to school counselors is that they target their client's current level of wellness and functioning, and attempt to assist them in reaching their optional levels of well-being. Counselors are "called" to facilitate the growth and development of all students through normative challenges as well as assist those who are experiencing more severe threats to their emotional well-being.

School counselors will embody values that support prevention when they target wellness as a focus (Myers & Sweeney, 2005). In addition to reflecting the school counselor's unique professional identity, emphasizing prevention efforts provides the best way to reduce the time-consuming need of one-on-one direct service as well as ensuring a reduction in rates of recidivism. By fostering students' social and emotional development, adaptive behavior, resiliency, rationality, and academic performance, the school counselor increases the students' abilities to navigate the challenges they encounter successfully and thus reduce the need for individual intervention.

The current chapter describes the many targets and tiers for prevention services. After reading the chapter, the reader should be able to

1. describe the unique wellness, developmental, and preventive focus for school counselor services;
2. define primary prevention;
3. define secondary prevention;
4. define tertiary prevention; and
5. explain why a focus on wellness, development, and prevention requires a school counselor's employment of consultation as a mode of service delivery.

Prevention: Multileveled

Prevention programming can be universal and implemented school-wide, and promote the development of a broad range of protective factors (Greenberg, 2010). Prevention measures also can be targeted to those at risk or even those already in the grips of crisis. In either case, the value of preventive approaches is that they target the development of competence and adaptive capacities, which in turn result in a reduction of future problems and interferences with our students' academic achievement and social and career development.

When considering the concept of prevention, one may assume that it is something in which the counselor is engaged that removes students from risk or completely insulates them from threats to their emotional well-being and academic performance. In one sense, this is true. However, prevention can take many forms and can be implemented at many levels.

Primary Prevention

Primary prevention efforts are universal in scope, addressing an entire population before the manifestation of any difficulty and thus attempting to stop problems before they emerge (McMahon, Mason, Daluga-Guenther, & Ruiz, 2014). These programs most often do not target specific stressors or life challenges but rather provide knowledge and skills that facilitate normative, healthy development. These programs are genuinely proactive and are delivered to the entire school, grade level, or specific classroom. The critical element defining a primary prevention program is that the identified population is not exhibiting difficulties at this time, and the programs are geared to further enhancing their ability to cope with normative challenges, should these occur.

Primary prevention programs are employed with an explicitly defined group (i.e., a specific class, a grade level, or an entire school). The programs are delivered before the emergences of any signs of problems or detrimental effects of current conditions. Consider the normative stress encountered by students transitioning from elementary to middle school or from middle to high school. These transitions can be, and typically are, stressful. Counselors who implement programs to reduce the stress or anxiety for all the new students, before they exhibit stress or anxiety reactions, are engaging in primary prevention. Without knowledge and skills on how to navigate their new environment as well as skills for stress management, the stress resulting from these natural transitions can interfere with the students' initial adjustment and academic functioning.

There are numerous examples of counselors engaging in primary prevention programming, often in the form of classroom guidance curriculum (see Table 3.1). The programs typically attempt to facilitate the students' development of the knowledge and skills needed to cope with the social and emotional changes that accompany the students' ongoing development, and that can challenge their ability to perform within the classroom. See Case Illustration 3.1 for a sample lesson focused on the opening vignette. While some efforts

---

Case Illustration 3.1
A Lesson on Conflict Resolution: Primary Prevention

Jasmine, the student in our opening vignette, has exhibited a tendency to react with explosive anger when situations are not as she wants them to be. It is clear that she could benefit from direct, one-to-one counseling. The counselor employing a preventive orientation realizes that while she is giving form to such low frustration tolerance and the resulting anger, other students could use practice in conflict resolution and anger management. With a primary prevention focus, the counselor would develop classroom guidance lessons that teach skills of anger and frustration management to all students before they face difficult situations. Just think of the decreased drama and discipline referrals once these students resolve their own issues—without dramatic outbursts! Teaching these skills before students face difficult and dangerous situations and increased peer pressure would be helpful to the students, parents, and school community.

The following is a sample of a classroom lesson on conflict resolution for the fifth-grade classes in Jasmine's school.

Grade & Time	5th grade; 35 minutes
Unit/Lesson	Conflict Resolution/Lesson 1 of 6
Goal	What is conflict?
Mindsets & Behaviors	Mindset Standards: **M-M.1.** Belief in development of whole self, including a healthy balance of mental, social, emotional, and physical well-being Behavior Standards: **B-SMS 2.** Demonstrate self-discipline and self-control **B-SMS 7.** Demonstrate effective coping skills when faced with a problem **B-SS 6.** Use effective collaboration and cooperation skills **B-SS 8.** Demonstrate advocacy skills and ability to assert self, when necessary (https://schoolcounselor.org/asca/media/asca/home/MindsetsBehaviors.pdf)

Objectives	Students will state two outcomes of conflict. Students will role play a scenario with conflict and use one of three appropriate strategies to work through the conflict. Students will explain their perspective to other students.
Materials	Sample video: https://www.brainpop.com/technology/digitalcitizenship/conflictresolution/
Activity	Use a video to introduce conflict and learn about perspective, coping, and compromise. Sample video: https://www.brainpop.com/technology/digitalcitizenship/conflictresolution/ Role play scenarios involving conflict.
Process Questions	Sample Questions: What could happen if the conflict was not settled? What could happen if someone's perspective is not known? What worked to resolve the conflict?
Evaluation	Students will complete all three objectives successfully.

attempt to promote competencies that result in an optimized development, others may be more targeted and focused on areas or at specific times in which the students' development and academic achievement may be particularly vulnerable.

Schools have adopted many primary prevention strategies geared to protecting the students' physical health; these strategies include, for example, the removal of dangerous products (e.g., asbestos) from our schools or requiring the use of safety equipment (e.g., a harness) when engaged in specific physical education activities (e.g., rope climbing). Just as these are important to safeguard the physical health of our students, other primary prevention strategies addressing our students' emotional well-being are also essential. The American School Counseling Association has identified mindsets and behaviors, such as making healthy choices, developing social skills, and utilizing resiliency strategies, that when used to guide lessons in classroom guidance programs serve primary prevention efforts (ASCA, 2014). Examples of School Counseling Primary Prevention Programming are abundant. Table 3.1 provides a sampling of such programs.

Secondary Prevention: Early Identification and Intervention

Often, a school counselor becomes aware of a student who is beginning to show signs that they are struggling. Some of these students present with conditions that would suggest that they are at higher risk of having difficulty or may be exhibiting early indicators of an emerging academic or psychosocial problem. When engaged in secondary prevention services, the school counselor attempts to intervene in a way that prevents the full development of a problem or shortens the duration and impact of that issue, preventing it from becoming more severe.

TABLE 3.1 **Sampling of School Counseling Primary Prevention Programs**

REFERENCES	TARGETED POPULATION	PROGRAM	FINDINGS
Brigman, G., & Webb., L (2003). Ready to learn: Teaching kindergarten students school success skills. *Journal of Educational Research, 96*, 286–292.	Kindergarten students	Ready to Learn, a kindergarten program designed to improve students learning skills before they enter first grade. Skills necessary for success in school include attending, listening, working cooperatively with others, and following directions.	At the end of the year, students in these experimental classrooms scored significantly better than comparable classes on measures of listening, comprehension, and behavior.
Espelage, D. L., Low, S., Polanin, J. R., & Brown, E. C. (2013). The impact of a middle school program to reduce aggression, victimization, and sexual violence. *Journal of Adolescent Health, 53*(2), 180–186.	Middle school students	Second Step: Student Success through Prevention is a program designed to reduce youth violence. Classroom lessons focus on empathy, anger management, impulse control, listening skills, problem-solving, bully prevention, and alcohol and drug prevention.	Sixth-grade students in schools that implemented the *Second Step* program were 42% less likely to say they were involved in physical aggression compared with sixth-graders in schools that did not implement the program.
Schroeder. B. A., Messina, A., Schroeder, D., Good, K., Barto, S., Saylor, J., & Masiello, M. (2012). The implementation of a statewide bullying prevention program: Preliminary findings from the field and the importance of coalitions. *Health Promotion Practice, 13*(4), 489–495. DOI: 10.1177/1524839910386887	Approximately 100,00 students in grades 3–12 from western and central Pennsylvania.	The Olweus Program aims to reduce school bullying. Specifically, this research looked for positive change in school climate by the end of the three-year implementation period as measured by students' perceptions of adult responses in bullying situations, the rate at which students actively intervene in support of their peers, the rate that students express fear of being bullied, and the students' perceptions as to how much they enjoy school.	Positive intervention results were seen for student reports of being bullied, bullying others, perceptions of adult responses to bullying, and attitudes about bullying.

In such prevention, the school counselor is responding after a problem has begun to manifest but before its full development, or recognizing there is a strong chance of a problem developing due to students being higher risk for some reason. The shortening of duration or the lessening of a problem's impact is the essence of secondary prevention. What it prevents, by way of its systematic early identification and early intervention, is the possible progression and duration of this type of problem and with that the development of more serious negative consequences. Early identification of at-risk students is an example of a secondary prevention strategy. Counselors, for example, can employ strategies to develop study techniques or social skills for those showing early signs of difficulty in these areas. The early introduction of interventions not only reduces the potential impact of these problems but it also helps to position the student for future success (Brigman, Webb, & Campbell, 2007). Case Illustration 3.2 depicts an example of a secondary prevention strategy.

Case Illustration 3.2
Jasmine Needs a Friend!

There have been plenty of complaints from the fifth-grade students regarding Jasmine's bossiness and rude talk. She is new to the school this year and does not yet appear to have connected with anyone enough to be considered a friend, or at least a buddy. As things are currently going, the counselor realizes that Jasmine may wind up alone during classroom group time and most certainly during lunch and recess. Such an experience is clearly distressing, especially given Jasmine's expressed desire to have friends and the sadness she feels about being alone. Such distress, if not addressed, will certainly interfere with her ability to attend and function in school.

Thinking of the levels of intervention and prevention, the counselor considers how she can support Jasmine in developing friendships. Jasmine's counselor has been teaching every fifth-grade class the principles of perspective and the skills of compromise; however, Jasmine appears to be at greater risk for not being able to use those skills on her own. The counselor decides that given Jasmine's goal of making friends, and knowing that she needs help with friendship skills, she will include her in a small counseling group. This would be considered a secondary prevention strategy. The counselor approaches Jasmine's teacher to collaborate on a good time to have the group and to check on recommendations for other students who have the same goal, as well as a student who can model appropriate friendship skills.

Supporting Jasmine in her quest to make a friend will help her feel more connected in the school and perhaps more willing to work on the skill deficits she is displaying. By including her in a small group, she can learn and practice the necessary skills with the counselor's guidance and reinforcement.

While there are many illustrations of counselors providing secondary prevention programs (see Table 3.2), some of the more dramatic programs are those targeting the early identification of students at risk for self-harm. One such approach involves providing teachers and staff as gatekeepers, with training on the indicators of potential high-risk students. As a secondary prevention program, gatekeeper training aims at improving the early identification of students at high risk for suicide and facilitating timely mental health referral (Brown, Wyman, Brinales, & Gibbons, 2007; Wyman et al., 2008).

Tertiary Prevention: Intervention with a Twist

Embracing an expanded, more ecological perspective on need and service does not mean that direct service, such as individual counseling of students, will no longer be a mainstay of the counselor's day. What is suggested, however, is that even when engaged in such direct contact, counselors will have an eye on the delivery of service that expands beyond remediation to facilitating development, wellness, and prevention.

TABLE 3.2 **Sampling of Secondary Prevention Programs within the School**

REFERENCES	TARGETED POPULATION	PROGRAM	FINDINGS
Brigman, G. A., Webb, L. D., & Campbell C. (2007). Building skills for school success: Improving the academic and social competence of students. *Professional School Counseling, 10*(3), 279–288.	Students at risk for academic difficulties in grades 5, 6, 8, and 9 from six schools were identified using state-mandated achievement tests in math and reading and a measure of social competence.	School counselor-led Student Success Skills, designed to teach academic, social, and self-management skills.	Students who received the intervention scored significantly higher in math achievement and showed substantial improvement in behavior.
Fabiano, G. A., Vujnovic, R. K., Pelham, W. E., Waschbusch, D. A., Massetti, G. M., Pariseau, M. E., Naylor, J., Yu, J., Robins, M., Carnefix, T., Greiner, A. R., & Volker, M. (2010). Enhancing the effectiveness of special education programming for children with attention deficit hyperactivity disorder using a daily report card. *School Psychology Review, 39*(2), 219–239.	Students identified with an Individual Education Plan (IEP) and diagnosed with attention deficit hyperactivity disorder in grades 1-6.	DRC included consultation with the teacher, checklists and goals, and communication with the parent to impact behavior and academic productivity.	Students who received a DRC exhibited positive effects for classroom functioning, IEP goal attainment, academic productivity, and disruptive behavior in the classroom.
Haydon, T., & Kroeger, S. D. (2016). Active supervision, precorrection, and explicit timing: A high school case study on classroom behavior. *Preventing School Failure, 60*(1), 70–78.	Students in grades 9 and 10 exhibiting problem and off-task behaviors.	Interventions included active supervision, precorrection or prompting, and explicit timing procedures.	Results showed decreased student problem behavior and decreased duration of transitions in instructional periods.

The final level of prevention programming is considered tertiary and seeks to reduce the negative impact of an event once the effect of that event has become apparent on a student or students. Tertiary prevention involves strategies that ensure that a student or group of students who are already being treated for some social-emotional or academic difficulty develop the competencies needed to not only return to a normal level of functioning but to do so in a way that helps to prevent relapse. Tertiary prevention moves beyond remediation to developing the knowledge and skills necessary to prevent reoccurrence or continual adverse effects of the original condition.

When approaching individual counseling with an eye toward prevention, counselors will incorporate an educational component that attempts to help the student understand the predisposing conditions, the types of precipitating events, and the mindset and behavior that can be employed to reduce their future negative impact. An example of this is the counselor who, when counseling a student who is experiencing emotional distress because of his gender identity or sexual orientation, helps that student gain a positive self-identity and feelings of self-worth. By reducing the student's feelings of vulnerability and increasing his resilience, the counselor is reducing the possibility that this student will experience shame or engage in risky behavior (Ryan, 2001). Table 3.3 provides a sampling of additional counseling strategies and methods that provide a tertiary preventive impact.

While each of the levels of prevention are distinct, quite often the issues that a counselor wishes to address can be attacked at all three prevention levels. A good example of such three-tiered approach is Positive Behavioral Intervention and Supports (PBIS) (Sugai, Horner, & McIntosh, 2016; Sugai & Horner, 2002; Sugai et al., 2000). At the level of primary prevention, this program emphasizes the teaching and reinforcing of appropriate behavior proactively and universally to all the students within the school. Some students who appear to have difficulties with peers or in following directions will receive additional support, even though those behaviors are not severe. The focus here is on preventing the possibility that they may develop into more disruptive behaviors in the future and thus efforts to prevent this (i.e., secondary prevention) are instituted. Finally, additional behavioral interventions are provided to those children exhibiting behavioral problems in an attempt to prevent them from getting worse (i.e., tertiary level prevention).

TABLE 3.3 **Tertiary Prevention: Moving Beyond Intervention**

REFERENCES	TARGETED POPULATION	PROGRAM	FINDINGS
Majeika, C. E., Walker, J. P., Hubbard, J. P., Steebe, J. M., Ferris, G. J., Oakes, W. P., & Lynne Lane, K. (2011). Improving on-task behavior using a functional assessment-based intervention in an inclusive high school setting. *Beyond Behavior, 20*(3), 55–66.	Single adolescent male in an inclusive high school, low academic GPA, high number of office discipline referrals (ODRs), and high ratings on the school's behavior screening.	A functional assessment-based intervention was conducted as a tertiary prevention measure.	Andrew achieved a relatively high percentage of on-task behavior upon the implementation of the individualized function-based intervention.
Graybill, E. C., Vinoski, E., Black, M., Varjas, K., Henrich, C., & Meyers, J. (2016). Examining the outcomes of including students with disabilities in a bullying/victimization intervention. *School Psychology Forum: Research in Practice, 10*(1), 4–15.	13 students with disabilities in grades 4–8 who identified as having high victimization scores.	Group sessions to learn empathy, and problem solving, and coping strategies. Some students had individual sessions only, or in combination with the group. Individual sessions included more in-depth information and were designed to reinforce knowledge and provide practice.	Students with disabilities increased their knowledge of bullying-related content, self-efficacy skills, coping skills, and self-reported ability to problem solve during bullying situations.
Yakubova, G., & Waganesh, Z. A. (2016). A problem-solving intervention using iPads to improve transition-related task performance of students with autism spectrum disorder. *Journal of Special Education Technology, 31*(2), 77–86.	Three male students diagnosed with autism spectrum disorder who are ready to transition out of high school.	Teaching transition-related tasks using point-of-view video modeling and use of a cue sheet.	Students had improved problem-solving skills and were able to generalize their skills in another setting.

Expanding the School Counselor's Role

To be successful at providing prevention services, the school counselor must not only see the issue through a systemic, ecological lens but also understand and employ the resources available within the system. The breadth of targets for intervention—ranging from adjusting school policy and procedures (primary prevention), to engaging others in early identification of those at risk (secondary), or even calling on others to assist in a student's reentry following remediation (tertiary)—highlight the fact that it will take more than one person, the counselor, to be effective.

To foster the development and wellness of our students and thus prevent many of the social-emotional challenges that may disrupt their academic achievement, school counselors must work more systemically (e.g., Dahir & Stone, 2009). It will be through engagement in coordinating, collaborating, and consulting with teachers, school administrators, parents, and at times other community service providers that school counselors will have their maximum impact.

Directions: Below you will find information that you have gathered about Jasmine. Using a preventive orientation, develop strategies that would have value as a primary, secondary, and tertiary prevention. An example has been provided in the chart below. You may find working with a practicing school counselor or professional colleague to be useful in completing this exercise.

As a school counselor who uses an ecological perspective, you have spent time talking with Jasmine and looking at her records, and you have discovered the following:

- She has an older sister who is bossy and demanding.
- Her parents work late and are not home for dinner or to help with homework.
- The family lives in a small home without many amenities and no close neighbors.
- Jasmine is in the free or reduced lunch program.
- She has been in a new school every year for the past four years.
- Jasmine and her sister are the only two people in the family who speak English.
- Jasmine rarely completes or hands in her homework.
- Other students complain about Jasmine's bossiness and won't include her at the lunch table, at recess, or in the classroom during group work.

Strategies for intervention and prevention for Jasmine:

	Classroom	Lunch/Recess	Peers	Family/Home
Tertiary	Consult with the ESL teacher for possible support for Jasmine.		One-on-one counseling for expression of feelings.	Liaison with community services for a computer.
Secondary		Small group during lunch to practice social skills.		
Primary	Lesson on creating a classroom community.			

Exercise 3.1 Many Levels of Support

Given its importance to the overall achievement of a counselor's mission, consultation as a primary mode of service delivery will serve as the remaining focus of the chapters to follow.

Summary

- Counselors are trained in and possess the skills necessary to intervene with those experiencing emotional and behavioral difficulties. By the nature of their professional identity, they are called to value the provision of preventive care over mere remediation.
- Prevention programming can be universal, implemented school-wide, and promote the development of a broad range of protective factors. Prevention measures can be targeted to those at risk or even those already in the grips of crisis.
- Primary prevention efforts are universal in scope, addressing an entire population before the manifestation of any difficulty and thus attempting to stop problems before they emerge.
- The American School Counseling Association has identified mindsets and behaviors, such as making healthy choices, developing social skills, and utilizing resiliency strategies, that when delivered as classroom guidance programs serve primary prevention efforts.
- Secondary prevention focuses on preventing an emerging problem from getting worse or having more significant adverse consequences.
- Tertiary prevention involves strategies that ensure a student or group of students who are already being treated for some social-emotional or academic difficulty develop the competencies needed to not only return to a normal level of functioning but to do so in a way that helps to prevent relapse.
- When targeting wellness, development, and prevention positions, school counselors employ consultation as a mode of service delivery to engage all stakeholders.

Additional Resources

Print

Brock, S., & Jimerson, S. R. (2012). *Best practices in school crisis prevention and intervention* (2nd ed). Bethesda, MD: National Association of School Psychologists.

Miller, D. N. (2011). *Child and adolescent suicidal behavior: School-based prevention, assessment, and intervention* (The Guilford Practical Intervention in the Schools Series). New York, NY: Guilford Press.

Web-Based

American School Counselor Association. (2014). *Mindsets and behaviors for student success: K–12 college-and-career-readiness standards for every student*. Alexandria, VA: Author. Retrieved from https://www.schoolcounselor.org/school-counselors/about-asca/mindsets-behaviors

Dimitt, C. (n.d.) Evidence-based practice resources for school counselors. Retrieved from http://www.kedc.org/sites/default/files/Zyromski%20-Evidence_Based%20Resources.pdf

Positive Behavioral Interventions and Support. (n.d.) Retrieved from http://www.pbis.org

UW-Stout University. (n.d.). Lesson plans/curriculum: School counseling and psychology. Retrieved from http://libguides.uwstout.edu/c.php?g=36557&p=232138

West Virginia Department of Education. (n.d.). Group lessons. Retrieved from http://wvde.state.wv.us/counselors/group-lessons.htmlm:

References

American School Counselor Association. (2014). *ASCA mindsets & behaviors for student success: K–12 college-and career-readiness standards for every student.* Alexandria, VA: Author.

American School Counselor Association. (2016). *The ASCA National Model implementation guide: Foundation, management and accountability.* Alexandria, VA: Author.

American School Counselor Association. (2017). *The role of the school counselor.* Alexandria, VA: Author.

Brigman, G., & Webb., L. (2003). Ready to learn: Teaching kindergarten students school success skills. *Journal of Educational Research, 96*, 286–292.

Brigman, G. A., Webb, L. D., & Campbell C. (2007). Building skills for school success: Improving the academic and social competence of student. *Professional School Counseling, 10*(3), 279–288.

Brown C. H., Wyman, P. A., Brinales, J. M., & Gibbons, R. D. (2007). The role of randomized trials in testing interventions for the prevention of youth suicide. *International Review of Psychiatry, 19*(6), 617–631.

Dahir, C. A., & Stone, C. B. (2009). School counselor accountability: The path to social justice and systemic change. *Journal of Counseling and Development, 87*(1), 12–20.

Espelage, D. L., Low, S., Polanin, J. R., & Brown, E. C. (2013). The impact of a middle school program to reduce aggression, victimization, and sexual violence. *Journal of Adolescent Health, 53*(2), 180–186.

Fabiano, G. A., Vujnovic, R. K., Pelham, W. E., Waschbusch, D. A., Massetti, G. M., Pariseau, M. E., Naylor, J., Yu, J., Robins, M., Carnefix, T., Greiner, A. R., & Volker, M. (2010). Enhancing the effectiveness of special education programming for children with attention deficit hyperactivity disorder using a daily report card. *School Psychology Review, 39*(2), 219–239.

Graybill, E. C., Vinoski, E., Black, M., Varjas, K., Henrich, C., & Meyers, J. (2016). Examining the outcomes of including students with disabilities in a bullying/victimization intervention. *School Psychology Forum: Research in Practice, 10*(1), 4–15.

Greenberg, M. T. (2010). School-based prevention: Current status and future challenges. *Effective Education, 2*, 27–52.

Haydon, T., & Kroeger, S. D. (2016). Active supervision, precorrection, and explicit timing: A high school case study on classroom behavior. *Preventing School Failure, 60*(1), 70–78.

Majeika, C. E., Walker, J. P., Hubbard, J. P., Steebe, J. M., Ferris, G. J., Oakes, W. P., & Lane, L. K. (2011). Improving on-task behavior using a functional assessment-based intervention in an inclusive high school setting. *Beyond Behavior, 20*(3), 55–66.

McMahon, H. G., Mason, E. C., Daluga-Guenther, N., & Ruiz, A. (2014). An ecological model of professional school counseling. *Journal of Counseling and Development, 92*(4), 459–471.

Myers, J. E., & Sweeney, T. J. (2005). Counseling for wellness: Theory, research, and practice. Alexandria, VA: American Counseling Association.

Ryan, C. (2001). Counseling lesbian, gay, and bisexual youths. In A. R. D'Augelli & C. J. Patterson (Eds.), *Lesbian, gay, and bisexual identities and youth: Psychological perspectives* (pp. 224–250). New York, NY: Oxford University Press.

Schroeder, B. A., Messina, A., Schroeder, D., Good, K., Barto, S., Saylor, J., & Masiello, M. (2012). The implementation of a statewide bullying prevention program: Preliminary findings from the field and the importance of coalitions. *Health Promotion Practice, 13*(4), 489–495. DOI: 10.1177/1524839910386887

Sugai, G., & Horner, R. (2002). The evolution of discipline practices: School-wide positive behavior supports. *Child and Family Behavior Therapy, 24*, 23–50.

Sugai, G., Horner, R. H., Dunlap, G., Hieneman, M., Nelson, C. M., Scott, T., Liaupsin, C., Sailor, W., Turnbull, A. P., Turnbull, H. R., Wickham, D., Wilcox, B., & Ruef, M. (2000). Applying positive behavior support and functional behavioral assessment in schools. *Journal of Positive Behavior Interventions, 2*(3), 131–143.

Sugai, G., Horner, R., & McIntosh, K. (2016). *Establishing a positive school-wide social culture. Multi-tiered systems of behavior support: The role of positive behavioral interventions and supports (PBIS) in education.* Retrieved from http://www.pbis.org/resource/1070/multi-tiered-systems-of-behavior-support-the-role-of-pbis-in-education

Witmer, J. M., & Granello, P. F. (2005). Wellness in counselor education and supervision. In J. E. Myers & T. J. Sweeney (Eds), *Counseling for wellness: Theory, research and practice* (pp. 261–271). Alexandria, VA: American Counseling Association.

Wyman, P. A., Brown, C.H., Inman, J., Cross, W., Schmeelk-Cone, K., Guo, J., & Pena, J. B. (2008). Randomized trial of a gatekeeper program for suicide prevention: 1-year impact on secondary school staff. *Journal of Consulting and Clinical Psychology, 76*(1), 104–115.

Yakubova, G., & Waganesh, Z.A. (2016). A problem-solving intervention using iPads to improve transition-related task performance of students with Autism Spectrum Disorder. *Journal of Special Education Technology, 31*(2), 77–86.

Section II

Consultation: A Paradigm for
School Counselor Services

CHAPTER 4

Consultation as Paradigm: More Than Just a Technique

"You really need to see Jasmine," the note from the music teacher Dr. Jameson said. But then again, he reacts as if everything were a crisis. I know he wants me to see Jasmine IMMEDIATELY, but I think I will try to see him first. Hopefully, by seeing him first, I may be able to understand what he expects me to do as well as share with him how we may be able to work together.

---- ○ ----

It is clear that Dr. Jameson is concerned. What may also be evident in the brief "referral" is that Dr. Jameson, at least at this juncture, expects our counselor to work directly with Jasmine to address his concern.

In reading this brief description of the counselor's reflections, we begin to see the counselor's valuing of responding to the referral, but doing so in a way that conveys to Dr. Jameson that his input is sought and valued. Meeting with Dr. Jameson, as you will soon discover, is more than merely the politically correct thing to do. It is more than a kind and caring response to a colleague in distress, but is the first step necessary to developing a collaborative consultation approach to the issue at hand. This first step to the process, if successful, will not only result in the intervention of this specific concern but will lay a foundation for the prevention of this and similar issues in the future.

As will be emphasized throughout this text, consultation is not just an additional technique. As presented here, consultation is a mode of service delivery, one that can serve as an umbrella for all other services provided by the school counselor. It is not a mere strategy or technique but a way of conceptualizing and delivering all the services offered by the school counselor. Granted, this may be somewhat of a paradigm shift for many school counselors, but it is one that, once embraced, will facilitate their provision of both intervention and prevention services to their schools.

The current chapter presents consultation as model of service delivery that allows school counselors to integrate all their roles and functions in a way that maximizes the impact of their services. After completing this chapter, the reader should be able to

1. define the unique characteristics of consultation as contrasted to individual counseling,
2. differentiate aspects or dimensions of the various activities and services deemed to be consultation, and
3. describe how each specific form of consulting would approach a single problem.

Consultation: An Operational Definition

The forms of service and interaction that have been grouped under the rubric of consultation are many and quite varied. The term *consultation* has been applied to activities as varied as the informal discussion between spouses or partners "consulting" their calendars to plan a dinner party, to the formal process of receiving advice or service from an expert with specialized training. In most cases, the colloquial definition of consultation is one of giving or receiving advice or service. Such a description fails to reflect the complexity of the consulting process or the potential impact of consultation, especially as applied to the school and the school counselor as consultant.

The term *consultation*, or *consulting*, is certainly something that is almost commonplace among professionals. However, seeking to identify a single operational definition of consultation that would be applicable across the spectrum of human services is not an easy task. As noted by Parsons & Kahn (2005), much of the difficulty stems from the fact that various practitioners and theorists tend to emphasize different elements of consultation in their definitions and approaches. However, cutting across these dimensions and specific foci are a set of core characteristics that, at a minimum, can serve as the operational components of this process called consultation. Parsons (1996) presented five characteristics that can serve as core facets of consultation: (a) a helping, (b) problem-solving process that involves a (c) voluntary, (d) triadic relationship of help-giver (the consultant), a help-seeker (the consultee), and another (the client) with the (e) dual purpose of both resolving the current problem and providing for the prevention of its reoccurrence.

Problem Solving Focus

Consultation is most often characterized as a problem-solving process in which the target of such problem solving is the work, or in the case of students, the achievement of the student as the client (Parsons & Kahn, 2005). Focusing consultation on "work-related issues" ensures that the consultant resists engaging in mental health counseling or psychotherapy with the consultee and focuses service to the consultee in a way that it improves the performance of the client. This is not to suggest that the consultee may not also need skills or new insights. What is being highlighted is that consultation, even when taking such a "consultee-centered" focus (see Chapter 11) emphasizes problem solving around issues of the client's performance as opposed to therapeutic personal insight and growth for the consultee.

Consider the situation in which a school counselor is making a classroom observation of a third-grader's disruptive behavior. The consultant can provide the teacher (i.e., consultee) insight if the feedback provided offers evidence that the teacher's attention to the student in response to the student's disruptive action is acting as a positive reinforcement, thus strengthening the acting out behavior. In this case, the consultee (i.e., classroom teacher) will gain insight and even develop new skills for class management, but this is secondary to the purpose of reducing the student's (i.e., client's) disruptive behavior.

The nature of the relationship with the consultee will require that the school counselor as consultant employ many of the same helping behaviors used in counseling (e.g., active listening, summarizations) while at the same time avoiding developing a personal, therapeutic contract with the consultee. While this may appear clear-cut and relatively simple, the truth is that it is not always easy to walk the fine line between consultative help and personal therapy.

Consider the following case of Allen T. Allen was a high school history teacher with 42 years of teaching experience. Allen requested the consultative services of the school psychologist because he was worried about a young boy in his class. Allen described Dennis as "a good boy, who last year was quite prompt in completing assignments. This year, however, Dennis has been frequently late with assignments and (I) must always give him extra time." Continuing, Allen stated: "I think he's going through some difficult times. His dad died only six months ago!"

As the consultant worked with Allen, two things became quite clear. First, the student, Dennis, was grieving the death of his father. However, his grief reaction appeared appropriate in both intensity and duration. Also, Dennis was involved in supportive counseling with his family, which seemed to be very useful. The second and perhaps more essential issue identified by the consultant was that Allen's objectivity and professional approach to Dennis had been compromised. Allen, by his admission, was overly solicitous of Dennis and provided him more freedom in meeting deadlines than he usually would allow. It became apparent that Dennis was responding to the extra time given him by making the most of it. It was also apparent that Allen's issues surrounding the delayed grieving of his own parents' deaths and the anticipatory grief connected to his upcoming retirement were interfering with his professional objectivity and ability to hold Dennis responsible for deadlines.

While the consultant needed to help Allen see the connection between his overreaction to Dennis and Dennis' lack of performance in class, it was imperative that he avoid focusing his energies and interventions on Allen and Allen's own delayed grief. This is not to suggest that recommendations to Allen to consider some individual work would be inappropriate. What is being presented is that the contracted nature of the consultation should remain on resolving the work-related problem of the client and not the therapeutic needs of the consultee. Knowing how to walk the fine line between work-related problem solving and personal therapy is essential for the counselor working from a consultative frame of reference.

Mutual and Voluntary

While consultation is often presented as a process involving the engagement of an "expert" in the form of the consultant, the most effective types of consultation are those that are collaborative and mutual with both the consultant and the consultee, bringing unique perspective and expertise to the problem resolution. The value of a mutually contributing model in which both the consultant and consultee approach the consultation as coequals, sharing in the ownership and responsibility for the consultation interaction and outcome, is emphasized throughout this text. But even when a less than an entirely collaborative relationship exists, there is value in consultee involvement and ownership to whatever extent possible.

Moving the relationship to one of mutual responsibility and shared ownership for the process and final content, while valuing individual differences in perspective and expertise, requires the counselor-consultant to develop additional interpersonal skills aimed at reducing consultee resistance and equalizing psychosocial power differentials. These skills are presented in Chapter 8.

Triadic Relationship

A distinguishing characteristic of consultation in relation to counseling is that consultation involves a triadic relationship (Parsons, 1996). The engagement of a consultee expands the helping relationship beyond the boundaries of helper (i.e., counselor, therapist) and "helpee" (i.e., client, patient). This consultee is the individual who has responsibility for the client's work-related behavior and is experiencing some concern or difficulty in relation to that client or that client's performance. Thus, a consultee could be a classroom teacher; a school administrator; a parent; or, in other settings, a supervisor or a manager. Exercise 4.1 will help further clarify the triadic nature of the consultation.

Unlike direct service models where a school counselor meets individually with the student (see Figure 4.1), consultation is a triadic form of service, meaning that the work to be accomplished will at some level involve the consultee in both the identification of the problem and problem-solving processes (see Figure 4.1).

It would not be uncommon, for example, for a school counselor to ask the classroom teacher for more data or for the school counselor to do an observation to gather more data that more clearly defines the student's difficulty. The consultant may review these data with the consultee (i.e., teacher), and together they may decide on an intervention that could be implemented by the teacher or one that engages the counselor more directly. The consultant who provides a plan for another (e.g., teacher, parent, administrator) to implement is employing a prescriptive mode of consultation (Figure 4.2).

Directions: For each of the following scenarios name the consultant, the consultee, and the client.

Example: Sheila, a third-grade teacher, is experiencing great difficulty getting Joel to refrain from calling out in class. She has gone to speak with Mr. Dino, the school counselor, knowing that he previously worked with Joel.

- Consultant: Mr. Dino
- Consultee: Sheila
- Client: Joel

Scenario 1: Reginald, the reading specialist at Elmwood Elementary, is approached by Al, the fourth-grade language arts teacher, who expresses a concern about one of his students, Louis, who appears to have difficulty following along in class.

- Consultant:
- Consultee:
- Client:

Scenario 2: Dr. Peterson, the school psychologist, asks to talk with Mrs. Hurd, who serves as Fatima's school counselor. Dr. Peterson has attempted on numerous occasions to engage Fatima but with no success. He has heard of the longstanding counseling relationship that Mrs. Hurd has with this student and is hoping she can provide some insight into what may be interfering with his attempts to create a helping relationship with her.

- Consultant:
- Consultee:
- Client:

Scenario 3: Dr. Toby, the principal of Hatfield High, approaches Len Forsythe, the supervisor of the counseling department, expressing her apprehension about needing to confront a teacher about a possible drinking problem. While Dr. Toby does not reveal the name of the teacher, she is very concerned about learning the most effective approach to such a confrontation and is hoping that Mr. Forsythe can help.

- Consultant:
- Consultee:
- Client:

Scenario 4: Luis, the principal of P.S. 142, contacts the local community mental health center to request assistance with providing some AIDS awareness programming for his senior high students.

- Consultant:
- Consultee:
- Client:

Exercise 4.1 Consultation: A Triadic Relationship

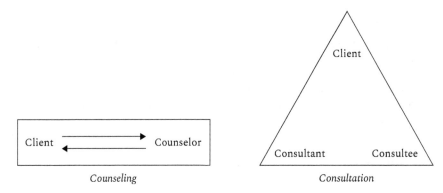

FIGURE 4.1   Direct and Indirect Service

Dashed line = problem identification
Solid line = delivery of intervention

FIGURE 4.2   Prescriptive Mode of Consultation

It is possible that after interacting with the consultee, the consultant may take on the role of the "implementer" of the intervention or prevention program. In this case, a provisional role is enacted by the consultant, and it would look like that presented in Figure 4.3.

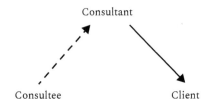

Broken line = problem identification
Solid line = intervention delivery

FIGURE 4.3   Provisional Mode of Consultation

While both prescriptive and provisional modes of service are valuable, the model of consultation emphasized here is one of collaboration (see Figure 4.4). It is a model which emphasizes mutual participation in both defining the problem and finding solutions. While an outcome of collaboration may be that one or the other party takes primary responsibility for implementing the program mutually developed, it is often the case that both the consultant and consultee have an active role in the solution process.

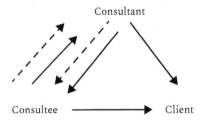

Consultant

Consultee   ⟶   Client

Dashed line = problem identification
Solid line = delivery of intervention

FIGURE 4.4   Collaboration Mode of Consultation

For further clarification, consider the case with which we opened the chapter. Perhaps as our consultant begins to meet with Dr. Jameson, it becomes clear that Dr. Jameson firmly believes he knows what the difficulty is and what needs to be done. Perhaps he is somewhat insistent on how the counselor-consultant should intervene. But even when such provisional service is requested, the counselor now working as a consultant will do more than just rush into a session with Jasmine. Recognizing the importance of the triadic relationship, the consultant, even when about to operate from a provisional mode, will attempt to engage the consultee (i.e., Dr. Jameson) in a dialogue about the case and all possible forms of intervention. The focus of this discussion is on having each party (i.e., consultant and consultee) share their perspective on the nature of the problem as well as what needs to be done.

Following this sharing and agreement, the consultant may, in fact, take the next step to employ some strategy with Jasmine. In this situation, the consultant is engaging in provisional consultation. But, let's assume that the consultant discussed Jasmine's case with Dr. Jameson before actually meeting with Jasmine. Further, if we believe that as a result of that meeting with Dr. Jameson, a couple of ideas that seemed best implemented by Dr. Jameson emerged, then the counselor-consultant would be "prescribing" for the consultee to implement. Perhaps, the consultant provided the consultee (i.e., Dr. Jameson) with a couple of steps to take that were designed to gather more "diagnostic" information, or even begin to remediate the situation. Under this condition, the consultant is working from a "prescriptive" mode of consultation.

These two modes are not exclusive. As collaborators in the problem identification and problem-solving processes, it would not be usual for both parties (i.e., consultant and consultee), after sharing their mutual perspectives and expertise, to come up with roles for both to perform. Through such a collaborative dialogue, a mutually agreed upon strategy for working with this problem may be derived that entails both the consultant and the consultee engaging in some way with Jasmine.

Case Illustration 4.1
Good Vibes for Dr. Jameson

The school counselor was able to set up a meeting with Dr. Jameson prior to her speaking with Jasmine. Dr. Jameson was both the part-time music teacher and the head teacher. He took both roles very seriously, and in this instance, he was very concerned that Jasmine would fail music class. He could not get her to engage in class or participate in group work without major complaints from her group members. The counselor knew that the art teacher had been successful in getting Jasmine to participate in class by assigning her the role of leader for her table. Using a prescriptive mode of consultation, she shared some strategies with Dr. Jameson that he could use to draw on Jasmine's desire to be in charge of her peers, and do so in a positive way.

Dr. Jameson was appreciative of the suggestions and said he would try to initiate a strategy for increased group participation. He then shared that Jasmine wasn't the only student who he had difficulty getting to engage by singing or playing an instrument. She was the only one in danger of failing, but it seemed there were other students who were hesitant to perform. The school counselor described a strategy that she called shaping, and said by setting up participation in smaller steps and then positively reinforcing those steps, the students may feel more comfortable taking a risk to participate. Dr. Jameson was excited about this idea but did not feel he understood the strategy well enough to do it well.

The counselor then used a provisional mode of consultation by setting up and implementing the shaping and reinforcement strategy for Dr. Jameson's class. The counselor followed up with Dr. Jameson several times over the next few weeks. The intervention worked so well that Dr. Jameson implemented it as a prevention strategy with the rest of his music classes. Dr. Jameson was so delighted with the outcome of the strategies, he requested that the counselor share them at the next faculty meeting.

The types and number of focal points for the helping relationship are undoubtedly multiplied once the service moves from dyadic, as in counseling, to triadic, as in consultation. The inclusion of this third party as a coparticipant in the problem-solving venture provides additional resources and perspective. The addition of this third party also requires the counselor-now-consultant to develop a new shift in focus and employ a unique set of skills previously unused in a direct service model. Understanding and coordinating multiple perspectives, different terminology, turf concerns, and power issues are but a few of the additional variables included in the dynamics when one moves to a consultative model of service delivery.

Dual Focus

One of the primary values of a consultation model of service delivery is that it does more than target the work problem for intervention. More than merely intervening to resolve a current work problem (remedial/intervention focus), consultation has as a second goal: the provision of some measure of preventive service (Parsons & Kahn, 2005; Parsons, 1996, Kurpius & Fuqua, 1993).

The Many and Varied Dimensions of Consultation

Consultation as a form of service delivery is used in many settings (e.g., school, hospitals, industry) and as such is often depicted in various ways. Parsons (1996) presented a model for categorizing the different types of consultation. This model, which is shown here in abbreviated form, classifies consultation along five dimensions: nature, problem-goal, theory, skills, and modes. While it is helpful to understand these various aspects, the actual value of consultation is maximized when these components are integrated into a flexible, multidimensional approach to consultation as is presented within this text.

Dimension I: The Nature of the Consult—Crises or Developmental

Consults that are of a crises nature are those in which the individual consultee or consultee system experiences pain or dysfunction and requests the consultant's assistance. For example, a school principal may seek help from the counselor-consultant following the sudden, unexpected death of a student. Under these conditions, the counselor-consultant must often respond quickly with little time to develop an extended process and would attempt to provide an intervention to bring the consultee and the consultee's system back to its previous level of functioning as quickly as possible. Because of the nature of the crisis and the pain experienced by the consultee, the consultant recommendations are quite often accepted with minimal resistance.

Other consultation services may come at a time of relative stability and focus on promoting growth and wellness, and increasing skills such as social skills, problem-solving skills, and stress management. Such a consult would be considered developmental, focusing on growth and prevention rather than pain reduction and remediation.

The absence of crises allows the consultant and the consultee the luxury of time to plan and implement the most growth-filled form of service. However, the same lack of pain and crises often reduces the felt need for such service. Thus, developmental consultation may be met with resistance. Overcoming this "if it ain't broke, don't fix it" mentality requires additional interpersonal marketing skills on the part of the consultant to enlist the consultee's cooperation and ownership of this developmental process.

Dimension II: Problem and Goal Definition Varying in Depth and Breadth

A second way various forms of consultation may be different is in the way the problems, and thus the specific goals, are defined. Problems can be conceptualized as varying in breadth and depth. The scope of a problem can be restricted to a single student or more broadly identified as involving a group or grade level, or perhaps even the entire school system. A problem can be defined as varying in depth, from a single issue to one involving multiple concerns, or from a surface problem to a more hidden or convoluted problem. Further, the problem can be defined as either one of a technical nature to one involving a human systems or process glitch.

Just as the problem definition can vary along breadth and depth dimensions, so can the goal statement and focus. Goals can be operationalized to involve changes in a person (client, consultee, etc.), a policy, or a system structure or process.

Dimension III: Theory and Assumptions

Like other forms of helping, the consulting process and focus will be guided and shaped by the consultant's operating set of assumptions or model of consultation. The role the consultant employs, the outcomes expected, and the strategies chosen reflect the consultant's assumptions and operative model. There are many consultation models and theoretical views (Brigman, Mullis, Webb, & White, 2005; Caplan & Caplan, 1999; Erford, 2014; Kampwirth & Powers, 2012); the following are three views, briefly described.

Mental Health Consultation

Popularized by Gerald Caplan (1970) and presented in its updated version (Caplan & Caplan, 1999; 2015), the mental health model of consultation emphasizes the value of a collaborative relationship with the consultee. For example, Caplan worked as consultant to a small staff of psychologists and social workers responsible for the mental health needs of immigrant children in Israel. His efforts were initially aimed at merely providing the staff (i.e., the consultees) with new techniques for coping with the problems they had identified with the children (i.e., the clients). Unlike a number of the earlier "expert" models, in which the consultant would diagnose the problem and provide authoritative, expert prescription, the keystone to Caplan's approach was the nonhierarchical or coordinate relationship that existed between the consultant and the consultee.

Caplan conceptualized the relationship between the consultee and the consultant as one of equals, wherein the consultant had no direct-line authority over the consultee. The mental health consultation model, while focusing on the client's (i.e., an individual, group, or organization) functioning, did so with emphasis given to the role of the consultee's knowledge, skill, and objectivity in relationship to both the remediation and prevention of the problem at hand. The basic premise was that increasing the knowledge, skills, or professional objectivity of the clinical staff would not only result in the amelioration of the presenting concern but also serve a preventive function in reducing the need for future consultation on similar type of issues.

Behavioral Consultation

A different set of assumptions about the targets for both problem identification and resolution can be found within the behavioral model of consultation (Bergan & Kratochwill, 1990; Sheridan & Kratochwill, 2008). Unlike the mental health model, behavioral consultation was founded on social learning theory and as such focused on the overt behaviors of the consultee and the client.

Operating from behavioral theory by emphasizing learning the influence of one's environment, school counselors performing from a behavioral consultant orientation often assume a directive role. They may be directly active in observing client behavior or client-consultee interaction and gathering descriptive data about the conditions and frequency of the particular problematic behavior. They will then prescribe an intervention and monitor the consultees' implementation of that prescription.

Organizational Consultation

Organizational consultants (Schein, 1988, 2009) gather data on a particular organization's functioning. The consultant may introduce some new technology and serve as a trainer or advisor in the use of these new technologies. Or, the consultant may focus on the current organizational structure and processes, and help the organization refine these structures and procedures to be more successful. The organizational consultant often plays the role of systems analyst, assessing the corporate culture of a company in order to prescribe ways to help the various parts work better as a whole, or may provide more direct, provisional service in the role of administrative coach, staff developer, and reorganization specialist.

Dimension IV: Consultant Skills Content or Process Expertise

While it is evident that consultation always involves some level of expertise, the level of emphasis on this expertise may vary from content/technical specialization to process knowledge and skill. From the role of content/technological expert, the consultant's goal is to provide the needed information, material, principles, or programs aimed at resolving the problem. The operative assumption underlying the role of content expert is that the current concern can be addressed by the direct application of specific knowledge or techniques. It is assumed that the consultant possesses the knowledge and methods that are needed and which the consultee lacks. Process consultation (Schein, 1989), on the other hand, involves working with a consultee and implementing a planned change process. The process consultant operates from the assumption that those within the system are unaware of the recurrent procedures that have been or could be significantly impacting their performance and may be the source of their current difficulties. The process consultant will attempt to increase the consultee's awareness and understanding of the nature and impact of their system's patterns or processes. The focus of the process consultation would be on those individual roles and functions, intergroup and intragroup dynamics, communication patterns, leadership styles, or decision-making mechanisms that appear problematic. The operational assumption is that through such increased awareness, the consultee will be able to adjust or in some way change the problematic process and thus increase the effectiveness or productivity of the system. The process consultant operates more as a facilitator than a director. The process consultant serves more as a coordinator and less as the expert problem resolver.

Dimension V: Modes of Consultation—Provisional, Prescriptive, Collaborative, Mediational

A fifth way to differentiate the various examples of consultation is to contrast consultation as a function of the particular role played by the consultant. Kurpius (1978) describes four modes of consultant behavior that could be used to differentiate consultation. While others have extended this model (Fox, Baker, & Gerler, 2017), the four original modes offered by Kurpius (1978) are described as follows.

In the provisional mode, the consultee retains full control of the focus of the consultation, and the consultant is expected to apply specialized knowledge (content and process expertise) to implement action plans toward the achievement of goals defined by the consultee. It is as if the consultant, while possessing specialized knowledge or skill, functions as an extension of the consultee, employing specialization in the manner that achieves the consultee's outcome objectives. In this form of consulting, the consultant defers to the consultee for determination of the problem and formulation of the desired outcome. In this role, two-way communication is limited (consultee initiates, consultant responds) and control rests with the consultee. The effectiveness of the consultant's intervention is strongly affected by the accuracy of the consultee's diagnosis of the problem and selection of the desired outcome.

An example of this might be when a school principal asks the school counselor to provide a faculty development workshop on a topic that the principal believes the faculty wants and needs. In this situation, the nature of the problem, the identified goals, and the desired outcomes are all defined by the principal. The success of the presentation is, therefore, not only dependent on the competencies of the counselor as the presenter but also on the accuracy of the need identified by the consultee (i.e., principal).

The prescriptive mode is somewhat reactive and crises focused in nature. In this form of consultation, the consult is typically initiated by the consultee, and usually out of a sense of need.

While the service provided may tap the consultant's content or process expertise, the focus of the role is for the consultant to serve as a diagnostician and a provider of prescriptions for intervention to the consultee. The application of the intervention is the responsibility of the consultee, who may be directed and guided by the consultant.

In the collaborative mode, the consultant assumes that joining the specialized knowledge and skill of the consultant coequally with those of the consultee will increase the accuracy of problem identification, and maximize intervention resources and approaches. It is assumed that through such an expansion of resource and perspective, the probability of effectiveness will be increased. In the collaborative mode, both the consultee and consultant play an active role. Responsibility for data gathering, analysis, goal setting, and intervention planning are shared. The responsibility for success and failure of the consult is also shared, and communication is two-way. As with the previous modes, the collaborative method is viewed as reactive, with the consultant being invited into the referral, typically because of the consultee's concern.

Finally, the consultant who is operating from a mediational role or mode will take a much more proactive stance than would be the case in any of the previously discussed ways. The consultant in the mediational mode will initiate the consultation contact with the consultee. Other authors refer to this mode of consultation as initiation mode (Baker, Robichaud, Westforth-Dietrich, Wells, & Schreck, 2009). Regardless of the title of the mode, in these instances the consultant will undertake the connection having recognized a recurrent problem before the consultee's recognition or experience of need. In this mode, the consultant will gather, analyze, and synthesize existing information as a way of defining the problem and develop an intervention plan for implementation.

When operating in a mediational mode, the consultant has to not only address the problem at hand but "sell" the need for intervention to the consultee. The consultant will have to demonstrate to the consultee the wisdom and value of the need for consultation since up to this point the consultee has been operating without crises or need. It is as if the consultant is trying to demonstrate the value of fixing something when the consultee feels that same something works and has worked well. Exercise 4.2 will help further clarify these varied modes of consultation.

Directions: Read the presenting issue and decide on which consultation mode you will proceed. Remember, you may change modes as data are gathered and goals change. An example has been provided for you.

Example: Mrs. Ida Know has asked for help with her freshman science class. The students are not producing work to the high standards she expects. She tells you this happens all the time with freshmen as she tries to whip them into shape for high school. However, this year seems to be worse than ever before. She has no idea what to do. You suggest that she survey the students to gather information about what they think would be helpful, and then together create a contract with them explaining the expectations and the positive and negative consequences of fulfilling them, or not.

This is an example of what mode of consultation? *prescriptive mode of consultation*

1. Mr. Ted. E. Bare comes to you in reference to a new student in his room. The student seems very apprehensive to participate during class discussions and won't interact with the other classmates. Together you decide on a goal of class participation, and each of you will implement strategies to help the new student. This is an example of what mode of consultation?

2. Ms. Sarah Nade consistently complains about the male students in her room, and their disrespectful and irresponsible behavior. Several of the students and their parents have expressed frustration with Ms. Nade's forgetfulness, losing assignments, and lack of understanding of preadolescent boys. You set up a meeting with Ms. Nade to increase her awareness of these issues and offer to work with her on strategies to remedy the situation. This is an example of what mode of consultation?

3. Ms. Ida Know from the example above is back in your office complaining that the strategies didn't work. You ask her to describe the process of how she implemented the strategies, and you find out that she didn't survey or talk to the students at all regarding what their needs were; she just made a contract with no input. When you ask her about this piece of the intervention, she replies that she has no time to make up a survey, and besides, she really doesn't know how to implement such a thing. You ask her if she would like you to create the survey and interpret the data and Ms. Know is thrilled, saying she would love that! This is an example of what mode of consultation?

Exercise 4.2 Are You in A Good Mode?

Summary

- Consultation is practiced in many settings (e.g., schools, mental health services, hospitals, industry) and presented as embodying a variety of roles and functions.
- Consistent with most definitions of consultation is that it is a voluntary, triadic relationship among consultant, consultee, and client.
- As presented here, consultation has a dual focus on both intervention (remediation) and prevention.
- The form of consultation can vary based upon the nature of the problem (i.e., crisis or developmental), the depth and breadth of the problem and goal, the consultant's skills set (i.e., content or process), and the mode of consultation employed (i.e., provisional, prescriptive, collaborative, meditational).

Additional Resources

Print

Dollarhide, C. T., & Saginak, K. A. (2012). *Comprehensive school counseling programs: K–12 delivery systems in action* (2nd ed.). Boston, MA: Pearson.

Erford, B. T. (2014). *Transforming the school counseling profession* (4th ed). Boston, MA: Pearson.

Web-Based

American School Counselor Association (ASCA). Retrieved from https://www.schoolcounselor.org/

https://www.emeraldinsight.com/doi/abs/10.1108/EUM0000000001132?journalCode=lodj

Warren, J. M., & Baker, S. B. (2013). School counselor consultation: Enhancing teacher performance through rational emotive-social behavioral consultation. In *Ideas and research you can use: VISTAS 2012*. Retrieved from http://www.counseling.org/knowledge-center/vistas

References

Baker, S., Robichaud, T., Westforth-Dietrich, V., Wells, S., & Schreck, R. (2009). School counselor consultation: A pathway to advocacy, collaboration, and leadership. *Professional School Counseling, 12*(3), 200–206.

Bergan, J. R., & Kratochwill, T.R. (1990). *Behavioral consultation and therapy*. New York, NY: Plenum Press.

Brigman, G., Mulls, F., Webb, L., & White, J. (2005). School counselor consultation: Developing skills for working effectively with parents, teachers and other school personnel. Hoboken, NJ: John Wiley & Sons.

Caplan, G. (1970). *The theory and practice of mental health consultation*. New York, NY: Basic Books.

Caplan, G., & Caplan, R. (1999). *Mental health consultation and collaboration*. Prospect Heights, IL: Waveland Press.

Caplan, G., & Caplan, R. (2015). *Mental health consultation and collaboration*. Long Grove, IL: Waveland Press.

Erford, B. T. (2014). Consultation, collaboration and encouraging parent involvement. In B. T. Erford (Ed), *Transforming the School Counseling Profession* (4th ed., pp. 303–324). Boston, MA: Pearson.

Fox, S. P., Baker, S. B., & Gerler, E. R. (2017). *School counseling in the 21st century*. New York, NY: Routledge.

Kampwirth, T. J., & Powers K. M. (2012). *Collaborative consultation in the schools* (4th ed.) Upper Saddle River, NJ: Pearson.

Kurpius, D. J. (1978). Consultation theory and process: An integrated model. *Personnel and Guidance Journal, 56*, 335–338.

Kurpius, D. J., & Fuqua, D. R. (1993). Introduction to the speed issues. *Journal of Counseling and Development, 71*, 596–697.

Parsons, R. D. (1996). *The skilled consultant*. Needham Heights, MA: Allyn & Bacon.

Parsons R. D., & Kahn, W. J. (2005). *The school counselor as consultant*. Belmont, CA: Brook/Cole.

Schein, E. H. (1988). *Process consultation* (2nd ed., Vol 1) Reading, MA: Addison-Wesley.

Schein, E. H. (1989). Process consultation as a general model of helping. *Consulting Psychology Bulletin, 41*, 3–15.

Schein, E. H. (2009). *Helping: How to offer, give, and receive help*. San Francisco, CA: Berrett-Koehler.

Sheridan, S. M., & Kratochwill, T. R. (2008). *Conjoint behavioral consultation: Promoting family-school connections and interventions* (2nd ed.). New York, NY: Plenum Press.

CHAPTER 5

A Multidimensional, Integrated
Model of Consulting

This has been so helpful. I've been working with Jasmine for over two months, and simply spending some time with Mrs. Lane gave me an entirely new perspective. I think approaching two fronts, with me working directly one-on-one and Mrs. Lane adjusting her classroom management style, is going to be a greater help to Jasmine.

———————————————— ○ ————————————————

These reflections of our elementary school counselor upon the benefits of consulting with Jasmine's teacher, Mrs. Lane, demonstrate the value of incorporating counselor services, even those involving direct-one-on-one counseling, under the umbrella of consultation. Not only has the counselor received an additional pair of hands to assist with Jasmine, but also Mrs. Lane's classroom perspective and expertise allow for an expansion of the number of techniques and strategies that can be applied, not just to this one student but perhaps for all students within Mrs. Lane's class.

The current chapter presents consultation as a model of service delivery that allows the counselor to integrate all her roles and functions in a way that maximizes the impact of her services. After completing this chapter, the reader should be able to

1. explain the value of viewing the elements of consultation as existing along a continuum;
2. describe the multidimensional model of consultation that allows for the integration of various consultant styles, modes of service delivery, and targets for change; and
3. identify decision criteria to guide the practicing consultant in the selection of the consultation type that is most appropriate to any given situation.

Integrating Perspectives—Nature, Focus, and Modes

The descriptive classifications of consultation as a mode of service delivery, discussed in Chapter 4, have value in highlighting a particular aspect or characteristic of a consult. These dimensions are typically presented in binary, either/or fashion as if any particular consult could only be in one form of the pairing (i.e., a crises consult rather than one targeting growth). While such a presentation may help clarify the types of elements that can be brought to a consult, the implied binary nature of the characteristics described is simply misleading when it comes to actual, effective consultation as practiced.

In practice, consultations rarely fit so neatly into such a binary grouping of elements. More often, a consultation involves a mix of a number of these dimensions. Further, it is not unusual for the nature, focus, and target of the consultation to change as it develops over time. Therefore, rather than attempting to develop unique camps of consultation, (e.g., crisis consultant vs. development consultant, or content consultant vs. process consultant) it is much more functional to view these elements as existing along a continuum in which all consults involve various weightings of each of these elements. Thus, for example, rather than seeing a consult as one of crisis or as one of growth and development, it is more effective to view each consult as falling along a continuum of "felt" need with crisis/pain at one end and growth/prevention at the other. With this perspective, all consultation, even those engaged out of crises, provides opportunity to stimulate growth, development, and prevention. Similarly, all consults, even those initiated with a focus on growth and development, where there is the absence of crisis, will prove more effective when the consultant can tie that growth to the client's and consultee's felt needs.

The position presented here, and previously expressed by Parsons & Kahn (2005), is that it is much more effective for the school counselor to view each consult as a multidimensional, integrated activity that takes its shape and distinctiveness by moving along a number of continua, reflecting (a) the consultee's degree of felt need, (b) the consultant's expertise, (c) the degrees of collaborative involvement, and (d) the expansiveness of impact targeted.

The following case (Case of Tommie) will be used throughout this section as a way of demonstrating each of the elements contributing to the unique nature of any one particular consult. As an instructional tool and reflection guide, we invite you to use Exercise 5.1 as you proceed through the chapter and consider the questions as you read through the case illustrations.

Case Illustration 5.1
The Case of Tommie

Referral

His teacher, Ms. Casey, referred Tommie to the counseling office. Tommie is in 5th grade. He lives at home with his mother (a corporate lawyer) and his father (a psychiatrist). Tommie has an older sister (Julie) who is a senior in high school and an older brother (Alex) who is attending Columbia University Law School.

Ms. Casey sent Tommie to the counselor with a note, which read "Tommie needs your help! He is a disturbed child. I found Tommie dropping his pencil in class in an attempt to look up the dress of the girl who sits behind him. I also found some drawings that I would be embarrassed to show you. Tommie is inattentive. He is always fidgeting in his seat, looking around in class, and doing things (like dropping his pencil) to get attention. I have tried talking to Tommie, I have kept him after school, I have spoken to his parents, and NOTHING works. It seems I spend more time calling out Tommie's name than teaching. Please help him to get it together!"

Observations

In meeting Tommie, you note that he is a very nice, mannerly, and articulate youth. Tommie "admits" that he was trying to look up the girl's dress but stated that "it's just a game, other guys do it too!" Tommie complained that Ms. Casey is always "on his case" and that she is really "boring."

In describing his home life, Tommie noted that he misses his older brother (who had been at home up until this past month). He explained that he has a small job (taking care of his neighbor's dogs) after school and it keeps him busy from the time he gets home (3:00 p.m.) until the time his mom comes home from work (4:15 p.m.). Tommie discussed the many hobbies and sports activities he enjoyed and noted that his dad had been the coach for both his soccer and baseball teams. Tommie has been described by other teachers as a "good kid" who is somewhat of an "itch."

About the Consultee

Ms. Casey has been a teacher for the past 27 years. Ms. Casey has taught grades K through 2 for most of her career. This is the first year she has taught 5th grade. Ms. Casey stated that "she loves teaching and wouldn't know what to do if [she] couldn't have her classroom."

She expressed concerns over the real possibility of being forced to retire, and as such, she wants to "demonstrate to the administration that [I] can be in complete control of [my] classroom." She noted that other children in her class have "discipline problems" and appear a bit "itchy." She noted, however, that she is concerned about referring these children for counseling, since "a good teacher should be able to handle her problems within the classroom!"

About the School

The school contains grades K through 5th, with a student population of 520 students. The school has 18 classroom teachers, three supplementary teachers, a school psychologist, a learning specialist, and two school counselors. Within the last five years, the community has grown significantly in size, educational background, and financial status. Most of the children come from homes in which both parents work in professional capacities, and the family expectations are that education will be valued and achieved.

The goals of the school are to "foster academic development, inspire pride in self and country, and to promote the development of self-control and responsible decision making." Informally, the school seems to value calmness, order, and neatness. The school employs a self-contained mode of classroom education, and as such, teachers are responsible for all subject curriculum (except for physical education).

Directions: As you review each of the continua and the elements used to define the particulars of a consult, review the questions below and consider how you might approach each of the factors described.

Consultee's degree of felt need	What are some possible outcomes if the consultant does not address the crisis end of the spectrum? The developmental/preventive end?
Consultant's expertise (content/process)	How might the consultant acting as content expert make an impact in this consultation? Process expert? What might occur if the consultant considers approaching this consult with only one lens of expertise?
Degree of collaborative involvement	How is this consult impacted if only working in a prescriptive mode? A provisional mode? What may occur if a collaborative mode is employed in this consult?
Expansiveness of impact targeted	What outcomes may be achieved with a greater number of targets addressed (student, teacher, system)? What may occur if the focus is narrower (student only)?

A Continuum of Felt Need

Most counselors have had the experience of working with a client or consultee who presents in the *state of crisis*. With their stability shaken, these consultees and clients are often quite open to any of the interventions proposed or help provided. Often, consultees or clients in such heightened states of pain or need have limited ability to fully contribute to the analyses of the problem or the development of the intervention. In this state of crisis, they may simply seek direction from the counselor-consultant.

For consultation to be truly effective in both addressing the crisis and providing elements of prevention, the counselor-consultant needs to understand that once the pain has been reduced or the crises averted, the task is still not complete. With the level of pain (i.e., crisis) experienced reduced and the consultee and/or client's return to stability, there is still value in continuing the work to foster growth and development. By doing so, the consultant can reduce the possibility of such a crisis returning or further develop the client's and/or consultee's ability to address similar conditions should they occur in the future. Thus, even when addressing a crisis, the effective school counselor-consultant sees the consult as existing along a continuum of felt need. With this as a perspective, the counselor-consultant attempts to engage across that continuum, having interventions tied to need reduction (away from crisis) while at the same time providing preventive value (toward development and growth).

For example, consider the first-year, nontenured teacher who is teaching honors English to graduating senior high school students. Assume that she runs into the counseling office yelling that she is ready to pull her hair out because these students don't listen. Given the apparent strong felt need of the moment, the counselor will address the crisis first and then turn her attention to areas for this teacher's professional growth. The teacher clearly needs to vent and have her sense of frustration "heard" and affirmed. The counselor will be empathic and supportive. When a sense of calm has been restored, the counselor helps the teacher develop a strategy that will help her return to class and continue with her classes. Once the crisis plan has been engaged, the counselor, working along with the teacher, will begin the process of working toward a developmental and preventative goal targeting an increase in the teacher's knowledge and skill in working with graduating seniors who may have a touch of "senioritis."

This same perspective applies when the consultation is one that is initiated with *growth or development, and prevention* as the targets and where there is low felt need. To be effective in this situation, the consultant needs to ensure that the services provided not only have a value in the future as a preventive measure but result in some immediate, concrete reduction of a current felt need. Without such a connection, the value of the consult may be missed, and the full participation on the part of the consultee may be absent. Thus, rather than approaching any one consultation contract as crises or developmental in nature, it is more effective to view each case existing on a continuum of crises or felt need (see Figure 5.1).

CRISIS FOCUS ◄──────► PREVENTION FOCUS

Extreme and immediate crisis, sense of a pressing need. Alleviating crises is the focus.

Addressing possible future difficulties, no immediately felt need. Development and growth are the focus.

FIGURE 5.1   Continuum of Felt Need

When the client's needs are strong, it is clear that development and prevention come secondary to reestablishing a level of stability and normalcy. On the other hand, when the need is minimal and the request is primarily on the developmental/preventive side of the continuum, it is important for the counselor-consultant to highlight the personal value to need satisfaction of the consultation in order to fully engage the client and consultee in the consultation. This will become clear as we return to our sample case of Tommie (see Case Illustration 5.2).

The consultee in this case, Ms. Casey, was experiencing an immediate need for intervention. However, conceptualizing the consult from only a crises orientation would have blinded the consultant from the preventive potential of the consultation. The consultant who viewed this interaction as one starting at the extreme left side of the felt need continuum will perceive the value of moving up the continuum toward the prevention end as the immediacy and severity of the need subsides. Thus, in addition to assuring Ms. Casey that something can be done to reduce Tommie's disruptive behaviors in her classroom, this consultant will also have an eye for prevention, looking for ways to assist this consultee to better cope with the demands of a new type of student population (i.e., fifth graders) in the future.

Case Illustration 5.2
Case Application—Tommie: Crises and/or Developmental

We can begin to more clearly see how consultants operating from either a crisis or developmental focal point would differentially approach a consult by reviewing the case of Tommie. A consultant operating from a crises frame of reference could consider all of the following in the case of Tommie. Ms. Casey is in need of assistance (in crises). Remediation for Ms. Casey's limited understanding of typical 5th-grade behavior or ineffectual classroom management skills seems appropriate. Intervening with Tommie, who is also in crises, being "bored" and in trouble with Ms. Casey, appears relevant. Working with Tommie and Ms. Casey perhaps in developing a behavioral contract aimed at increasing his time on task and positive classroom behavior seems to be a potentially useful plan for crises consultation.

Even though the referral was made in a crisis, a consultant with a developmental orientation may see other potential problems that need addressing. A consultant approaching this situation from a more developmental perspective may target each of the following as points for preventive programming:

- Teacher in-service and preparation, especially in light of new grade level assignments
- Retirement planning and transitional support
- After school programming
- Sexual development education curriculum

A Continuum of Content-Process Expertise

For the school counselor to be an effective consultant, she will need to not only possess unique knowledge and skills that she can share with the consultee and client, but she will also need to be able to assist the consultee and the client to engage their own resources, insights, and talents in the resolution of this issue and in its future prevention. In this way, the counselor-consultant will engage both content and process expertise in affecting change. The degree of emphasis, be it on providing content or technical assistance or in facilitating the engagement of the consultee's and/or client's resources, will be dependent on the nature of the consultation. However, it is only the emphasis that will vary. The effective school counselor-consultant will employ technical or content expertise as well as process expertise in all consultations if they are to result in both remediation and prevention. The counselor-consultant will use technical (content) expertise to provide unique perspective and alternative strategies while at the same time facilitating the optimal operations of the processes currently in place (see Figure 5.2).

TECHNICAL EXPERTISE (SPECIALIZATION)	PROCESS EXPERTISE
Provides new materials, programs, equipment, methods etc. and assists in application.	Assists the consultee to analyze and adjust existing materials and procedures.

FIGURE 5.2   Content-Process Expertise—Need for both

A number of elements (e.g., consultee's need, original consultation contract, consultee's expectations) can be used to determine which end of the "expertise" continuum the consultant will initially emphasize. However, the point for consideration is that regardless of the level of emphasis, both technical and process expertise is important. Simply put, if the counselor has nothing new to offer—that is, if there is no real content or technical expertise—then why would the consultee bother? Similarly, without fostering the consultee's understanding and awareness of the process by which the problem emerged, or the processes that are available to the consultee for reducing the likelihood of this problem reoccurring, hopes of prevention may be blocked. Both content and process expertise are essential to effective consultation.

Again, considering the case of Tommie (see Case Illustration 5.3), it is apparent that a consultant skilled in behavioral techniques (content expertise) could certainly provide

---

Case Illustration 5.3
Case Application—Tommie: A Technical or Process Approach

A consultant approaching the case of Tommie has a number of targets that she could address (Tommie, Ms. Casey, the classroom, etc.) from a number of theoretical perspectives. But regardless of the goal or the conceptual model, the consultant could emphasize either content/technical expertise or process expertise.

The content expert may:

1. Provide Ms. Casey with a specific set of behavior modification recommendations
2. Offer a "packaged" in-service program for teachers regarding classroom management, preadolescent sexuality
3. Suggest to the school board or building principal the inclusion of a sexual development education component to the curriculum
4. Propose the development of an after-school program for students who may be going home to an empty house

Regardless of the target or the model, the content expert consultant brings to the situation a formulated set of principles, techniques, strategies, or programs which she believes has value to the current difficulty.

The process consultant, while attempting to bring expertise to the resolution of the problem at hand, will approach it with a different focus. As such she may:

1. Assist Ms. Casey in reviewing her current classroom management decisions and procedures in an attempt to increase her awareness of how these processes may be impacting the current difficulty
2. Create a faculty ad hoc group who will begin to discuss common professional concerns and generate possible actions to be taken (which may include the development of in-service training)
3. Review with the relevant administrators the operating procedures guiding teacher/grade-level placement, teacher evaluation processes, or retirement programming, with the possibility of changing policy or initiating a mentor program as needed

a specific remedial program for the client to be applied by either the consultee as part of her classroom management or the consultant or by both. Similarly, from a process orientation, the consultant could support and facilitate the consultee's own analysis of the situation, along with her own identification of the specific factors characterizing her classroom process that may contribute to the current problem.

Given the high level of experienced stress, the history of her own unsuccessful interventions, and the expectation that the consultant will "help him get it together," the consultant working with Ms. Casey may elect to start by providing a number of specific, technical steps to be taken. For example, the consultant could remove Tommie from the classroom and begin a behavioral contract system with him that focuses upon his attending behavior. In addition to such "technical" intervention, the consultant will want to help Ms. Casey identify elements in her own style and classroom process and the impact these may have on the behavior of her students, including Tommie. Further, the consultant, acting as a process expert, may facilitate her understanding of this impact and the possible modification to her teaching style that would augment the work the consultant is doing with Tommie. In this way, a consultant is employing both content/technical expertise and process expertise in the delivery of the service.

A Continuum of Collaboration

Regardless of the role to be played by the consultant, be that the provider of service or perhaps the prescriber of the service to be implemented by the consultee, engaging the consultee in a process that is collaborative will prove most effective. As previously discussed, collaboration is one mode of consultation along with prescriptive, provisional, and mediational modes. Rather than viewing collaboration as a unique mode of consultation, one distinct from these other modes, it is much more effective to view all consultation, be it prescriptive, provisional, or meditational in nature, as reflecting and engaging some degree of collaboration.

Collaboration should be viewed as a style of consultation, one that has value regardless of the nature or mode of consultation (Baker, Robichaud, Westforth-Dietrich, Wells, & Schreck, 2009; Parsons & Kahn, 2005). From this perspective, it appears that the least collaborative mode of consulting would be that in which the consultant provides specialized services (i.e., provisional mode), whereas the most collaborative form of consultation would be one in which the consultant and consultee engage in a coordinate relationship, mutually sharing diagnostic observation and coequally owning and developing intervention strategies. These two positions are identified as idealized poles at the extremes of the collaborative continuum, with the reality falling somewhere in between.

While serving in a provisional role, the consultant with a collaborative style seeks out the consultee's input into the specifics of what is to be provided as well as values the need to provide educative and preventive feedback to the consultee. Similarly, the consultant operating from a prescriptive stance values and employs collaborative skills to ensure that not only does the consultee understand the prescription but also values and "owns" the prescribed plan. Without such understanding and ownership, the prescribed plan will have little chance for success.

PROVISIONAL SERVICE ◄─────────► COORDINATE SERVICES

The consultant takes direction from the consultee and serves as the provider of the identified service.

The consultant and consultee coequally participate in the identification of the problem, and the creation of the interventions.

FIGURE 5.3   Continuum of Collaborative Style

The point to be made is that collaboration, as a style and process of consultation, will maximize the intervention and prevention value of the consult by engaging the consultee as much as possible, whether the focus is on prescription, provision, or mediation (see Figure 5.3).

To be effective the counselor-consultant will attempt to maximize the mutuality of input and ownership, and therefore includes elements of collaboration into each consult. This would appear to be true in the case of Tommie (see Case Illustration 5.4)

Case Illustration 5.4
Case Application—Four Modes for Tommie

To more fully appreciate the role of differentiation suggested by the previous discussion around modes of consultation, consider how a consultant might work from a provisional, prescriptive, collaborative, or mediational mode in order to service Ms. Casey.

Provisional: As an added pair of hands, the consultant might take Ms. Casey's request to "please help him to get it together" literally. As such, the provisional consultant may meet with Ms. Casey to more concretely identify what she sees as the problem and what she wants the consultant to do with Tommie. Perhaps Ms. Casey wants Tommie removed from her classroom since he is such a disruption. She may also want the consultant to see that his parents get Tommie professional help. Should the consultant modify Tommie's schedule to place him in another class and speak to the parents about professional counseling for Tommie, the consultant would be operating from a provisional mode.

Prescriptive: Being that Ms. Casey is in crisis, the consultant may respond to her need by providing suggestions on what to do with Tommie. Perhaps after getting a better understanding of the nature of the problem, the prescriptive consultant might suggest the following:

1. Ms. Casey could refer Tommie to a RTI or team meeting
2. Ms. Casey could use movies and lessons on respecting each other (provided by the consultant) as a way of helping the class modify inappropriate behavior
3. Instruct Ms. Casey to review material (provided by the consultant) on the behavior modification principles of extinction, shaping, and reinforcement so that she would be more competent and confident in applying these principles to shape Tommie's behavior

Collaborative: While each of the recommendations either enacted by the consultant in the provisional mode or provided to Ms. Casey in the prescriptive mode may have value, they were generated from only one source (either the consultee or the consultant). As a result of this unidirectional action, understanding and complete ownership of the interventions may not be shared and a second potential resource went untapped. The collaborative consultant will attempt to work with Ms. Casey to come to a joint agreement regarding the nature of the problem. As a result of their discussions, Ms. Casey and the consultant may agree that while Tommie is most likely neither an evil child nor a child with a sexual problem, his behavior in class is somewhat disruptive and should be modified. Further, from a sharing of principles of what could be done (from the consultant) and the identification of the natural conditions of the classroom environment and the procedures that have already been applied (from the consultee), a new, situation-specific application of the behavioral principles may emerge to which both the consultant and consultee had input and ownership.

Mediational: Even though the consultant has been asked to intervene in the case of Tommie and thus is reacting to a crisis, the conditions of the referral also provide a number of targets from a mediational consultation. While the immediate concern of Ms. Casey is Tommie, it is clear that the process of teacher evaluation and the eventuality of her retirement also loom as future stressors that may negatively impact her professional performance and the performance of her students. The mediational consultant will attempt to elevate Ms. Casey's awareness of the potentially detrimental effects of these possible stressors and help her begin to plan methods for reducing the harmful stress of these events and increasing her ability to cope and adjust to such stress.

The consultant in this case may want to enter the relationship with Ms. Casey at the level of provisional service, since that is what she is requesting, but would attempt to maximize the active involvement of Ms. Casey along the entire process. Including Ms. Casey's input into this process not only increases the probability of developing a successful intervention plan, one which is adapted to and reflective of the unique characteristics of the client, the consultee and the system, but also provides the avenue through which preventive programming could be initiated.

A Continuum of Student-Client Engagement

While all consultation has the goal of serving the client, the degree to which the methods employed directly involve client contact can range from a great deal to none. At one end of this continuum of client engagement we would see the counselor-consultant providing direct service to the student. Perhaps this would be a case where a teacher sent a student to the counselor because of the student's ongoing disruptive behavior within the class. The nature of the referral clearly engages the counselor in direct, one-on-one services with the student. However, as a counselor-consultant, this counselor will also reach out and work in coordination with the referring teacher to not only gather a better understanding of the nature of the issue and the conditions that may surround the disruptive behavior but to also understand the possibilities for engaging the consultee in the intervention process. This would be an example of a client-focused consultation, engaging both client and consultee within the process (see Chapter 10). At the other end of this continuum, a counselor-consultant may attempt to

CONSULTATION

DIRECT SERVICE
(ONE-TO-ONE COUNSELING) ←————————→ INDIRECT SERVICE

Client-Focused Consultation: Emphasis on intervention/remediation and tertiary prevention.

System Focused Consultation: Emphasis on prevention.

FIGURE 5.4   Expanded Focus

resolve the anger displayed by a student, not by working with the student directly but rather by engaging with administrators to change policies, procedures, and even the physical structure of the building in order to decrease the student's level of frustration and anger that results from being blocked in his ability to get to his classes on time (see Figure 5.4).

As suggested in Figure 5.4, client-focused consultation (Chapter 10) involves the highest level of direct client engagement, whereas targeting changes within the system (Chapter 12) while still attempting to affect client change will do so with no direct client contact and as such has the least amount of direct client engagement. Each of these levels requires specific diagnostic and intervention skills and as such will be discussed in greater detail in later chapters (see Chapters 10–12).

As the consultant engages more indirect modes of service delivery to the client, the potential for having an impact that expands beyond the specific student is increased. The expansive impact can be more fully illustrated by once again returning to our case of Tommie (Case Illustration 5.5).

Case Illustration 5.5
Case Application—Tommie: Many Targets, Many Goals

Again, a review of the case of Tommie (Case Illustration 5.1) might clarify this issue of how a consult could be differentially defined and approached along this dimension of problem and goal conceptualization.

In reviewing the case of Tommie, it may appear obvious that the breadth of the focus of the referral could be narrowed and restricted to working directly with Tommie or defined more broadly to include working with Ms. Casey's entire 5th grade. Further, goals may be established and intervention procedures employed that attempt to produce changes in various targets. The breadth of the intervention and purpose may be limited to an individual—for example, modifying Tommie's inattentive behavior or increasing Ms. Casey's classroom management skills. Goals and interventions could also be expanded to include changes within a group; educating the students in Ms. Casey's class about the issues of preadolescent development is one example. Or, even more broadly defined goals could include the development of institutional policies and procedures that would protect against inappropriate teacher-grade assignments or provide a system of supports for preretirement planning, peer mentoring for new assignments, curriculum change, or in-service training on child development or behavior management strategies.

Where to Start? Deciding on Form and Focus of Consultation

In assuming an integrated, multidimensional approach to consultation, the consultant enters a consultation relationship without a predetermined, fixed plan of operation. The consultant will be flexible and responsive to both the demands and the opportunities of the situation, shifting the consult in terms of its nature, focus, content, and mode, thereby sliding, if you will, along each of the continuums described above.

It is hoped that this conceptualization of consultation along these various continua will serve as a cognitive map to employ when engaging in any one consultation contract. For example, in a student-client focused consultation (Chapter 10), one that may have originated with a client problem (crisis) and a consultee who is seeking direct services (i.e., provisional and remedial), the consultant employing a multidimensional, integrated model of consulting can identify opportunities for preventive programming by targeting the changes for the consultee and/or the system to implement (i.e., prescriptive and preventive).

With so many modes of operation and points of focus possible, one may soon become overwhelmed with the role of consultant. To be effective, the consultant needs to be able to select the level of service (e.g., student-client focused, consultee focused, system focused) and the form of consulting (i.e., degree of collaboration) that will provide the greatest degree of immediate remediation and provide the highest level of prevention potential.

While there are no hard and fast rules to direct a consultant in her decisions, there are a number of considerations that could be used as guidelines when selecting the form and level of a consultation. The process of selecting a form and focus for a particular consult will be influenced by (a) the nature of the consultation contract, (b) the definition of the problem and goal, (c) the consultant's orientation, and (d) the consultee style. Each of these elements must be considered when choosing a mode, style, and focus for a consult. As such, each of these elements is described below and is expanded upon in later chapters.

The Contract as a Defining Element

It may seem obvious but the consultant's form of operation will be at least initially defined by the nature and limits of the consulting contract. The school counselor must be sensitive to requirements of the contract that defines the counselor's role and function within that system. Regardless of whether this is a formal, written contract or merely an implicit agreement between the counselor and the principal or representative of the school system, the contract establishes a number of conditions that must guide the counselor-as-consultant's choices. This may be considered a type of "informed consent" for consultation.

When reviewing the expectations of role and function, it is important to identify the degree to which the administration is open to the school-counselor employing a more indirect, consultative form of service delivery. The expectations and sanctioned forms of performing the counselor's duties will help establish the level of consultation (i.e., student-client focused, consultee focused, or system focused) that are allowed and that are preferred.

With this in mind, it is suggested that consultants approach contract formulation as an opportunity for intervention and education. Whenever possible, it is important to establish a broad-based contract that includes the consultant engaging in:

- Direct client and consultee contact along with indirect (systems) services
- Provision of services of both crises and preventive nature
- Emphasizing the value of a collaborative mode of consulting along with specifying the specific expectation of these collaborative relationships

Clearly, establishing such a broad base will allow for more flexibility in decision-making on the part of the consultant. Such an initial contract is ideal, and often the school counselor-consultant may have to work within less than ideal parameters. As will become evident throughout the remaining chapters, the process of consulting is fluid, and the effective consultant will continue to look for opportunities to reenter and even renegotiate the consultative contract so as to allow and value efforts to engage in preventive activities with systemic impact. Skills for such renegotiation and shaping the role of counselor-as-consultant will be discussed in the upcoming chapters.

The Nature of the Problem and Goal

In an ideal world, the mode of consultation, form of intervention, and style of consultation employed should all be responsive to the nature of the presenting problem, along with the nature and conditions of the goal(s) desired. However, there are many ways to conceptualize a presenting complaint. Any one presenting concern can be defined or conceptualized as one calling for student-client focused, consultee focused, or even systems focused consultation.

Thus, while the consultant could possibly define both the problem and the goal at a number of levels, with each level helping to determine the nature and direction of the consultation, the consultant needs to adjust this conceptualization in order to make it coordinate with the conceptualization and expectations held by the consultee. While there may be an optimal way of defining this or that problem and the subsequent goals, it is more important to present the problems and goals in ways that the consultee can embrace, moving from the "real" toward the "ideal" as much as possible. In the example of our disruptive student, the counselor-consultant may feel it is best for both remediation and prevention to work directly with the consultee and focus on developing different classroom management skills. However, if the consultee is fixated on the student needing to see the counselor for direct, one-on-one service, it is more effective for the counselor to engage the student directly and attempt to provide some prescription (e.g., tweaking management style) to the consultee as support for the direct service.

Consultant Orientation

As counselors, we need to be aware of our professional orientation and our worldview. We also need to be sensitive to alternative perspectives. This is especially true for the school counselor serving as counselor-consultant. It is important to remember that consultation is a triadic relationship, one occurring within a specific system and culture. The consultant needs to be aware of her own orientation and values, and be sensitive to the possibility that this professional orientation and perspective can shape the way she defines a problem and its intervention.

As consultant, the school counselor also needs to be cautious to ensure that the strategies employed address the needs of the client and those of consultee and are not merely those selected from the comfort level of the consultant. It is essential for the school counselor as consultant to be aware and respectful of the values of the client, the consultee, and the system in which they function.

Consultee Experience, Expectations, and Style

A final consideration when attempting to formulate the "what" and "how" of a consult is to identify the consultee's previous experience with consultation and how this may shape his current expectations. It is also important to understand the consultee's understanding and view of this problem, the strategies for solution, and his role in the process. Finally, as with all forms of professional helping, it is important for the counselor-consultant to understand the consultee's interpersonal and professional style so as to parallel these as much as possible within the process of consulting. The uniqueness of the consulting relationship, and the communication and dynamics involved, will be discussed in more detail in Chapter 7.

Summary

- Consultation is a multidimensional, integrated activity that takes its shape and distinctiveness by moving along a number of continua, reflecting (a) the consultee's degree of felt need, (b) the consultant's expertise, (c) the degrees of collaborative involvement, and (d) the degree of student-client engagement.
- In assuming an integrated, multidimensional approach to consultation, the consultant enters a consultation relationship without a predetermined, fixed plan of operation.
- The consultant will be flexible and responsive to both the demands and the opportunities of the situation, shifting the consult in terms of its nature, focus, content, and mode.
- Effective consultants select the level of service (e.g., student-client focused, consultee focused, system focused) and the form of consulting (i.e., degree of collaboration) which will provide the greatest degree of immediate remediation and provide the highest level of prevention potential.
- The process of selecting a form and focus for a particular consult will be influenced by (a) the nature of the consultation contract, (b) the definition of the problem and goal, (c) the consultant's orientation, and (d) the consultee style.

Additional Resources
Print

Brown, D., Pryzwansky, W. B., & Schulte, A. C. (2011). *Psychological consultation and collaboration: Introduction to theory and practice* (7th ed.). Boston, MA: Pearson.

Caplan, G., & Caplan, R. (1999). *Mental health consultation and collaboration.* Prospect Heights, Il: Waveland Press.

Dougherty, A. M. (2014). *Psychological consultation and collaboration in school and community settings* (6th ed). Belmont, CA: Brooks Cole.

Web-Based

Missouri Department of Elementary and Secondary Education. (2015). *Professional school counselor consultation guide: A professional school counselor's guide to consulting and collaborating.* Retrieved from https://dese.mo.gov/college-career-readiness/school-counseling/responsive-services

Pereza-Diltz, D. M., Moe, J. L., & Mason, K. L. (2011). An exploratory study in school counselor consultation engagement. *Journal of School Counseling, 9*(13). Retrieved from http://jsc.montana.edu/articles/v9n13.pdf

References

Baker, S., Robichaud, T., Westforth-Dietrich, V., Wells, S., & Schreck, R. (2009). School counselor consultation: A pathway to advocacy, collaboration, and leadership. *Professional School Counseling, 12*(3), 200–206.

Parsons, R. D., & Kahn, W. (2005). *The school counselor as consultant.* Belmont, CA: Thomson Brooks/Cole.

CHAPTER 6

The Process of Consultation

Well, miracles can happen. I finally got Jasmine's math teacher, Mr. B., to meet with me. I know he's got a lot going on but I really want him to work with me in trying to decide what, if anything, needs to be done for Jasmine in math class. I really need to think about this first meeting. This first meeting is key if I am going to be able to establish a collaborative relationship, one that will continue throughout the entire process. I need to really do some planning for that meeting.

———————————— ○ ————————————

The process of consulting employs many of the same skills evidenced in any counseling dynamic. From the establishment of a working alliance, through termination and the engagement of steps to ensure maintenance, consultation is at its roots, a helping process.

The current chapter will describe the stages of action characterizing the consultation process and the communication skills essential to achieving the desired outcomes. The chapter will also highlight the various forms of resistance one may expect to encounter, their source, and ways to navigate through them. Specifically, after reading this chapter, you will be able to

1. describe each of the six stages of consultation;
2. describe the focus and concerns to address at each of stage of consultation; and
3. explain the specific forms of verbal and nonverbal communication employed to develop and maintain a collaborative, mutual, and nonhierarchical consultation relationship.

Stages of Consultation

The process of consultation involves a series of specific and recognizable tasks or, if you will, stages of action. While these tasks are presented as if they were separate experiences following in a neat linear order, such is not the case in the world of application. In practice, the consultation process will often cycle in and out of various stages. Thus, while portraying each stage in a discrete, linear fashion makes it easier for this book presentation, it is not to be assumed that these stages will occur in neat, discrete, or invariant order within one's professional practice.

Stage 1/Pre-entry: Creating Conditions for Successful Consultation

As with any service provided by a school counselor, consultation requires careful consideration and planning. This planning and preparation starts well before the reception of the first request for service.

Establishing Norms and Expectations

The systemic norms that exist in a school system prescribe the expectations for the counselor's role and function in resolving school problems and achieving certain outcomes. The counselor-consultant needs to makes it clear that she approaches her duties from a collaborative perspective.

Implied in this norm is the school-wide belief that everyone who experiences a concern about a student and is making a referral to the counselor is, in fact, referring themselves as the one seeking assistance in the resolution of the situation. This is a very subtle yet important point. Whereas a teacher may assume that he is referring a student to the counselor, a school counselor engaging a consultant orientation will view the situation as a referral from and about the teacher. Yes, there is a student of concern, but in fact it is the teacher who is seeking the counselor assistance. For example, in our case of Dr. Jameson, he asked the school counselor to see Jasmine as quickly as possible. Implied in Dr. Jameson's referral is the expectation that the school counselor will take over the change process, and that Dr. Jameson's role in the process ends with the referral. The counselor in this illustration was acutely aware of the challenge. Thus, instead of seeing Jasmine for counseling or observing/diagnosing her functioning directly, the school counselor wisely chose to schedule a meeting with Dr. Jameson to discuss the referral and build a collaborative, working relationship. By meeting with Dr. Jameson first, the school counselor established the critical norms that are the foundation of collaborative consultation.

Pre-entry Considerations

Creating conditions for collaboration is the goal of pre-entry. Collaboration is developed, first of all, by informing the consultee that the counselor is a resource and not the resolution. Second, the counselor must establish and maintain an efficient and timely referral procedure that is accessible to and understood by every consumer of counseling services. Third, in every occasion that an individual refers herself to the counselor for help with a third party (i.e., the client), she needs to understand and expect that the counselor will meet with her first and that she is committing herself to a consultation relationship. Exercise 6.1 will help you consider how you may establish these norms and expectations.

Directions: To facilitate both the access to and the work with the school counselor-as-consultant, a number of pre-entry norms and expectations need to be established. Review the targets for pre-entry consideration listed below and consider steps that can be taken to achieve these goals. It may be beneficial to discuss this exercise with a practicing school counselor.

Targets: Pre-entry norm or expectation	Steps to be taken to address Target
Establishing an understanding of the difference between a consultation and a direct counseling model of service	How do teachers, parents, staff, etc. know about a consultation model? Examples: Pamphlet explaining consultation Relaying information at a faculty meeting _____ _____
Using a referral system	How do you receive referrals? Examples: Electronic or paper form Secure mailbox _____ _____
Establishing yourself as a welcoming and reliable resource	What steps and processes are employed to present yourself as a professional resource? Examples: Building rapport and trust Being flexible and helpful _____ _____

Exercise 6.1 Pre-entry Norms and Expectations

Stage 2/Entry: Establishing the Contract for Consultation

The first meeting between counselor-consultant and consultee shapes the formation of the working relationship. Each party in the consult brings a host of expectations about how the process will proceed; the criteria that will determine success and failure; and the role and function performed by the consultant, consultee, and client. How do we want to work together? What expertise and expectations do each of us bring to our cooperative problem solving and decision-making? These are the questions to be addressed as the parties enter the consultation process.

During this initial stage, it is important for the counselor-consultant to demonstrate relationship building skills, including the demonstration of accurate empathy and a non-judgmental disposition (see Table 6.1). It is important for the consultee to express her story and feel heard and understood by the consultant.

Another focus during this entry stage is for the consultant to provide clear and acceptable guidelines for when, where, how, and why the consult is to occur. The following key points are to be addressed when structuring the consultation relationship:

- Emphasize that the outcome objective of the consult is a resolution of the consultee's concern.
- Explain that, when possible, the process leading to that outcome will involve a working partnership (collaboration) between the consultant and consultee.
- Decide upon convenient times and locations for the meeting. Frequently, the best location for the meeting is in the work environment of the consultee. This increases the comfort of the consultee and sensitizes the consultant to the working conditions of the consultee.
- Each meeting will be structured with a specific purpose and agenda and can be initiated by either the consultant or consultee.
- The consultee brings valuable (expert) knowledge about the client and the environment in which the consultee and client are working. The consultant's expertise may be technical or in the facilitation of change processes. The optimal success of the consult will require the expertise of both parties.
- Any decision for the consultant to work directly with the client (for diagnostic or remedial purposes) will be made collaboratively by the consultee and consultant.
- The professional ethics of confidentiality (and privileged communication where appropriate) apply to the consultant-consultee relationship just as it would in individual counseling. The exceptions to confidentiality under Duty to Warn considerations equally apply in consultation. The consultee should be informed that whenever a threat to the consultee or client is evident, this information must be reported to the appropriate authorities (e.g., the school principal) for action.
- These structuring points can be codified into a written contract that can be discussed and signed by the consultant and consultee.

Stage 3/Exploration: Defining the Problem and Its History

As noted by Newman et al., (2017), consultants need to resist the consultee's efforts to get a "quick fix." It is essential that consultants take time to gather the data needed to accurately define the problem before rushing to intervention. This is especially true when the consultee approaches consultation from within a crisis mode.

By the time a consultee has made a referral to the school counselor, the consultee has already invested time and effort into resolving the problem. It is important for the consultant to gain a thorough understanding of the consultee's perspective on the "problem at hand" as well as the steps that he has taken to resolve the issue. Not only should the consultee's efforts be affirmed but the consultee's experience can provide the consultant will valuable information as she attempts to develop an approach to resolving the issue.

Consider the counselor who begins working with a student without having sufficient information about the student's issue and how it's an issue for the teacher. Neither the counselor not the student may know why the student is sitting in the counseling office, prompting frustration and lack of any progress, and possibly sending a message to the teacher that the counselor is not helpful at all.

During this stage, the consultant will engage those communication skills found in all helping relationships during the time of problem identification (see Parsons & Zhang, 2014). The consultant will continue to engage active reflective listening but will also employ open questions, clarifications, and summarizations as a way of assisting in the understanding of the problem. The consultee will be encouraged to describe the problem or concern as it currently exists, the relevant background and history of the problem, and all successful and unsuccessful previous efforts at problem resolution.

Gathering and Organizing the Data

Consultees will disclose a great deal of information as they "tell their story." Sometimes their exposition will be clear and well organized. When this is not the case and the consultee's description is somewhat confusing, incomplete, incongruent, or even inaccurate, the consultant should attempt to gather data that will better define the nature of the problem and the conditions contributing to its maintenance.

As with all efforts employed throughout consultation, the method for collecting data and the rationale for its collection should be collaboratively understood and embraced by both the consultant and consultee.

Stage 4/ Outcome Goals and Objectives: Moving Toward Solutions

With the consensual validation of the problem achieved, the focus of the collaboration will move from the identification of "What is happening now?" to an articulation of "How do we want things to be?" At this point, the consultation moves into the formulation of outcome goals and objectives.

In attempting to define the desired outcome for the consultation, the consultant can ask the consultee to respond to questions such as: How would you like things to be? How will you know if our consultation is successful? How could you tell if the problem no longer existed?

The Creation of Desired Outcome Goals

Outcome goals are typically presented as broad, general statements describing some desired end state. The following are typical examples of broad goal statements:

1. I'd like Frank to get along better with others.
2. Kulina needs to take more responsibility for her work.
3. I wish Todd and Jason would stop picking on Lorraine and Cheryl. They should just be kind and respectful to them.
4. Yolanda hates school. I wish she looked forward to going to school each morning.
5. Ms. Franklin's class would do so much better if she used effective classroom management.
6. We need a policy and set of procedures for dealing with bullies.

These goals lack a number of the characteristics associated with effective, achievable goals (see Parsons & Zhang, 2014). First, effective goals are specific rather than vague statements such as those listed. Second, effective goals are presented in positive terms, stating what the consultee would like to have happen or occur more frequently. Third, a critical criterion for any effective outcome goal is that it describes what the client (or consultee) will be doing as opposed to what the client will not be doing. One helpful approach in applying these criteria is to use the "Dead Person" standard. If a dead person can perform the stated outcome, then the outcome needs to be restated in doing terms. For example, if our first goal were stated as "I wish Frank would stop fighting with others," it would not meet the Dead Person criterion. A dead person could easily "stop fighting with others." In fact, a dead person never fights with others. Outcome goals need to describe the presence of something rather than the absence of something. Our third goal example, "I wish Todd and Jason would stop picking on Lorraine and Cheryl" clearly violates this criterion. If Todd and Jason were dead, they would most certainly stop picking on Lorraine and Cheryl. The next sentence, however, rectifies the violation by stating the desired outcome in the positive: "They should just be kind and respectful to them." Being kind and respectful are behaviors that Todd and Jason can do, and these new behaviors can be modeled, taught, and reinforced. And our goal for Frank might be expressed this way: "I would like to see Frank use coping strategies when he's angry." However, as you will see below, there may be other behavior to consider for Frank, hence the importance of gathering as much information about the issue as possible.

Translating Goals into Objectives

While broadly stated outcome goals begin to frame the desired outcome of a consultation, it is in reframing these goals into objectives that focus begins to emerge. Objectives describe the concrete evidence that each goal has been attained. As the concrete measure of goal attainment, the objective offers a clear, unambiguous direction for change as well as a valid means for assessing accountability for our efforts. As accountability is an important part of a comprehensive school counseling program, the data we gather from specific, measurable, realistic, and time-specified objectives are important not only to the counselor's job but also to recognizing the success of the intervention and consultation (ASCA, 2012).

Since any single goal can have multiple pieces of evidence supporting its achievement, goals typically translate into many objectives. Returning to our goals for Frank, we see that the first goal is for Frank to get along better with others. If we assume that Frank is a seven-year-old second grader (and knowledge of his age and grade will help us to formulate developmentally appropriate objectives), we can develop the following objectives and concrete manifestations of that broad goal. Frank could demonstrate getting along better with others by (a) actively participating in a language arts cooperative group activity, (b) sitting and communicating with a peer at lunch, (c) sharing play equipment with his peers at recess, and (d) expressing his needs as requests and accepting compromise. When displayed by Frank, each of these four actions provides evidence that Frank is truly "getting along with others" (i.e., Goal 1). Exercise 6.2 presents five outcome goals and asks you to formulate at least two objectives for each goal.

Directions: Formulate two objectives for the following outcome goal statements.

Goal 1. I (principal is consultee) would like the new students who transfer into our school during the year to make quick and successful adjustments.

Goal 2. I (teacher is consultee) don't like the way my Latino and African American students get along in my class. I wish they could get along and support each other.

Goal 3. I (teacher is consultee) wish the parents of my students would give them more academic support and discipline at home.

Goal 4. I (parent is consultee) have a hard time getting through to Mr. Simon (teacher). I wish he had a better understanding and more compassion about my son's learning disabilities.

Goal 5. These kids are unruly on my bus. I (bus driver is consultee) wish they would settle down and behave themselves so I can drive the bus.

Sub-Objectives: Building Upon Small Increments of Change

Once outcome objectives have been established, it is helpful to match the client's (or consultee's) current behavior with those desired outcomes. It is not uncommon to find a large gap between "what is" and "what is desired." Goal scaling is a strategy identified as useful in such a situation (Parsons, 2009a).

Goal scaling would involve the creation of a continuum, where one end of the scale, labeled as 10, represents the complete achievement of the goal. The other end of the scale represents the lowest level goal presence and is labeled 0. The next step to the process is to place the client's current behavior on the continuum in relation to the ultimate desired outcome. For example, if we scaled Frank's baseline behavior and outcome objectives along a continuum of 1 (Frank at his absolute worst) to 10 (Frank's outcome objectives), we might place Frank's current behavior at the level of 3. Any expectation that Frank will quickly perform at the level of 10 is unrealistic, and to pursue such a drastic change only sets up Frank and the consult for failure.

However, Frank may be able to demonstrate progress to the level of 4, which, in this illustration, is defined as observing him sitting quietly with his language arts cooperative group, eating lunch at the same table as his peers, shooting baskets with a peer and the recess aide, and asking his teachers for help in meeting his immediate needs. Although these behaviors do not demonstrate ultimate success for Frank and the consult, these sub-objectives are attainable and provide evidence of change in the right direction.

Reaching Consensus on Goals and Objectives

Once outcome objectives have been formulated, it is important that the consultant and consultee demonstrate a clear understanding and consensus of agreement for those outcomes. Mutual understanding and consensus are essential for the implementation of the change strategies. Unresolved differences about desired outcome objectives will impede

further collaboration and the success of the consult, while informed consensus will reinforce the collaboration, empower consultant and consultee alike, and build the foundation
for subsequent stages of the consultation.

Stage 5/Strategy Development and Implementation

With consensual agreement about the baseline and desired outcome, the consultant and
consultee are ready to address the question "What can be done to facilitate a process of
change that will move the client from baseline to the desired outcome objectives?" The
wording of this question is quite deliberate and warrants some analysis.

The first part of the question asks "What can be done?" This phrasing is meant to be
inclusive of every resource available that can help in the change process. It doesn't ask
"What can I (consultant) do?" Nor does it ask "What can you (consultee) do?" It doesn't
even ask "What can we (consultant and consultee) do?" By keeping the question inclusive,
it presumes a collaborative effort to creatively mobilize resources and strategies that will
create (facilitate) conditions for change. The initial question also presumes that change
will be a process that will move the client (and consultee) to the desired outcome. When
developing strategies, it is important to consider a few simple guidelines, described next.

Don't Reinvent the Wheel

When consultees refer to a consultant for help, they frequently feel that they have exhausted
all their ideas and resources for helping a problematic client. While the consultee may
experience a sense of failure and even hopelessness, the truth is that these same consultees
have experienced considerable success with others. As they review the current situation
and concern, it would be useful to help them revisit past success with other clients, even
if the strategies used were unique to that situation. For instance, Mr. Spitoli, Frank's sec-
ond-grade teacher, might have continually tried to lecture Frank about the value of sharing
and cooperation, only to see Frank withdraw further from others.

Coincidentally, the previous year a new student, Jerome, had enrolled in Mr. Spitoli's
class at mid-year and experienced social adjustment problems. One winter day, Jerome and
another popular student were feeling slightly ill and requested to stay in their classroom
during lunch and recess. Mr. Spitoli agreed to let the two boys eat their lunch in the classroom with him. As the lunch progressed, the two boys enjoyed a lively conversation, and
by the close of recess, Jerome had established a friendship that flourished and expanded
to other students for the remainder of the year. The opportunity for Jerome to interact
with only one student, who possessed considerable friendship and support skills, within
the safe confines of his classroom and with the support of Mr. Spitoli, enabled him to take
social risks and experience the joy of friendship and acceptance. With the help of his new
friend, Jerome's school adjustment was smooth and successful.

Unfortunately, a year later Mr. Spitoli failed to link his success with Jerome with the
problems that he was experiencing with Frank. It was only when the consultant asked him
when he had successfully worked with socially withdrawn students that he remembered
Jerome. As a result of linking a past success with a comparable, current concern, Mr. Spitoli

and the consultant were able to formulate a strategy involving a series of classroom lunches attended by Frank, a socially skilled and supportive peer, and Mr. Spitoli.

Using an Organizing Schema to Connect Diagnosis to Strategy Development

Just as the organizing schema should provide the framework for defining the problem to be addressed, it should also inform the construction of change strategies. For example, if the consultant employed a behavioral model to assess the problem, not only would the performance of a functional behavioral assessment provide the basis for defining the problem, but these data would also serve to give shape to the intervention strategy to be employed (Parsons, 2009b).

As applied with our case illustration of Frank, the consultant and consultee may introduce antecedents that make it safe and easy for Frank to "try out" some of his social skills. Frank's attempts at engaging would then be reinforced by way of the positive responses from his peer and the verbal praise from his teacher. Similarly, Mr. Spitoli could further facilitate Frank's attempts at social interaction by introducing a socially adept peer into the classroom lunches who would serve as a model for desired behavior.

Sometimes, More Is Better

In working with the consultee to identify strategies to employ, it is helpful to be creative and generate as many viable change strategies as possible. These strategies should target those that are to be implemented by both the consultee and consultant. This would be the case when, for example, working with a socially withdrawn client, the consultee adjusts her curriculum employing more team activities and the consultant, working with the same client, engages social-training interventions. Exercise 6.3 provides you with the opportunity to practice developing strategies tied to goals.

Directions: For this exercise, two colleagues or students will work together using the goals and objectives that were formulated in Exercise 6.2. The task is to review these goals and objectives and generate at least two forms of intervention, one employed by the consultee and one employed by the consultant (the school counselor).

To extend the exercise, consider an intervention that directly services the client, one that directly services the consultee, and one that services the system.

Exercise 6.3 Strategy Development and Implementation

Stage 6/Maintenance: Sustaining the Trajectory of Change

How are we doing? Are we on track to meeting our objectives? What changes have occurred? What changes still need to be made? Considering questions such as these serves as a guide to the ongoing monitoring of the effectiveness of the consultation. As the change process proceeds and strategies are formulated and employed, it is important to assess and document changes exhibited by the client and consultee. Translating outcome goals into objectives help to make assessment methodology clear. Moreover, the actual assessment procedures employed, such as observation, testing, interviewing, and surveying, will be shared by both parties in the consult.

These data attesting to change, or the absence of change, will be brought to each consultation for analyses and decision-making. When the data reveal that the trajectory of change is on track, the consult will adjust focus to be on the maintenance of successful strategies. During the maintenance phase, it is important for the consultant to provide recognition of the consultee's efforts and contributions. This recognition is helpful in facilitating the consultee's adoption of an internal locus of control regarding the process and outcome. This internalization of control is essential if the consultee is to feel empowered to act proactively and autonomously in the future.

At times the data will be disappointing, suggesting that our strategies need to be tweaked, revamped, or reconstructed entirely. Slower than expected change may indicate minor revisions in existing strategies or an agreement to lower expectations and increase patience. When the change occurs in the desired direction at a slower pace, it is often prudent to celebrate even the smallest increments of change while motivating everyone involved to stay on track and expect (look for) even more change.

When the data reveal no change or perhaps harmful effects, the following questions are helpful to answer:

- Was the real problem identified and defined?
- Could other factors, not identified during the exploration phase, be contributing to the problem?
- Could sources of resistance be operating that could mitigate change?
- Were systemic forces supportive of change mobilized?
- Were opposing forces addressed?
- Were the goals and objectives appropriate for the client, consultee, and the system?
- Were strategies created and implemented appropriate and reasonable?
- Were the strategies employed in the manner as designed?

By addressing these questions together, the consultant and consultee can review the consultation process. The answers will suggest minor or major changes to be considered collaboratively. Problem solving and decision-making about any aspect of the consultation must be the purview of both parties in the consult, with modifications in the process both expected and welcomed. Through the frequent overview of the consultation process and the contributions of each member of the consult, the foundation for successful termination is created.

Stage 7/Termination: Linking Past, Present, and Future

At some point in the consultation process, the review of the data will confirm the achievement of the outcome objectives. Or, the existing data will show sufficient progress, prompting the consultant and consultee to consider termination of the consult. In either instance, the decision to terminate should be consensual. In moving toward termination of the consultation, it is important for the consultant to engage the consultee around the following questions:

1. What did we accomplish?
2. How did we do it?
3. What did each of us contribute?
4. What actions can be taken to sustain the progress made?
5. What did we learn for the future?

By answering these five questions collaboratively, the consultant will have the opportunity to review and reinforce successful elements of the change process as well as the method employed to guide the process.

Communication Skills Essential to Collaboration

Like all forms of helping communication skills, those fostering the development of a collaborative helping relationship are essential to the mediation of consultation outcomes (Erchul, Grissom, Getty, & Bennett, 2014; Newman, Guiney, & Barrett, 2017). As is obvious, the effective use of helping communications, including open-ended questions, reflections, summarization, and even confrontation (see Parsons & Zhang, 2014), are fundamental to the development of an effective consultation relationship.

However, the collaborative nature of that relationship invites the use of additional communication skills. As noted, a collaborative relationship is one in which there is a mutual, nonhierarchical relationship where both the consultant and consultee participate and coequally own the results of the interaction. Maintaining this mutual, nonhierarchical, and coparticipative relationship is not always easy. The effective consultant will be aware of potential pitfalls as well as the forms of communication that facilitate a collaborative interaction.

Communicating to Foster Mutual, Nonhierarchical Involvement

The consultant, as an expert in the specific form of problem solving desired by the consultee, is responsible for the direction of the interaction. However, while retaining this control, the effective consultant employs nonverbal and verbal techniques aimed at developing and maintaining a sense of mutuality within the relationship.

Employing Nonverbals

One interviewing technique suggested by Gerald Caplan (Caplan & Caplan, 1993) is to sit beside, as opposed to opposite, the consultee. This positioning gives nonverbal support to the psychological tone the consultant is trying to attain. In sitting side-by-side, the message conveyed is that this consultation will be an "elbow-to-elbow," mutual problem-solving venture. Rather than sitting across from one another in a role of problem teller (i.e., the consultee) and problem solver (i.e., the consultant), the side-by-side posture suggests a mutuality to both the understanding and resolution of the problem.

Verbally Communicating a Desire for Nonhierarchical, Mutual Involvement

In addition to directly asking and encouraging the consultee to freely and actively contribute to the consultation process, the consultant can actively engage the consultee by the judicious use of questions. The use of questions is a primary tool for engaging the consultee in the consultation (Caplan & Caplan, 1993). Rather than giving immediate advice and direction, the consultant seeking to maintain a collaborative relationship will attempt to engage the consultee in joint "pondering" over the nature of the problem at hand as well as the options available for intervention. This invitation to the consultee to join with the consultant in pondering, reflecting, and considering the issues at hand is important to the development of the collaborative relationship. The consultant, seeking collaboration, must resist the tendency to provide solutions, directions, and answers. Rather than directing and resolving, the consultant seeking collaboration will ask questions. Asking questions such as "I wonder if...," "Do you have any ideas about...," and "Any suggestions for..." elicits active participation by the consultee and creates the sense of mutuality within the relationship.

Another technique to build a collaborative relationship is to engage in "we" language rather than "I" language (Rosenfield, 2012). The use of "we" not only highlights the shared, coequal relationship and engagement in the process of consultation but also builds a bond and cohesiveness between consultant and consultee.

The importance of engaging in both verbal and nonverbal communication of a nonhierarchical nature is illustrated in Case Illustration 6.1.

Case Illustration 6.1
Handling Power Differentials

The Background

Tom is a counselor working for an agency that contracts services to schools. He has been requested to attend a child study team meeting at a local school. Tom has been fortunate to have inherited a significant amount of family money, and for this meeting he wore a $1000 handmade suit, Italian shoes, and exquisite gold jewelry. Tom parked his European sports car in the visitor's spot. He exited his car carrying his monogrammed Gucci attaché case.

Entering the building, Tom noted that while everyone was neatly groomed, the dress was informal. All the members of the team dressed in sweaters or casual blouses and slacks. The principal was wearing a corduroy sports coat, open-collar shirt, and khaki pants. Being aware of the obvious differences in dress and the potential that such may convey a less than a nonhierarchical relationship, Tom made the following adjustments in an attempt to lessen the status and power differentials.

1. Rather than making physical gestures, such as straightening French cuffs on the shirt to highlight the fact that the shirt was handmade and the cufflinks had real diamonds, he decided to remove the coat ASAP, undo his tie, and roll up his sleeves.
2. Instead of placing his Gucci attaché on top of the table, he kept it on the floor and brought materials up to table without the gold pen or leather binder.

3. He was very mindful not to make hand gestures that would highlight his manicured fingernails and his Rolex watch.
4. Finally, remaining professional in tone and language, he attempted to incorporate words and images employed by the consultee.

It certainly would have been advisable for our consultant, Tom, to have done some homework regarding the culture and manner of dress for the setting in which he was about to consult. It becomes clear that even when artifacts of power and status are present, the consultant can do some things to de-emphasize the power differential they may suggest.

Integrating Stages, Purpose, and Communication Skills

Now that we have looked at the purposes of consultation and the communication skills required of the consultant in achieving those purposes, it is helpful to place both purposes and skills within the context of the consultation process. The following matrix, which was

TABLE 6.1 **Communication Skills in Consultation**

STAGES	PURPOSES	SKILLS
Pre-entry	Provide Information	Written/Verbal Directives
Entry	Provide Information Support & Reassure Persuade & Influence Empathy & Rapport Instruction	Written/Verbal Directives Open & Closed Questions All Reflective Listening
Exploration	Obtain Information Provide Information Affirm & Reinforce Empathy & Rapport Creative Data Gather Instruction	All Active Listening Tacting Leads Summarization
Goal Formulation	Obtain Information Affirm & Reinforce Persuade & Influence Creative Data Gather Instruction	All Active Listening Tacting Leads Summarization Written/Verbal Directives
Strategy Develop & Implement	Obtain Information Provide Information Creative Data Gather Persuade & Influence Instruction	All Active Listening Tacting Leads Written/Verbal Directives
Maintenance	Provide Information Obtain Information Affirm & Reinforce	All Active Listening Written/Verbal Directives
Termination	Affirm & Reinforce Obtain Information Instruction	All Active Listening Summarization Written/Verbal Directives

first presented by Parsons and Kahn (2005), attempts to link the purposes, communication skills, and stages. Although the matrix can only provide a general overview of these connections, it should help you to appreciate that the communication skills of the consultant are varied, complex, and always purposeful.

Summary

- The process of consultation involves a series of specific and recognizable tasks or stages of action.
- The consultation process will often cycle in and out of various stages rather than neatly proceed through each in a linear fashion.
- The pre-entry is where norms and expectations of a collaborative relationship are addressed.
- At entry, the consultant and consultee will define the specific contract for consultation, including the nature of the mutual relationship and the desired outcomes.
- Once engaged in the consultation, the consultee and consultant will explore the presenting concern and its history as well as the previous strategies employed to address the issue.
- Goals and outcomes are developed, agreed upon, and formulated in a way that promotes their assessment.
- All strategies developed reflect the contribution and perspective of both the consultee and the consultant.
- Throughout the stages of consultation, the use of fundamental helping skills along with verbal and nonverbal conveyance of a collaborative relationship is essential to success.

Additional Resources

Print

Green, B. L., Everheart, M., Gordon, L., & Gettman, M. G. (2006). Characteristics of effective mental health consultation in early childhood settings. *Topics in Early Childhood Special Education, 26*(3), 142–152.

Kampwirth, T. J. (2006). *Collaborative consultation in the schools.* (3rd ed.). Upper Saddle River, NJ: Merrill.

Rosenfield, S. (2004). Consultation as dialogue: The right words at the right time. In N. M. Lambert, I. Hylander, & J. H. Sandoval (Eds.), *Consultee-centered consultation: Improving the quality of professional services in organizations* (pp. 337–347). Mahwah, NJ: Erlbaum.

Web-Based

Jhangiani, R., & Tarry, H. (2014). Changing attitudes through persuasion. In C. Stangor, *Principles of Social Psychology: 1st International Edition.* Retrieved from https://opentextbc.ca/socialpsychology/chapter/changing-attitudes-through-persuasion/

School Psychologist Files. (2018). *Consultation.* Retrieved from http://schoolpsychologistfiles.com/consultation/

References

American School Counselor Association (ASCA). (2012). *The ASCA national model: A framework for comprehensive school counseling programs* (3rd ed.). Alexandria, VA: Author.

Caplan, G., & Caplan. R. (1993). *Mental health consultation and collaboration*. San Francisco, CA: Jossey-Bass.

Erchul, W. P., Grissom, P. F., Getty, K. C., & Bennett, M. S. (2014). Researching interpersonal influence within school consultation: Social power base and relational communication perspectives. In W. P. Erchul & S. M. Sheridan (Eds.), *Handbook of research in school consultation* (2nd ed., pp. 349–385). New York, NY: Routledge.

Newman, D. S., Guiney, M. C., & Barrett, C. A. (2017). Language in consultation: The Effect of affect and verb tense. *Psychology in the Schools, 54*(6), 624–639.

Newman, D. S., McKenney, E. L. W., Silva, A. E., Clare, M., Salmon, D., & Jackson, S. (2017). A qualitative meta-synthesis of consultation process research: What we know and where to go. *Journal of Educational and Psychological Consultation, 27*, 13–51.

Parsons, R. D. (2009a). *Thinking and acting like a solution-focused school counselor*. Thousand Oaks, CA: Corwin.

Parsons, R. D. (2009b). *Thinking and acting like a behavioral school counselor*. Thousand Oaks, CA: Corwin.

Parsons, R. D., & Kahn, W. J. (2005). *The school counselor as consultant*. Belmont, CA: Thomson/Brooks-Cole.

Parsons, R. D., & Zhang, N. (2014). *Becoming a skilled counselor*. Thousand Oaks, CA: SAGE.

Rosenfield, S. (Ed.). (2012). *Becoming a school consultant: Lessons learned*. New York, NY: Routledge.

CHAPTER 7

Counselors as Agents for Change

I just got back from the ASCA conference and the message was loud and clear. As school counselors, we need to step up and lead. We need to advocate for all students and we need to actively create change that removes barriers to our students' success. It's easier to recognize when someone like Jasmine needs help because she's acting out, but I need to look out for all students! The conference was exhilarating...but scary, as well.

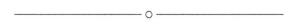

These opening reflections of a school counselor, while highlighting the need to be an agent of change, fail to note that she has been a change agent throughout her career. Perhaps when we think of school counselors, our first thoughts may not take us to an image of an agent of change, and yet upon reflection, that is exactly what we are. The student who is in pain and who seeks assistance from a counselor clearly expects that things will be different (better) as a result of their interaction with the school counselor. The same is true for the parent or teacher who reaches out to the school counselor in regards to a student of concern. Whether specifying it directly or not, change is what is desired, and change is and has been that which is offered by the school counselor.

Placed within the context of the school counselor as consultant, one who operates from an ecological systemic view, the focus and breadth of change is expanded. No longer will the counselor-consultant be satisfied with "adjusting" the client to the circumstance but rather will attempt to adjust the circumstance in support of the client and all others functioning within that context. As such, by definition the effective counselor-consultant will affect change in the client, the consultee, the school, and the community (American School Counselor Association (ASCA), 2012; Center for School Counseling Outcome Research and Evaluation (CSCORE), 2011; Chen-Hayes, 2007; Holcomb-McCoy & Chen-Hayes, 2011; National Office for School Counselor Advocacy (NOSCA), 2011).

The current chapter provides a look at the dynamics involved in the process of instituting innovation and change within an organization or system. The chapter will highlight the role of the consultant as one of change agent and innovator. Further, the chapter will discuss the basis of resistance often encountered by agents of change and provide a model for initiating change in the face of such potential resistance.

After completing this chapter, the reader should be able to

1. explain how the role of consultant is inevitably one of change and innovation;
2. describe how consultation is a process advocating for both the system and the client;
3. explain the basis for system resistance to change; and
4. describe the principles of diffusion of innovation, which may help to reduce resistance and facilitate change.

Inevitably Impacting the System

In Chapter 2, we introduced the idea that the effective school counselor employed an ecological, systemic perspective when providing service to students. We further affirmed the position offered by the Education Trust (2009) that the role of the school counselor is to reduce environmental and institutional barriers that impede student academic success.

Such an ecological, systemic orientation by its very nature suggests that the work of a school counselor with any one student will have an additional impact on the system in which that student is attempting to function.

It is assumed that the student's behavior and academic achievement occurs within the context of his psycho-social-physical environment. As such, to be effective, the school counselor-consultant needs to focus not just on the student's intrapersonal dynamics but also on the extrapersonal factors (e.g., the role of the consultee, the tasks assigned, and the environment) contributing to the existence and maintenance of the current problem.

Members of the school, along with the processes, structures, procedures, and products found within the school as a system, are by definition interdependent. Therefore, efforts taken to effect change in the student-as client, or the teacher as consultee, or any one of these processes or structure elements will effect change within the system as a whole. Changes that impact more than a client are said to effect a greater breadth of change.

For example, consider the situation in which our counselor-consultant helps a student develop assertiveness skills. By providing this student with the skills and belief structures needed to assert her needs, the counselor is impacting the system. Just consider how her change in attitude and behavior will impact her relationships with friends, family, teachers, and other people who are significant in her life. Or, consider the situation in which a counselor runs a group on nonviolent conflict resolution. What happens when these students attempt to use their problem-solving skills when encountering a disagreement with a teacher or an administrator? Providing these capabilities to one element of the system, the students set in motion the wheels of change within the system.

Perhaps when you think of organizational change or system innovation, you envision massive reallocation of resources or realignment of structures and processes. While such a focus on the exosystem is at times warranted and may feel outside of the competency of the school counselor, system change comes in many forms, some less dramatic, less encompassing than others, and many falling clearly within the skill and job domain of our school counselor-consultant. To be a leader and an agent of change is the directive given by the American School Counseling Association (2012; 2003). Counselors are directed to serve as advocates focusing on (a) eliminating barriers impeding students' development, (b) creating opportunities to learn for all students, (c) ensuring access to a quality school curriculum, (d) collaborating with others within and outside the school to help students meet their needs, and (e) promoting positive systemic change in schools (ASCA, 2014).

Advocating for Client *and* System

School counselors are sometimes given a difficult choice when presented with the question of who is their client. Are they there to help the student or is their primary responsibility to serve the school? Often it seems that counselors are expected to "fit" the student into the system or, if that is not possible, perhaps arrange for the removal or placement of this student. At other times, the counselor is presented as the advocate and in a more derogatory fashion the "bleeding heart" for the struggling student who wants everyone else to accommodate the student. This may place the counselor into an adversarial position with teachers and administrators.

Presenting the issue as either the student or the school is truly a false dichotomy. The counselor-as-consultant need not be in an adversarial role pitted against the "system." It is possible to be an advocate for both the student-client and the school system. Advocating for the student is advocating for the system *if* we assume the system's mission, that is, its reason for existence, is to educate and facilitate the development of its student population.

Advocate and Adversary?

It is not unusual for one to assume that an advocate for one party or position is by definition the adversary of another party or position. The role of an advocate is often presented as one that promotes a position that benefits some while being to the detriment of others. The advocate in this orientation attempts to gain advantage for her constituency at the expense of some others. When applied to the school counselor as consultant, such a perspective would lead one to conclude that the counselor-consultant's efforts on behalf of her student will come at the expense of the teacher and administration. The teacher will have to adjust their approach to teaching and classroom management. Or, the administration will have to provide additional services. This perspective places the school counselor-consultant in an adversarial role with others within the school and will ultimately prove detrimental to the student and the effectiveness of the counselor-consultant.

The question, of course, is whether the school counselor's advocacy by definition places him within an adversarial role with others within the system. The answer is no. The school counselor can be an advocate, can even be adversarial, when what he is advocating for is the embodiment and fulfillment of the school's mission, its purpose, and its clear goals.

Advocate for the Mission

The school counselor as a consultant will serve as an advocate, not for individual student's likes and dislikes but rather, as noted by ASCA (2012; 2003), for the elimination of barriers impeding students' development and the creation of opportunities to learn for all students. This role for the counselor is in line with the reason our schools exist, that is, the creation of opportunities for student academic achievement and development.

The model of consultation presented here does not oppose the client with others in the system. It is not a matter of student versus teacher or teacher versus administration. The student-client is an interdependent part of the system, just as the consultee is a part of the system. Change in the client, change in the consultee, or change in the process and structure of the system are all innovations in the system and, if aimed at facilitating the school's achievement of its purpose and goals, are not adversarial (Parsons, 1996). Each is intended to better serve the system as well as all of those involved as they attempt to fulfill the mission of that system. Consultation, as presented here, is advocacy for both client and system. Such a point of advocacy can be seen in the efforts of one sixth grade counselor (Case Illustration 7.1).

Case Illustration 7.1
Mission Accomplished?

Mr. Starkey is the physical education teacher at Liberty Middle School. He is very proud of his program and how the curriculum includes an emphasis on teamwork. The school and district mission statements both highlight the value of "developing responsible and collaborative students," and he strives to create a community feeling in his classes.

Mr. Starkey went to see Mr. Clifton, the sixth-grade school counselor, about Zack, a student in his class. Mr. Starkey explained that Zack's grade was dropping because he was not coming to gym in his gym clothes. Mr. Starkey thought that perhaps Zack was refusing to change in the locker room with the others, betting that he was the smallest student in the sixth grade. Mr. Starkey was confused about Zack's resistance since he felt that he developed a safe and team-oriented environment. Mr. Clifton asked if Mr. Starkey had spoken to Zack in regard to the issue, and Mr. Starkey responded that he had not yet done so but would be happy to talk to him that very afternoon.

When Mr. Starkey checked in with Zack, he learned to his surprise that it wasn't an issue about his size but rather that Zack had difficulty using the combination lock in the locker rooms. Zack has poor fine motor skills and a form of dyslexia, which causes him to see blurry and inaccurate letters and numbers. Upon hearing this information, the counselor, Mr. Clifton, went to the principal to ask if the type of lock could be changed in order for Zack, and other students who may have difficulty using the combination lock, to more easily and fully participate in physical education class. Mr. Clifton made the point that not only would this change be an appropriate modification for students with disabilities but it would also be responsive in supporting the achievement of the school (and district) mission by enabling the students to be more self-responsible.

TABLE 7.1   **Using MTSS**

School counselors are involved with the development and implementation of a multitiered support system, continually collaborating with others to identify student need and remove barriers to learning. Using the information from Case Illustration 7.1, the following table shows an example of how MTSS may be utilized.

SUPPORT TIER	EXAMPLE OF SUPPORT
Tier 1: Preventive interventions for all students	Orientation for all students to practice opening locks. Supplying easy-access locks for all students.
Tier 2: Interventions for students at some risk	Small group counseling for assertion training for Zack and other students who need to self-advocate.
Tier 3: Intensive, individual interventions for students at high risk	Exploration of other unknown barriers Zack may be encountering due to his disabilities to prevent academic failure.

Collaborating with school personnel and parents, and advocating to remove barriers so all students have an equitable education, is a mainstay for school counselors (ASCA, 2014). The model of consultation described here lends itself to fulfilling these charges using the frameworks for intervention implementation referred to as multitiered support systems (MTSS) and one of its subsystems, response to intervention (RTI). An example of these initiatives using the information in Case Illustration 7.1 is shown in Table 7.1.

When Goals Conflict

The idea of the counselor as an advocate for system and client is based on the assumption that the goals of the system and those of the individual are not antagonistic. In this situation, the consultant who is facilitating the development and healthy functioning of the individual within the system is also increasing the health of the system. Further, by improving the organizational structure and processes so they are more in line and in service of the mission, it is assumed that the goals of the individual will find a context that is more supportive and facilitative.

Although it is desirable for a consultant to work with systems in which he feels congruent with both mission and goals, sometimes this is either not possible or not readily apparent. When the consultee or systems members are actively engaged in unethical or illegal behaviors, then clearly the consultant must confront these behaviors and terminate contracts when they are not ceased.

Although very few counselors will experience situations in which there is a gross violation of ethical or legal principles, many may encounter systems in which the goals and processes, while not so radically incongruent with their own, may create conflict between the organization and the individuals within, as seen in Case 7.1. Such conflict interferes with the system's goal attainment. Change in the individual, the system, or both is needed, and change that results in reduced conflict and increased harmony is the type of goal-directed change suggested here.

At times, the school counselor as a consultant will advocate for system change. When, for example, the school's functioning, decision-making, and communication processes are incongruent with its own mission and goals, the counselor-consultant acting as a change agent will address these incongruences. Helping those in administration realign the way the system is operating to bring the system in line with its goals will have a positive impact on all of those within the system, including the student or students of concern.

Resistance: Change Is Not Always Easy

Whether it is the individual student, a teacher, an administrator, or the system as a whole, surrendering the way things are done and adopting a new approach is not comfortable and at times is outright resisted (Burke, 2008; Boohene & Williams, 2012). To facilitate change, regardless of the level at which the resistance is encountered (i.e., client or system), the school counselor as consultant needs to understand the fundamental conditions supporting resistance and be skilled in the employment of principles that facilitate the adoption of change and the diffusion of innovation.

Some common reasons for resistance to change within organizations include felt loss and desire for self-preservation, threats to power or influence, personal cost and inconvenience, and fear of the unknown (Lunenburg & Ornstein, 2008; Mullins, 2005; Robbins & Judge, 2009).

Resistance as Self-Preservation

As counselors, we all can attest to the resistance we often encounter when attempting to help students develop a new perspective or set of behaviors. Even when their current approach is less than optimal and may even be causing them discomfort, letting go of what is done and embracing a new approach is not always easy. This same sense of maintaining the status quo as a form of resistance to change can be seen when attempting to stimulate change within a system.

Systems, like individuals, develop a pattern that has come to serve, or at least has previously served, its needs. These processes and, in the case of systems, the structures that support these processes become that which is expected, even when they become less than useful. There is in systems, as in individuals, a desire to maintain stability, a homeostasis, and as a result, a reluctance, if not outright resistance, to surrendering the old for the new is often encountered by those attempting to invite systemic change.

In looking at a system, it becomes clear that over time the system employs its resources for two ends. Some energy and resources are deployed to continue its mission-driven activities. Other resources, however, are redirected to maintain the system's structure and function. With the goals of self-maintenance or system preservation in mind, systems create organizational structures, role definitions, formal lines of communications, and a variety of procedures and policies aimed at keeping the style of operation and current character in its present form and configuration. Thus, where once change, adaptation, and flexibility were the rules of the day, now innovation, experimentation, and change are not only ignored but actively resisted. Change is viewed as a threat not just to the organization's stability but to its very identity, it's very existence. Any force, person, or idea that would indicate that the existing system is changed, be it as minute as expanding or modifying a job definition or as complicated as decentralizing the form of management or modifying curriculum, will run contrary to this self-maintenance goal and evoke system self-preservation resistance.

Specific Conditions Stimulating Resistance

While any change may evoke a self-preservation response and thus system resistance, four specific conditions can actively evoke system resistance. These conditions involve change that threatens the balance of power, suggests the risk of sunken costs, creates miscommunications, or challenges group norms (Kast & Rosenzweig, 1974). Understanding and ameliorating these conditions is essential if the counselor-consultant is to be an effective agent of change.

Threats to the Balance of Power

A primary source of resistance is the fear that innovation will upset the balance of power between the various subgroups existing within the system. Consider the situation where the counselor-as-consultant attempts to promote a change in the way children with special needs are included in the school's curriculum and activities. If the innovation is perceived as giving those faculty and staff in special education added resources or power to direct curriculum, it may arouse resistance from faculty and staff in general education departments. This resistance may be further supported by parents who view a shift in the utilization of school resources, and therefore tax dollars, to the needs of particular children to be a cost and detriment to other children.

Innovations that appear to be to the benefit of all members of the system, or innovations that require the least amount of loss of power to any one, will be the innovations that meet the least resistance. Counselors working from a consultation perspective need to be sensitive to the different constituencies within the system and the perceived impact their recommendations and innovations may have on each constituent's role, function, and power.

Sunk Costs

In systems such as schools where resources are limited, there is always concern over the way these limited resources, be they time, energy or capital, are to be utilized. Thus, a consultant seeking to introduce change and innovation may be perceived as expending school resources on a yet to be proven program or process. From this perspective, it is viewed as a cost without return. Without a clear sign of the payoff this innovation will accrue, these costs that are real and immediate are viewed as sunken, without return. Naturally, such a perception of cost without a return will stimulate resistance.

The counselor-consultant seeking to stimulate change and innovation needs to be sensitive to this type of "cost" perception. With this in mind, the counselor-consultant needs to introduce change in a way that keeps costs, including tangible costs such as expenditure of resources and time as well as psychological costs including stress, frustration, and anxiety, to a minimum. The successful consultant will be able to demonstrate real, concrete, and, where possible, immediate payoffs or returns on the investment in change. With such a reduction of cost and the experience of gains, resistance will be reduced.

Miscommunications

Quite often the individuals who are aware of the need (and potential benefit of change) fail to communicate the need and nature of the change in ways that can be understood and accepted by others within the system. Rumors, miscommunication, and conflicting data elevate system anxiety and confusion and, with it, increased resistance (Lewis, 2000). It is not unusual to hear that a counselor's request to visit a classroom to observe a student is a ruse for evaluating the teacher or that a counselor who is attempting to facilitate the inclusion of a student with special needs into a particular class is in fact attempting to open the floodgates and eventually move all the children with unique needs to that classroom.

These misperceptions need to be corrected, and steps need to be taken early in consultation to reduce the possibility of their occurrence. It is important for the consultant to communicate the need, the purpose, and the process of the consultation to all involved (Lewis, 1999). With a fuller understanding of the need and what the process will entail, misunderstanding and needless anxiety will be reduced and with it a reduction in resistance.

Protecting Tradition

A fourth source of resistance to innovation stems from a desire to maintain and defend tradition. In many schools, the culture is rich with history. The way things are done have long historical roots, and often those within the system value the way things are done, just because it is the way we always have done it. A tradition is a powerful base for resistance. Change is a risk, especially if the traditional way of doing things has worked pretty well, but when change is viewed as a challenge to a procedure that has become normative, almost sacred, resistance will be maximized.

Quite often, the original reason for a particular process or procedure may have long passed, and in fact, those involved with the original decision to employ such a process or procedure may no longer be around, yet tradition can dictate that it be continued. It is not so much that the process is viewed as having much value; it is simply that the process is a part of the system's identity or "the way we do things." Tampering with this process may be mistakenly interpreted as tampering with the system's identity and thus elicit system resistance.

For example, consider the experience of Mr. Alverston, the ninth-grade counselor at Eagleville High. Mr. Alverston is in his first year at Eagleville, having worked in a nearby district for the past seven years. Over the course of his first semester, Mr. Alverston became aware of a large number of students who were being suspended. It appears that Eagleville is known for its "no-nonsense" approach to discipline. Further, the previous dean of students (who retired last year) had developed a strict disciplinary code, which included the use of internal and external suspensions for a variety of offenses.

In working with some of the students, Mr. Alverston began to realize that this strict approach, while perhaps having some value for some students, was impacting many of the students in a very negative way. Students who had previously not demonstrated a history of school offenses were developing a negative, hostile attitude to what they perceived to be an overly oppressive system.

In an attempt to reduce this negative perception among students as well as reduce this high rate of suspension, Mr. Alverston attempted to incorporate a peer court system, which he had found extremely effective at his previous school. The proposal included a process where students who were facing suspension could have the option to go to Student Court rather than directly to the dean of students. For those choosing the Student Court, their case would be reviewed by a select body of their peers, and if found in violation, the court of peers would assign some form of consequence. These consequences could include those previously dictated under the code of conduct; a referral to the dean of students; or the assignment of the student to do some form of school-based service.

Mr. Alverston suggested that rather than simply removing the students from classes, as was the procedure with in-house and external suspension, it would be more productive to assign these violators to prosocial activities, such as tutoring, helping with the recycling of school refuse, or participating in one of the school's after school programs. Mr. Alverston suggested that this Student Court approach would help the students understand the value of the school code and give them opportunities to engage in prosocial activity rather than merely being removed from the school, which for some was a positive experience.

While the proposal was well thought out, Mr. Alverston immediately began to experience resistance, not just from the dean of students, but from the principal and most of the faculty. When asked what the point of objection was, most were hard pressed to provide an answer other than to simply state that the dean of students always enforced the code.

For the counselor-consultant confronted with resistance based in tradition, the goal is not to compete with tradition or in any way attempt to demean the status quo. Instead, the consultant should attempt to offer change as an alternative or suggest a minor adjustment that can be used to affirm the value of the traditional way (Brown, Blackurn, & Powell, 1979). In this situation, where the dean of students had traditionally been the court of no appeal, returning power to the dean would be essential. Thus, Mr. Alverston revised the original proposal, suggesting that rather than the counselor or the students deciding on who would have the opportunity to have their case heard by the Student Court, it would be up to the dean of students. Further, Mr. Alverston proposed that this option could be employed for those students having minor offenses and that such a process may reduce the amount of time the dean had to spend with these cases, allowing him more time and energy for the more serious cases. While this was but a small step in modifying the discipline system at Eagleville High, it was an introduction of innovation that no longer threatened the tradition of empowering the dean of students as the school's disciplinarian and as such was accepted as a pilot program.

Even though school counselors have the creativity and insight to develop wonderful programs for remediating and even preventing potentially problematic situations, it must be remembered that these programs are only as good as their implementation. Further, for a program to be successfully applied, it must be embraced by those responsible for its implementation. Therefore, to be successful, a counselor-consultant will not only need to recognize sources of resistance but will also need to employ techniques and strategies that engage all significant players in the ownership of the suggested changes and thus reduce these forms of resistance.

Promoting Innovation

As an agent of change, the school counselor operates within two different systems. The first system is that which currently exists. It is the way things currently operate, and it is the one that the counselor is seeking to change. The second system is that which the counselor is attempting to create. It may only be a system with a minor adjustment or change from that which is, but it is a change, and it is different than the status quo.

This second system is envisioned to have a way of operating that will make it more effective than that which is or will in some way reduce the problem currently encountered by the counselor operating within the old system. But for this change to be effectively implemented, the counselor-consultant needs to act as the bridge between these two systems of "what is" and "what is hoped." The consultant will need to employ strategies and techniques that reduce the system's resistance to innovation and bring these systems in line so that the new information, program, or process can be disseminated and accepted.

There are a variety of models of planned change (Argyris, 1970; Bartunek & Louis, 1988; Ellsworth, 2000; French & Bell, 1990; Mohrman, Mohrman, Ledord, Cummings, Lawler & Associates, 1989; Schmuck & Runkel, 1985). However, five principles culled from the classical work of Rogers and Shoemaker (1971) appear to be particularly useful for the school-counselor attempting to introduce innovation and change. The principles are (1) keep innovations culturally compatible, (2) introduce change in small steps, (3) align change with opinion leaders, (4) increase consultant power and value, and (5) move in a crisis.

Principle 1: Keep Innovation Culturally Compatible

Acting as a bridge between the old system of status quo and that of innovation, the counselor-consultant needs to understand the original system's norms and values. Further, the consultant seeking to diffuse innovation needs to shape and form the innovation in ways that make it compatible with these existing norms and values (Eldridge, 2001). To introduce change that is compatible to the existing system culture, the counselor-consultant needs to shape that innovation in a way that

1. is in line with the mission and purpose of the system;
2. at a minimum, approximates the operating values and norms; and
3. is sensitive to the unique internal and external forces or pressures impacting the system, as well as to the unique history and tradition that may be affected by the change.

Case 7.2 (Dwayne, the Attention Seeker) will help to more fully demonstrate the importance of this principle.

Case Illustration 7.2
Dwayne, the Attention Seeker

The fifth-grade teacher at J. R. Turnball Elementary School requested to meet with the counselor. It appeared that over the course of the last five weeks, Dwayne, a fifth-grade student, had been calling out in class and making inappropriate "animal noises." The teacher, Ms. Zaborowski, reported employing a number of techniques to stop Dwayne but all have proven unsuccessful. The teacher noted that she has (1) verbally chastised Dwayne when he called out, (2) kept him in at recess, (3) made him take his seat out in the hallway, and (4) even threatened to send him to the principal.

In observing the class, the counselor-consultant noted that Dwayne was isolated from the rest of his classmates. Whereas the other class members worked in groups on learning projects, Dwayne sat at his desk working on individual worksheets. When asked as to the reason for this classroom arrangement, the teacher reported that this was a result of Dwayne's disruptive behavior in the learning groups.

The counselor-consultant also observed that the teacher, who was in her first year of teaching, exhibited a lot of energy and enthusiasm, going from table to table to work with the different groups of students. However, it was only when Dwayne called out or made an "animal noise" that she would attend to him.

Following upon these observations, the consultant suggested to the teacher that Dwayne was simply seeking attention and that her chastising and negative attending were actually reinforcing Dwayne's inappropriate behavior. The consultant recommended that the teacher begin to ignore Dwayne's inappropriate behavior (as a process of extinction) and begin to praise Dwayne when he was working on his worksheets (as an attempt to shape appropriate behavior). The teacher understood the concepts of shaping, extinction, and reinforcement, and said she would try.

The recommendation failed. Dwayne's behavior grew more disruptive, and the teacher lost confidence in the consultant. When the consultant followed up on the recommendation, she found that the teacher failed to stick with the "agreed-upon plan."

In order to understand what happened, one needs to understand the basic profile of the system in which the innovation was introduced.

Ms. Z's fifth-grade class was in a private elementary school. Among the many things the school valued and attempted to promote were respect, self-control, obedience to authority, order, and compliance. Further, a norm operating within the system was that each classroom and its management was the responsibility of its teacher and that a good class (and thus a good teacher) was one in which the children were quietly working on tasks, and the teacher was actively in control. The intervention recommended by the counselor-consultant, while theoretically sound, has a number of unique dimensions that seem incompatible with the culture of this school and therefore made the recommendation unacceptable to the consultee (i.e., Ms. Z).

Behavior that was intermittently reinforced and that is now undergoing an extinction process at first tends to increase in frequency and intensity. As such, the recommendation made by the consultant to ignore Dwayne's inappropriate behavior led to an increase in the disruptive behavior. This rise in Dwayne's calling out was in direct violation of the norm of working quietly. Further, the fact that compliance, obedience, and authority are valued, and the teacher is expected to be in control, appeared to run contrary to the consultant's request for the teacher to ignore (or as she explained, "do nothing") when Dwayne acted out. Because of the felt incompatibility of the innovation with the norms and values of her own system's culture, the teacher simply failed to follow through.

Exercise 7.1 provides you with practice in creating interventions that are culturally compatible with the target system.

Directions: Below you will find a brief case presentation. After analyzing the presenting concerns along with the description of a number of specific system characteristics, review each of the intervention plans suggested. With a colleague, classmate, or supervisor, discuss the degree to which each intervention is compatible or incompatible with the current system profile. Which of the interventions provided would be most compatible? Could you create a fourth intervention that would be even more compatible and thus more likely to be accepted?

Problem:

In general, there is increasing tension and conflict between faculty serving general education and those in special education. The schools' faculty were feeling unsupported by the administration and were now contemplating union action.

Situation:

School A is a middle school located in an upper-middle-class, suburban district. School A has a long-standing history of both academic and athletic excellence. The school is proud of its large number of AP students, its state athletic championships, and a three-year track record of placing in the top 1% on state standardized testing.

The district has a strong teacher's union, and the teachers have enjoyed support from parents in each incident of their contract negotiations. Parents have been very supportive, given the academic and athletic achievements that have been made. All previous contract negotiations have been quite amicable, with all involved working for the betterment of the students and the maintaining of the highest quality. Up to this year, the relationship among various departments, as well as between faculty and staff, has been highly supportive.

At the beginning of the school year, the faculty were informed by the principal that the district was implementing "full inclusion" policies, and as a result, many if not most of the general education faculty would now have classrooms in which students with special needs would be included. Faculty were further informed that the inclusion policy being adopted provided for full participation in academics and all extracurricular activities. The principal stated that this was policy and as such it was up to the faculty "to make this

Exercise 7.1 Innovation as Culturally Compatible

happen." Faculty were also informed that a number of specialists had been hired by the district to serve as curricular advisers and consultants to the general education teachers. The principal directed the faculty to "work with" these advisers.

Throughout the first two months of school, a number of conflicts arose. Parents confronted teachers with concerns about anticipated drops in academic and athletic excellence. Parents of children with special needs were upset that some teachers failed to meet the children's needs. As a result, the faculty felt in the middle being damned if they did and damned if they didn't. Further, the faculty felt unsupported, abandoned by the administration, who kept reiterating that it was their (the faculty) job to make it work!

Faculty began to take out their frustrations on the consultants. They refused to meet with consultants and began to "blame" the consultants for anything that went wrong. Rumors suggesting that this was just the beginning and that their school would eventually become a special education center started to be circulated. With this increasing tension, the faculty meetings became gripe sessions with the focus on the intrusion of these "specialists" in our school. Faculty expressed resentment about having to change their curriculum and in general their way of doing things, which previously had proven successful. Many faculty threatened to make this an issue for union action.

Recommendations:

1. Have a town meeting at which the faculty and parents can voice their concerns to the superintendent.
2. Have the school principal meet with those faculty refusing or resisting the process and confront them with the reality of the district's decision, and the choices they have and their consequences.
3. Develop strategic work groups composed of faculty, consultants, parents, and administration to develop strategies for effectively maintaining levels of excellence and meeting the needs of all children.
4. Develop a representative body of school administration, teachers, and parents to pressure the central office to reconsider their decision and reduce the breadth of their inclusion plan.
5. Use the union as an agent for negotiation with the administration, and make this a matter of contract renegotiation.
6. (Write your recommendation.)

Exercise 7.1 Innovation as Culturally Compatible

Principle 2: Introducing Change in Small Steps (Shaping)

Although attempting to present innovation as culturally compatible, the reality is that any innovation, by definition, alters the way an organization will function and can never be completely compatible with the existing culture. Thus, in addition to introducing change that is most compatible to existing values and culture, innovation must be presented in ways that are perceived as tolerable and only minimally disruptive to the status quo.

Radical adjustments or changes are more likely to be met with resistance than those requiring small steps. Systems, like individuals, can be shaped toward change. Introducing the elements of innovations as small approximations of the ultimate desired goal may help to reduce the resistance to the innovation. Weick (1984), for example, found that a sequence of small wins (i.e., a measurable outcome of moderate importance), set up a pattern that can "attract allies, deter opponents and lower resistance" (p. 43).

Research suggests that innovations proving most acceptable will be those that (1) require the least amount of change, (2) require the least amount of resource expenditure, (3) require the least amount of adaptation of roles or development of skills and knowledge, and (4) prove least disruptive to the organization's schema or frame of reference (Bartunek & Moch, 1987; Torbert, 1985).

Change that is least disruptive to day-to-day functioning will be change that elicits the least resistance. Thus, changing the way morning messages are delivered will be less disruptive and therefore less resisted by faculty than changing the scope and sequence of a curriculum. The introduction of broader, more involved levels of change are more likely to elicit anxiety and thus system resistance. This doesn't mean a counselor-consultant should forgo addressing big issues and broad innovation. Rather, it is important to realize that it is more effective to move toward these broad outcomes through a series of small steps (i.e., shaping) rather than attempting to implement one broad and complicated pro-gram of change. Exercise 7.2 will help assist you in using the concepts of shaping in the development of an intervention plan.

Exercise 7.2 Change in Small Steps

Directions: For each of the following scenarios, use the principle of shaping to move the system in small steps toward the ultimate goal. Your task is to generate a subgoal that may help you begin the process of innovation while at the same time attempts to be least disrup-tive to the existing system. Discuss this intervention with colleague, classmate, or super-visor, attempting to identify points that may stimulate system resistance to its adaptation.

Scenario A: Over the course of the summer, P.S. 27 has been wired for high-speed In-ternet and in-house computer networking. The principal wants to have faculty place all lesson plans, attendance, and grading on the computer central network. He feels this will provide him easy access to information should a parent request data about a child or a specific teacher. The faculty has had neither prewarning nor preparation for this "com-puterization" of the school.

Goal: Place all curricula, lessons plans, attendance, and grading on central database

Subgoal: _____

Scenario B: The Oslo School counseling departments are attempting to move to a con-sultation model of service delivery. Faculty and administration have historically referred students (only) to counseling and expected these students to receive direct, one-on-one counseling services.

Goal: To use counselors as consultants, operating from a triadic, indirect model of service delivery. Counselors will expand the target for their services to include students, faculty, administrators, and the system.

Subgoal: _____

Principle 3: Align Innovation with Opinion Leaders

Another principle to follow when attempting to diffuse innovation and enhance the possibility that suggested changes will be embraced is to focus energy on aligning with the system's opinion leader(s) (Beer & Spector, 1993; Gray, 1984; Lippitt, 1982). The benefit of aligning innovation with opinion leaders is that those within a system who are respected and valued are given more leeway in "violating" group norms. The introduction of innovation is by definition a variance from the existing norm. Thus, once aligned to these opinion leaders, the variation appears somewhat sanctioned and thus more acceptable.

Opinion leaders are not always those individuals who occupy the formal positions of power, such as a department chair or principal. The counselor-consultant needs to be alert to identify those who appear most influential within the system, regardless of their formal role or title. Further, the counselor-consultant would do well to forge alliances with these formal or informal leaders.

Identification of and alignment with such opinion leaders often happens by engaging in the informal mechanisms and rituals in a system. Quite often, eating lunch at the same time as those who appear to be the opinion leaders or engaging in committee work, formal social activities, and informal gatherings (after work volleyball or end of the week happy hour, etc.) can provide the mechanism by which the counselor can come to know and be known by the opinion leader(s). While there are no hard and fast criteria for how to identify an opinion leader, any evidence that a person exerts influence over the functioning of the group's attitudes and behavior would be indicative of an opinion leader. Sometimes simply paying attention at faculty meetings may give the counselor the clues needed to identify the opinion leaders in the school. Exercise 7.3 may help you in identifying the opinion leaders in your current situation.

Principle 4: Increasing Value and Power as Consultant

Just as innovation and change may be more acceptable when presented by an opinion leader, a school counselor who is perceived as having special value to the system will be more effective in introducing change. This perception of value to those within the system can be enhanced by (1) doing something and (2) increasing social power.

Do Something

Quite often, the counselor, especially one new to a system, may face an uphill battle when attempting to gain respect and value. Without a history of demonstrated effectiveness to draw upon, the counselor-consultant may feel like he has to constantly "sell" his services. Under these conditions, the school counselor would do well to engage in any role or function that would be received as having real, practical value to the members of the system (Willing, 2002). The concept of doing something is not restricted to the realm of the esoteric nor the strictly professional. Quite often a counselor-consultant can begin to be perceived as valuable after serving a very practical function. Consider the following case illustration.

Directions: The following can be employed at a faculty meeting, workgroup meeting, or any gathering of members of your system where decisions are made. Identify by name and, where appropriate, formal title or role four individuals who are active in that group. Place a check mark under the name of the individual who most exemplifies the indicators listed. Next, share your observation with another member of that same group. Covalidation may be indicative of the identification of the group's opinion leader.

Name of Group: _____

	Name/Role	Name/Role	Name/Role	Name/Role
Indicator:				
1. Keeps the group on task				
2. Sets direction for group				
3. Most directly influences mood or tone of group				
4. Tends to be the most listened to				
5. Most often sought out for advice				
6. Individual with whom others wish most to relate				
7. Perceived as most important to the group				
8. Most often sought out at breaks in the group meeting				
9. Individual whose absence would be most missed				
10. Seen as the prime resource for the group				

Exercise 7.3 Opinion Leaders

Mr. R. was a counselor assigned to work in a particular inner-city elementary school. The school had a history of bad experiences with previous counselors and, as a result, members of the school were nonresponsive to Mr. R.'s attempts to work with the teachers and staff. Mr. R. attempted a number of different approaches such as sharing interesting articles he had read, going to faculty meetings, and contributing to discussions, but nothing seemed to break through the resistance. In spite of his professional competence and sophistication, the event which resulted in breaking through the resistance involved his driving ability.

The school had scheduled a day at the zoo for the lower grades (1–3) as a reward for children's participation in a Read-a-thon. As might be anticipated, the children were extremely excited about the day, and teachers, while somewhat apprehensive about monitoring the children, all felt it would be a wonderful experience. Because of a mix-up with insurance paperwork, the bus company contracted to transport the children the half mile to the zoo canceled on the morning of the planned trip. As fate (?) might have it, Mr. R. was licensed to drive a school bus, and he volunteered to transport the children (a total of five trips both ways). Further, he suggested calling the central office to see if a small bus could be made available to the school. Not only was his suggestion successful, but his willingness to roll up his sleeves to help with this problem, along with the rapport he demonstrated with the children as he transported them to the zoo, impressed the teachers and parents involved and resulted in a lowering of their resistance to working with him.

As a consultant, one would naturally seek to be valued for professional competence. With time, the effective counselor-consultant will, in fact, gain power and acceptance as his interventions prove effective. However, as illustrated in the previous case example, while a counselor-consultant may want to gain "value" as a result of his demonstrated professional competence, quite often he may find that an increase in his perceived value comes as a result of meeting any of the system's felt needs, even when those needs require practical, rather than professional, knowledge and skill.

Increase Value by Increasing Social Power

At first, counselors may feel some resistance to the idea of employing social power to influence another. As mental health providers and as educators, we do exert power in service to others. We must engage power if we are to be effective. The power that we are speaking of is that which provides the ability to influence another person's attitudes or behavior. For example, encouraging a student to expand her perspective on an issue or adjust her way of responding to specific situations are times that, as a school counselor, one is exerting social power, the power to influence.

There are many forms of social power. In a now classic look at power, French and Raven (1959) identified the following types of social power:

a. Coercive power is the ability to reward and/or punish another.
b. Legitimate or traditional power is the power which stems from society's sanctioning of a person's role and authority to control the attitudes and behavior of another, as may be the case with a parent or public official.
c. Informational power is that power accrued because the information that is provided by one person is viewed as highly relevant and useful by another person.
d. Expert power is the power that we associate to a person who is perceived as having specialized knowledge and skill that is valued or necessary by another. This is similar to informational power except that the focus is on the person (the expert) and not merely on the information available through that person.
e. Referent or identification power is the power to influence that accrues to a person because he is attractive, a person with whom another wants to like and be liked by—in short, a role model. Most often in referent power, this individual is viewed as having characteristics similar to or desired by the second person.

When considering increasing a school counselor's social power within a system, and as such strengthen his ability to introduce change, two of the above forms of power—expert and referent—appear most appropriate.

Expert Power. The very nature of asking the counselor-consultant for assistance would suggest that the consultant is perceived as having some form of expertise, and thus expert power. When the counselor-consultant's particular knowledge or skill proves useful to those within the client-system (e.g., the client, the consultee, administration), then the consultant's value and resultant power are increased. And as might be assumed, as the consultant's value and power increase, resistance to the consultant and his innovations should decrease (Lines, 2007; Erchul, Grissom, & Getty, 2008).

Research demonstrates that the perception of expertise and the resulting assignment of expert power to another can be enhanced by indications of advanced education, relevant experience, and higher social status; awards, citations, and affiliation with prestigious institutions are example indicators (Martin, 1978). Therefore, school counselors attempting to increase their expert power should find ways to communicate their experience and education and highlight factors that could increase their perceived social status. This, for example, could take the form of sharing information about articles they have written, testimonials received from other consultees, special awards or recognitions received, or even the sharing of special information or materials gathered at professional meetings. In addition to these general indicators of expertise, a consultant seeking to effect change should develop a small number of content areas of real expertise over and above his general knowledge and competency, and develop means of sharing or demonstrating this experience by, for example, offering faculty or parent workshops or teaching classroom lessons.

Expert power is clearly a useful tool for effecting change. However, since consultation as presented here is viewed as a collaborative effort, the counselor-consultant, while exuding expertise, must at the same time remain approachable. As a collaborative process, the consultee needs to feel as if she can approach the consultant and work openly with him. Thus, in addition to having specialized knowledge and skill, which makes the consultant "different" from the consultee, the consultant must also exhibit conditions that facilitate rapport and connectedness with the consultee (Caplan, 1970; Dinkmeyer & Carlson, 1973; Parsons & Meyers, 1984). In fact, relying solely on expert power may be detrimental to the effectiveness of the consultant in that it places the consultant in a one-up position, inviting the consultee to anticipate prescription or provision from the "expert" consultant. Bennis, Benne, and Chin (1969) noted that "the extent to which a change agent is successful (that is, influential) is dependent on the degree to which he is perceived as susceptible to influence by the client" (p. 148). Thus, one could argue that the more a consultant is perceived as the "expert," the less the consultant may be perceived as open to influence by the consultee. Therefore, while exhibiting some expert power, it is important to develop the collegial relationship, one in which the consultant is perceived as coequal, approachable, and susceptible to consultee influence (Parsons 1996, p. 66). Under these conditions, a second form of power, referent power, seems to hold special value.

Referent Power. When the consultee perceives the consultant as manifesting feelings, attitudes, interests, and behaviors similar to his own or to those that he would like to possess, the consultant has referent power. A consultant's effectiveness will be enhanced when he shares certain values, personal characteristics, behaviors, background experiences, knowledge, and interest with the consultee. Being able to relate to the local sports teams or political scene, sharing a common cultural background, or simply enjoying the same type of food, music, or entertainment may increase one's referent power.

As with all helping relationships, the consultant needs to engage empathically and nonjudgmentally with the consultee. However, to enhance his social power, the consultant also needs to provide appropriate and parallel self-disclosures, which increase the consultant's referent power. Increasing referent power is often best achieved in informal settings such as the lunchroom, after work, social contexts, break rooms, or even walking into school in the morning.

Blending and Balancing Power. The use of expert and referent power might at first appear somewhat incompatible since it is difficult to highlight one's unique expertise while at the same time emphasizing one's similarity. A proper blending of expert and referent power is what is called for if one is to engage in collaborative consultation. Research suggests that too much "expertise" reduces one's attractive value, and logic dictates that too much referent power, where the consultee sees the consultant as having the same expertise and knowledge as they do, will result in the consultee not seeking the consultant's advice (Kelleher, Riley-Tillman, & Power, 2008). Thus, the consultant who has accrued a good deal of referent power will benefit from emphasizing his expertise. This is often the case where a counselor who previously had spent years as a teacher then steps into the new position of counselor-consultant. In this transition, it is important for the counselor-consultant to engage in those actions that emphasize his newly acquired knowledge and skills. Under these conditions, it may be important for the consultant to publicize recent professional involvement or scholarship; communicate knowledge of relevant information, even using professional jargon; and demonstrate competency in specific areas of expertise, perhaps by providing in-service training.

On the other hand, the consultant who is perceived as "expert" will do well to balance this perception by highlighting points of commonality between himself and his consultee. This may especially be true for the counselor-consultant new to the system or one who is called in from outside or another system. While their presence in the school may have been preceded by information regarding previous training and experience, and perhaps even testimonials of success, the *person* of the consultant is still an unknown. Under these conditions, the counselor-consultant would do well to spend time in the informal settings getting known, and getting to know the consultee and the members of that system.

Demonstrating practical and immediate usefulness (i.e., doing something) along with developing expert and referent power are useful tools for the consultant seeking to decrease resistance and diffuse innovation. Exercise 7.4 will help the reader more fully understand the concepts described and begin to concretely apply these concepts.

Part I Directions: Below is a description of a presenting complaint along with the characteristics of the consultee and the system involved in this consult. After reading the descriptions, answer the questions that follow. It would be beneficial for you to share your response with a colleague, classmate, or supervisor since each consultant differs in both areas of expertise and referent abilities and thus will most likely respond differently to the opportunities presented.

Presenting Complaint:

The consultee (Dr. Seronita Torres) is principal of Elwood Good Alternative High School. She comes to you with a problem she is having with one of her students. The student, Regina, is an 18-year-old senior. Regina is an I.V. drug user (heroin) who was court-assigned to the alternative high school. In addition to her drug involvement, Regina has been living on the streets for the past 3 months and recently has met a man (age 31) whom she feels she loves. Regina told Dr. Torres that she was considering secretly trapping her boyfriend into marriage by becoming pregnant. Dr. Torres has attempted to get Regina to see the potential danger involved with her decisions, but nothing she has said appears effective. Dr. Torres admitted that she does not know what to do with Regina and would really like your assistance.

Consultee & Consultee Setting:

Dr. Torres is a 57-year-old principal with a doctorate in education from the University of Mexico and a master's in counseling (having been a counselor for 8 years, prior to becoming a principal). Dr. Torres has been in this country 18 months and has been working at her current position for only 9 weeks. She states that she feels somewhat "out of her element" working in her current setting.

The school services a poor, inner city population of identified SED students. Most of the students are either Hispanic Americans or African Americans. Dr. Torres revealed that she has limited knowledge and experience working with this population and that she took this position as a temporary post while she gained experience as a principal. Dr. Torres noted that she was able to get the job because of her political connections.

Dr. Torres comes from a very affluent and influential family in Mexico City. She expressed her difficulty with truly understanding the experience of the people with whom she works given her background, which included private schooling, extensive family affiliations, and "strict Catholic values." Dr. Torres also expressed her interest in and concern about the role and future of females within the Hispanic culture, and she is very politically active on women's rights.

You are the first counselor to be used by the staff at the school. Previously, all mental health services were out-serviced. It is clear that while Dr. Torres wants some assistance, she is also very concerned about how her peers and supervisors may perceive her if they know she sought consultation.

Consider each of the following and discuss in as concrete terms as possible.

1. Expert Power: What specific area of expertise do you bring to this situation? How might you convey this expertise to Dr. Torres and to the other staff, as a way of diffusing the potential resistance to your presence?
2. Referent Power: Identify at least two areas of dissimilarity and two areas of similarity between yourself and Dr. Torres. What elements could you highlight as a way of eliciting referent power? How would you reduce the perception of difference?
3. Do Something: Given the concerns expressed by Dr. Torres, what one, immediate thing would you do in order to demonstrate your value?

Exercise 7.4 Increasing Power and Value

Principle 5: Move in a Crisis

The old adage "if it ain't broke, don't fix it" bodes poorly for those of us with a focus on prevention. When systems are at points of equilibrium and stability and are not experiencing pain, resistance to change will be at its maximum. Thus, a final principle of diffusion of innovation is to be alert to signs of instability and disequilibrium as opportunities for diffusing innovation. The directive for the school counselor-consultant is to be prepared and move in a crisis.

Crisis, by definition, is a disruption to normal functioning. When experiencing a crisis, individuals and systems are placed into a disequilibrium, and what results are feelings of imbalance and urgency. Previous methods of operation or coping are overwhelmed and ineffective, thus making systems and individuals more receptive to approaches that will rapidly reestablish stability, even if those approaches are innovative.

For example, consider the impact that recent incidents of school violence and sensational news stories have had on creating a multitude of safe schools and at-risk initiatives. One local school district installed expensive security systems within its school, even though the district was facing fiscal crises. Similarly, numerous schools have implemented zero tolerance policies in regards to school violence and the use of "terroristic" language. Other schools have trained teachers and staff in lockdown procedures. All of these innovations, disruptive as they were to the previous, normal way of operating, were rapidly implemented with little resistance. The ability to diffuse this type of change was facilitated by the crisis nature of the times.

The school counselor seeking to act as an agent of change needs to be sensitive to points of disequilibrium and be able to respond at moments of these crises. Consider the case of Ms. L. Jackson, a counselor at a rural elementary school. After attending a professional conference, Postvention: Responding to School Suicide, Ms. Jackson returned and developed a proposal for a postvention response plan for her school. The plan outlined the steps to be taken and the community resources that could be brought in for support. While her program was well developed and in line with the sample programs she acquired at the conference, the principal and the school board were resistant to even considering such a program. The general feeling was that these programs are needed in urban schools where, as the principal explained, "these type of things [suicide] happen...but not here!"

Over the course of the next two years, Ms. Jackson attempted to reshape her proposal so that it might be more palatable to administration, but to no avail. Sadly, it was the joint suicides of two sixth grade students that moved the system to adopt her program.

On a Monday in October, the school returned to the news that two sixth grade students had committed suicide the previous Sunday. The school was thrown into absolute chaos. Students and teachers flooded Ms. Jackson's office, showing signs of shock. Parents hysterically called the school and attempted to remove their children. And, the principal was completely frustrated by her inability to gain any direction from the central office as to what steps she should take.

Ms. Jackson stepped into this crisis and gained permission to contact her community resources and begin the procedures that she had attempted to implement two years prior. While no hard data were collected, it may be fair to assume that the existence of a well thought-out program and this counselor's ability to make contact with community mental health providers, who were able to come to school to provide immediate crisis counseling for all, helped this school community avoid even further disaster.

Being able to move in a crisis means that a counselor has anticipated possible crises and has, in a preventive step, developed responses and programs that could reduce the potential impact of these destabilizing events. The hope, of course, is that these prevention programs can be embraced prior to crisis. In order to facilitate a systems acceptance of such programs prior to an actual crisis, the counselor can use data reflecting trends or other systems experiences as a way of elevating awareness of the real possibility and existence of threats. If successful, these data will produce the disequilibrium that can allow innovation.

For example, the consultant who provides a principal with demographic data and fiscal projections pointing to the declining tax base for the school district may find that these data serve as the stimulus for consideration of modifying the way counseling services are delivered within the school. Or, the school counselor attempting to introduce a peer mediation program may find it helpful to present data showing (a) the increase in number of incidents of student conflicts, (b) the increased amount of time spent by teachers and the vice principal in resolving student conflict (time taken away from other, more professional duties), and (c) the predicted increase in student conflict that may result as a function of an upcoming merger with a previous rival school. These data may help to elevate the principal's "felt" pain to the point where the discomfort of change appears to be a less than the potential costs (in terms of student conflict) of nonchange.

While we may like to believe that good ideas can simply stand on their merit alone, when it comes to change, we agree with Kurpius, Brack, Brack, and Dunn (1993) that it is the belief "that one's pain is reducible that is critical to implementing the motivation to change" (p. 424). Exercise 7.5 will help to clarify this point of moving in a crisis.

Summary

- A consultant not only intervenes with the client but does so in ways that impact the extrapersonal variables affecting the client.
- The preventive, extrapersonal focus of consultation will result in system change.
- The counselor-consultant is truly an agent of change, working to bring the system goals and individual goals into harmony in order to reflect the mission for which they have come together.
- Systems have developed a number of mechanisms through which they attempt to maintain the status quo and thus by definition resist any form of change that may be perceived as threatening to the balance of power, the utilization of resources, or simply the existing state of functioning.
- Innovation and change are most readily embraced when a number of principles are taken into consideration, including (1) keep innovation culturally compatible; (2) introduce innovation in small steps, shaping; (3) align innovation with system opinion leaders; (4) increase consultant's value and power within the system; and (5) introduce change at times of system crises.

Part I Directions: For each of the following scenarios identify:

a: the felt, or perceived, area of crisis; and

b: how you as consultant could use that as a point of diffusing innovation and an aid to reaching the listed goal.

Scenario 1:

Conditions: The consultee is a high school principal. Her school has recently experienced an increase in student population and faculty as a result of it absorbing the students and faculty from a neighboring school that was forced to close. Recent student conflict (gang fights) has stimulated the principal to call you in to provide "assertive discipline training" for the teachers "so that they can learn to intervene before problems emerge."

Problem: Besides the student problem with assimilating, the faculties from both schools were exhibiting symptoms of burnout. Faculty from the school that had closed had not adequately grieved the loss of their school and its tradition. The host faculty felt resentment toward the new faculty and anger at the crowding caused by their presence. The host faculty were also somewhat jealous of the attention the new faculty were receiving. Both faculties reported feeling disempowered, having not been consulted or even advised about the move until the very last moment.

Goal: To reduce the faculties' feelings of disenfranchisement and facilitate faculty ownership and decision-making around the steps to be taken to develop a blended identity of the two schools.

Consultant Strategy: _____

_____

Scenario 2:

Middle School Counseling Department. While there are no immediate problems that the chair or the other counselors have reported, you observe that the amount of work, as well as the complexity and severity of the cases managed, has clearly increased over the course of the last year.

Problem (identify potential problem area):

_____
_____

Goal (identify change in the current operation that may prevent the problem from developing):

_____
_____

Strategy (identify how you, as counselor-consultant, could reframe the lack of pain to encourage change):

_____

Exercise 7.5 Highlighting and Moving in a Crisis

Additional Resources

Print

Cialdini, R. B., & Goldstein, N. J. (2004). Social influence: Compliance and conformity. *Annual Review of Psychology,* 55, 591–621.

Gysbers, N. C. (2001). School guidance and counseling in the 21st century: Remember the past into the future. *Professional School Counseling,* 5(2), 96–105.

Web-Based

Shallcross, L. (2010). Managing resistant clients. *Counseling Today.* Retrieved from https://ct.counseling.org/2010/02/managing-resistant-clients/

Sink, C. A., & Ockerman, M. S. (2016). School counselors and a multi-tiered system of supports: Cultivating systemic change and equitable outcomes. *Professional Counselor,* 6(3), v–ix. Retrieved from http://tpcjournal.nbcc.org

References

American School Counselor Association. (2003). *The ASCA national model: A framework for comprehensive school counseling programs.* Alexandria, VA: Author.

American School Counselor Association. (2012). *The ASCA national model: A framework for comprehensive school counseling programs* (3rd ed.). Alexandria, VA: Author.

American School Counselor Association (ASCA), (2014). *The school counselor and multitiered system of supports.* Retrieved from https://www.schoolcounselor.org/asca/media/asca/PositionStatements/PS_Multitiered-SupportSystem.pdf

Argyris, C. (1970). *Intervention theory and method: A behavioral science view.* Reading, MA: Addison-Wesley.

Bartunek, J., & Moch, M. (1987). First-order, second-order and third-order change and organizational development interventions: A cognitive approach. *Journal of Applied Behavioral Science,* 23(4), 483–500.

Bartunek, J.M., & Louis, M. R. (1988) The interplay of organization development and organization transformation. In W. A. Pasmore & R. W. Woodman (Eds.), *Research in organizational change and development* (Vol 2, pp. 97–134). Greenwich, CT: JAI Press.

Beer, M., & Spector, B. (1993). Organizational diagnosis: Its role in organizational consultation. *Journal of Counseling and Development,* 71, 642–650.

Bennis, W. G., Benne, K. D., & Chin, R. (Eds.) (1969). *The Planning of Change.* New York, NY: Holt, Rinehart & Winston.

Boohene, R., & Williams A. A. (2012). Resistance to organizational change: A case study of Oti Yeboah Complex Limited. *International Business and Management,* 4(1), 135–145.

Brown, D., Blackurn, J. E., & Powell, W. C. (1979), *Consultation.* Boston. MA: Allyn & Bacon.

Burke, W. W. (2008). *Organization change: Theory and practice.* London, UK: SAGE.

Caplan, G. (1970). *The theory and practice of mental health consultation.* New York, NY: Basic Books.

Center for School Counseling Outcome Research and Evaluation. (2011). Mission statement. Retrieved from http://www.umass.edu/schoolcounseling/about-us.php

Chen-Hayes, S. F. (2007). The ACCESS Questionnaire: Assessing K–12 school counseling programs and interventions to ensure equity and success for every student. *Counseling and Human Development* 39, 1–10.

Dinkmeyer, D., & Carlson, J. (1973). *Consulting: Facilitating human potential and change processes.* Columbus, OH: Merrill.

Education Trust, National Center for Transforming School Counseling. (2012). Scope of the work. Retrieved from http://www.edtrust.org/sites/edtrust.org/ files/Scope of the Work_1.pdf

Eldridge, C. R. (2001). Organizational congruent values: Effects on attitudes for planned change and innovation in a production environment. *Dissertation Abstracts,* No. AAI3028847. Ann Arbor, MI: UMI.

Ellsworth, J. B. (2000). Surviving change: A survey of educational change models. *ERIC,* ED443417.

Erchul, W. P., Grissom, P. F., & Getty, K. C. (2008). Studying interpersonal influence within school consultation: Social power base and relational communication perspectives. In W. P. Erchul & S. M. Sheridan (Eds.), *Handbook of research in school consultation* (pp. 293–322). New York, NY: Taylor & Francis Group/Routledge.

French, W. L., & Bell, C. H., Jr. (1990). *Organization development* (4th ed.) Englewood Cliffs, NJ: Prentice Hall.

French, J. R. P., Jr., & Raven, B. (1959). The bases of social power. In D. Cartwright (Ed.), *Studies in social power*. Ann Arbor: University of Michigan Institute of Social Research.

Gray, J. L., (1984). *Supervision: An applied behavioral science approach to managing people*. Boston, MA: Kent Publishers.

Holcomb-McCoy, C., & Chen-Hayes, S. F. (2011). Culturally competent school counselors: Affirming diversity by challenging oppression. In B. T. Erford (Ed.), *Transforming the school counseling profession* (3rd ed., pp. 90–109). Boston, MA: Pearson

Kast, F. Z., & Rosensweig, J. E. (1974). *Organization and management: A systems approach* (2nd ed.). New York, NY: McGraw-Hill.

Kelleher, C., Riley-Tillman, T., & Power, T. J. (2008). An initial comparison of collaborative and expert-driven consultation on treatment integrity. *Journal of Educational and Psychological Consultation, 18*, 294–324.

Kurpius, D. J., Brack, G., Brack, C. J., & Dunn, L. B. (1993). Maturation of systems consultation: Subtle issues inherent in the model. *Journal of Mental Health Counseling, 15*(4), 414–429.

Lewis, L. K. (1999) Disseminating information and soliciting input during planned organizational change: Implementers' targets, sources, and channels for communicating. *Management Communication Quarterly, 13*(1), 43–75.

Lewis, L. K. (2000). "Blindsided by that one" and "I saw that one coming": The relative anticipation and occurrence of communication problems and other problems in implementers' insight. *Journal of Applied Communication Research, 28*(1), 44–67.

Lines, R. (2007). Using power to install strategy: The relationship between expert power, position power, influence tactic and implementation success. *Journal of Change Management, 7*(2), 143–170.

Lippitt, G. (1982). Developing HRD and OD, the profession and the professional. *Training and Development, 36*, 67–74.

Lunenburg, F. C., & Ornstein, A. C. (2008). *Educational administration: Concepts and practices*. Belmont, CA: Wadsworth.

Martin, R. (1978). Expert and referent power: A framework for understanding and maximizing consultation effectiveness. *Journal of School Psychology, 16*(1), 49–55.

Mohrman, A. M., Jr., Mohrman, S. A., Ledford, G. E., Jr., Cummings, T., Lawler, E. E., III, & Associates. (1989). *Large-scale organizational change*. San Francisco, CA: Jossey-Bass.

Mullins, L. J. (2005). *Management and organisational behavior*. New York, NY: Prentice Hall/Financial Times.

National Office for School Counselor Advocacy. (NOSCA). (2011). *Eight components of college and career readiness counseling*. Retrieved from http://advocacy.collegeboard.org/college-preparation-access/national-office-school-counselor-advocacy-nosca/news/8-components-college

Parsons, R. (1996). *The skilled consultant*. Needham Heights, MA: Allyn and Bacon.

Parsons, R., & Meyers, J. (1984). *Developing consultation skills*. San Francisco, CA: Jossey-Bass.

Robbins, S. P., & Judge, T. A. (2009). *Organizational behavior*. Upper Saddle River, NJ: Prentice Hall.

Rogers, E. M., & Shoemaker, F. F. (1971). *Communication of innovations*. New York, NY: Free Press.

Schmuck, R. A., & Runkel, P. J. (1985). *The handbook of organizational development in schools* (3rd ed.) Palo Alto, CA: Mayfield.

Torbert, W. (1985). On-line reframing. *Organizational Dynamics, 14*(1), 60–79.

Weick, K. E. (1984). Small wins. *American Psychologist, 39*(1), 40–49.

Willing, L. F. (2002). Making difficult change. *Fire Engineering, 155*(8), 81–84.

CHAPTER 8

Working With Resistance

I don't get it. Mr. B., Jasmine's math teacher, said that he wanted to work with me and I feel like I'm using all my communication skills, but every time we get started he seems to have something else he has to do or some "yes, but" kind of response. This is getting frustrating. If it wasn't going to help Jasmine, I'd just as soon tell him to forget it!

——————————— ○ ———————————

It may be hard for a consultant to accept that even though her intentions may be pure, her ideas reasonable, and her communication clear, resistance may still be encountered! And, like the frustration expressed by our illustrated consultant, counselor-consultants who are ill prepared to work with resistance may choose to terminate the relationship or attempt to employ power to push through consultee resistance. In either case, the outcome of the consult is doomed, and future consultation relationship with that consultee may no longer be possible. While consultee resistance can be experienced as frustrating, it need not be viewed as an adversarial something to overcome, something to defeat.

A consultee's resistance to consultation may be a direct reflection of the nature of the consultative process, the characteristics of the consultant, or the unique character of the consultee. In any case, it may prove to be an essential element to the consultation dynamic and needs to be understood and embraced. Accepting and working with resistance can lead a consultant to understand the consultee better. Working with the consultee's resistance can result in the development of a more productive collaborative relationship. Therefore, to be effective, a consultant needs to maintain her emotional objectivity when confronted with resistance. The effective consultant needs to employ her understanding of the nature of resistance along with her skills to work with, rather than push through, consultee resistance.

The information and exercises provided in this chapter will assist the reader to develop the understanding and consultative skills needed for effectively working with consultee resistance. After completing this chapter, the reader should be able to

1. recognize the existence and source(s) of resistance, including those originating with the consultee, the consultant, or the consulting relationship;

2. embrace resistance as part of the growth and change process (rather than as a personal attack);
3. see the consulting relationship as an invaluable resource to the consultation and as such accept the resistance as an opportunity for gaining increased clarity and direction in the relationship;
4. employ strategies to work with resistance, including assisting the consultee in identifying the emotional concerns or uncertainties that may be the foundation for her resistance; and
5. develop preventive strategies aimed at reducing the risk of resistance.

Understanding the Sources of Resistance

Resistance is any behavior that thwarts the probability of a successful process or outcome and reflects the consultee's failure to participate constructively in the process of consultation (Dougherty, 2000).

In consultation, this often manifests as a consultee's failure to actively engage in the problem-solving process (Piersel & Gutkin, 1983). Resistance can be either an overt or a covert process (Butler, Weaver, Doggett, & Watson, 2002) but either way can negatively affect the consultation dynamic and outcome (Sterling-Turner, Watson, Wildmon, Watkins, & Little, 2001). Thus, understanding the bases for a consultee's resistance is an essential first step to the process of working with consultee resistance.

It may be difficult to comprehend that even when the change being suggested would result in a desired outcome, a consultee and, as will be discussed later, a consultee's system may resist such change. But the truth is that even when the reasons and expected outcomes are positive, resistance to change can be experienced (Boohene & Williams, 2012). A number of authors have conceptualized and described the many causes for resistance (e.g., Brown, Pryzwansky & Schulte, 2006; Dougherty, Dougherty & Purcell, 1991; Robbins & Judge, 2009).

While the specifics of these categorizations may vary, they all seem to suggest that resistance is an emotional response to a perceived or real threat. The source of that threat can lie within (1) the actual demands encountered as a result of the consultation, (2) the consultee's personal issues and concerns, (3) the consultant's style, or (4) the nature of the consulting relationship and dynamic established. It is important for the consultant to discern the source of this threat so that it can be best addressed.

Resistance: Often a Reasonable Response

While the consultant experiencing resistance may simply want to give up or force through the process, assuming it to be unreasonable, it is important to understand that sometimes consultee resistance may, in fact, be a reasonable response to unrealistic and costly demands.

Consultee resistance can be a protective response to what is to be too risky or too dangerous. Under these situations, resistance may be done to preserve the consultee or the consultee's system. Consider the case where a teacher, serving as the consultee, is directed to "confront" and "stand-up" to the aggressive gang leader who is disrupting her class.

The consultee may find such a suggestion threatening to her well-being and safety and thus "resist" the consultant's recommendation. To resist when reflecting a desire to reduce risk and ensure safety is probably reasonable. Understanding the real potential danger and possible costs can help the consultant reformulate the recommendations so that they are more readily embraced and enacted by the consultee.

Resistance—A Response to Consultant Insensitivity

While the potential for danger is not always dramatic, resistance does, at a minimum, indicate that the consultee is feeling uncomfortable. It is not unusual to find that this discomfort is in direct response to a consultant's insensitivity and lack of empathy for the consultee. Consider the case of the overly "competent" consultant.

Case Illustration 8.1
The Overly "Competent" Consultant

A counselor-consultant, new to a school and eager to demonstrate his competence, was thrilled to receive a request for assistance from a well-liked and respected first-grade teacher. Ms. L. asked the consultant to assist her with, Ryan, one of her "troublesome" first graders. She noted that over the course of the last five weeks, Ryan's behavior had become increasingly disruptive to the class. According to Ms. L., Ryan began by calling out in class (without raising his hand and waiting to be recognized) but has since escalated his disruptive behavior to the point where he now "throws books up to the front of the room!" After listening to Ms. L.'s brief description, the consultant thanked her for her confidence in him and asked if he could visit the classroom to observe Ryan in action.

The next day, the consultant stopped in to observe Ms. L.'s class. What he noticed was that Ms. L. was a very creative, animated, and apparently interested teacher. Her classroom was brightly decorated, and the children were working at one of five learning stations located around the space. The children appeared very involved and attentive to the particular tasks they found at each learning station. Ms. L. was enthusiastically "bouncing" from station to station, both lending support and providing extensive verbal reinforcement.

In this environment of active, cooperative learning was Ryan. He was isolated from the other children and the learning stations, and was sitting at his desk fiddling with his pencil while his was supposed to be working on individual worksheets. Ms. L. stated that Ryan tended to be too disruptive in the small groups and thus was given personal seat work during these periods of cooperative learning.

As the consultant observed the class interaction, he noted that Ryan rarely focused on the task at hand and instead would get up and sharpen his pencil; roll around on the floor; or wait until Ms. L. was engrossed in discussion or demonstration at one of the learning stations, when he would then reach under his desk, select a book, and promptly throw it to the front of the room. The sudden loud noise startled everyone in the room and resulted in Ms. L. coming over to Ryan and reprimanding him for his behavior. The consultant observed this scene played out four more times in the span of twenty minutes. Feeling his observations confirmed his initial hypotheses about what needed to be done, the consultant excused himself and informed Ms. L. that he would provide her feedback at her lunch period (which was in about thirty minutes).

During the interim, the consultant went to his office, where he promptly typed a proposal for extinguishing this attention-seeking behavior along with detailed instruction on how to employ teacher attention to shape Ryan's positive behavior. The plan was comprehensive, providing step-by-step instruction on the shaping process along with some supportive references and recommended readings on extinction and shaping. It was indeed a paper worthy of any graduate student.

The consultant met with Ms. L., handed her the paper, and suggested that after she read it, she could contact him if she had any questions. However, he was sure that things would work out fine as long as she followed the recommendations. Fine!

The result of this insensitive display of pomposity was that the recommended program failed miserably. Ryan became more disruptive in his attention-seeking behavior. Ms. L. became more frustrated with Ryan, stopped the implementation of the plan, and reported to her fellow teachers that the consultant's plan "made things worse!" Further, she swore to her colleagues that she would never consult with "that guy" again.

As you most likely recognize, the problem in this illustration was not in the plan but in the planner, not in the product but in the process. This consultant's style created a situation in which the consultee felt insulted, unheard, humiliated, and angry. A consultee's resistance can, therefore, reflect a perceived devaluing and a general lack of trust rather than a negative response to the plan that is developed (Slonski-Fowler & Truscott 2004; Spratt, Shucksmith, Philip, & Watson, 2006).

Resistance is often an indirect way for the consultee to express discomfort with the consultant or the consultation process. The ability to recognize this indirect expression of distress and to discern the basis (rational or ill-founded) upon which it rests is essential to successfully working through the dynamics of consultation.

Resistance—A Reaction to Consultee Issues and Concerns

As noted above, resistance is at one level an emotional response to a perceived or real threat. Often, the source of the threat, while initially placed on the consultant, the consultation relationship, or the specific recommendations or processes encountered, stems from the consultee's issues. Four such concerns, (1) negative or conflicting expectations, (2) concerns regarding control, (3) feelings of vulnerability, and (4) anxiety around problem finding and problem solving, are discussed in some detail.

Negative and Conflicting Expectations

Brown et al. (2006) highlighted the value of the consultee's preconceptions or "expectations" as a significant contributor to the success of a consultation contract. They noted the importance of gaining congruency between the expectations of the consultee and those of the consultant as it contributes to the successful outcome. As such, identifying and working with consultee expectations should be a focus during the early stages of contracting and the identification of the problem under consideration (Brown, et al., 2006).

The consultee's negative expectations about the need or potential costs of consultation can serve as the foundation for his resistance (Gonzalez, Nelson, Gutkin, & Shwery, 2004). The consultee may also exhibit resistance because of differing perceptions and expectations (Thornberg, 2014). In addition, the consultee may not agree with the consultant that a problem exists or that one exists at a level of severity necessitating this consultation (Cautilli, Riley-Tillman, Axelrod, & Hineline, 2005). Or, in those situations where there is agreement on the existence and nature of the problem, differing expectations and perspectives regarding the strategies or even the goals to be achieved may serve as the source of resistance (Slonski-Fowler & Truscott, 2004; Spratt et al., 2006).

Resistance will be less when the consultant's expectations regarding the nature of the problem, the goal to be achieved, and the specific recommendations are compatible with that of the consultee (Knoff, 2013). It is vital that the consultation contract reflect the congruence of both consultant and consultee expectations regarding consultation process and outcome (Kurpius, Fuqua, & Rozecki, 1993).

Even with such agreement of need, goals, and strategies, the consultee may exhibit resistance as a simple result of his negative expectations regarding time, resource, or energy cost that may be incurred as a result of engaging in consultation (Gonzales et al., 2004). This seems especially true for individuals who are overwhelmed or are experiencing burnout. These individuals may just not have the energy to participate in the change that is anticipated will result from the consultation. They may see the consultation as one added burden to an already overburdened agenda (Friend & Bauwens, 1988).

In attempting to address this last point regarding potential costs, the consultant needs to keep in mind that the smaller the change required and the more that change is culturally (and personally) compatible with the consultee, the less resistance one should encounter. Further, the more rapidly the consultant can identify the consultee's motivations and needs and enter the relationship at a level that will satisfy at least one of these motivational states, the more payoff will be experienced by the consultee, and thus the less resistance encountered (Parsons & Meyers, 1984). For example, when working with a consultee who is experiencing burnout and crises around a particular client, a consultant can reduce or even prevent resistance by providing immediate relief through the provisional modality (even if it is short-term). Stepping in with hands-on assistance or removing an extremely disruptive client may prove more useful in reducing resistance than would engaging the consultee in a lengthy data-gathering process. Requiring the overburdened consultee to collect data or learn new intervention techniques would increase the consultee's expectations that such a relationship will be too costly and thus should be resisted.

The counselor-consultant who is experiencing consultee resistance as a result of adverse expectations regarding need, goal, strategies, or value (i.e., cost-payoff benefit) will have to clarify and (re)establish specific elements of a collaborative consultation contract. Specifically, the consultant would need to

1. provide or review for the consultee the rationale and potential benefits of using consultation, highlighting the preventive value;
2. re-emphasize the confidential nature of the relationship;
3. reiterate the consultee's right and responsibility to accept, modify, or reject the recommendations and the freedom to renegotiate or terminate the contract at any time; and
4. clarify the goal and direction that is mutually acceptable.

Exercise 8.1 provides an opportunity for you to recognize and develop strategies for working through consultee negative and conflicting expectations.

Exercise 8.1 Recognizing and Working Through Negative and Conflicting Expectations

Directions: Since there may be multiple approaches to working with resistance, it would be beneficial to work this exercise with a colleague, supervisor, or mentor. For each of the following scenarios you are to:

1. identify a possible negative and conflicting expectation that may serve as a source of consultee resistance and
2. suggest the specific strategy you may employ to reduce or prevent this potential source of resistance.

Sample: The consultant, Ms. Eberly, is a counselor at a senior high school. She receives a call from, Gail, the social studies department chair.

Gail: (voice is cracking, shaking) "I would like to talk with you. I could (starts to cry), could use your advice. I (long pause) have a situation with Helen, our new teacher. I am really worried (crying), I think I blew it!" (In the background the consultant hears Helen, yelling about taking Gail to the union representative).

Recognizing the consultee was in crisis, the possibility that the consultee was feeling vulnerability and out of control, and the real pressure of Helen threatening the consultee, the following scenario ensues:

1. The consultant decides to go to Gail's office rather than having Gail come to her room (reduce cost) and reduces Gail's feeling of vulnerability by not exposing her to others she may encounter coming to her office.
2. Entering Gail's office, the consultant decides to ask Helen if she would be kind enough to sit in an outer room while she speaks with Gail alone rather than attempting to mediate in the situation (hands-on, meeting needs to reduce attack, serves as payoff).
3. The consultant speaks to Gail rather than asking Gail what happened (reduced costs of possible vulnerability and provides emotional support and consultation refocus, which serve as need satisfier.)

Consultant: "Gail, I can see you are very upset and Helen sounded angry. Helen is in the outer office, and she's calming down. I let her know I will talk with her and that we can probably resolve whatever the problem is. She seems to be okay with that. I know you are concerned that you blew it, but it may not be that bad. Together I am sure we can work something out. Let's talk about it."

4. Having reduced the immediate crises (separating Helen and calming Gail), the consultant begins the problem identifying and resolving processes.

> *"Perhaps you could tell me a little about the problem and what you would like to have happen. I feel that if we work together on this, we probably can figure out what to do."*

Practice Scenario 1: The principal (consultee) asks that you consult with Ms. Hopkins (client), the 10th grade English teacher. Ms. Hopkins is in her last year of teaching and is scheduled to retire at the end of this year. The principal has had a number of parent complaints about her inability to manage her classroom. He is concerned that perhaps Ms. Hopkins is simply too old and may need to be removed; however, he is hoping that you can assist her to develop some new classroom management techniques.

Before you contact Ms. Hopkins, she approaches you and asks that you work with Drew, a "real problem child." From Ms. Hopkins perspective, Drew is the source of all the problems in her class.

For Reflection and Decision

1. What are the possible negative and conflicting expectations that may serve as sources of consultee resistance?
2. What specific strategy might you employ to reduce or prevent these potential sources of resistance?

Practice Scenario 2: Maxine is a bright, conscientious, 33-year-old assistant principal. She had been at the school only six months when the sudden resignation of the building principal served to elevate her to that post. She is the first woman to have achieved this position in this school and has been in the position only three months. You are the chair of the counseling department, and she requests a meeting with you.

At the meeting, Maxine appears upset, but with great effort, controls her emotions and explains that she feels that the assistant vice principals and other department chairs (all men) show little respect and often make inappropriate comments, some seemingly discriminatory. They also seem to be teaming up to make her look bad. She wants you to speak with them, to find some excuse to provide a workshop on the changing laws regarding harassment, diversity, et cetera. She believes they'll get the message. And one more request: You can't let on that she requested it!

For Reflection and Decision

1. What are the possible negative and conflicting expectations that may serve as sources of consultee resistance?
2. What specific strategy might be employed to reduce or prevent these potential sources of resistance?

Concerns Regarding Control

Resistance often reflects the consultee's concern about losing control or, at a minimum, being perceived as without control (Wynne, 2002). According to reactance theory (Nugent, 2013), when one feels forced into a certain behavior, they will react against the coercion. Often the form of that reaction is an increase in the behavior that is now restrained.

Block (1981) noted that since control with one's job is often the mark of success within the organization, the more power, responsibility, and authority an individual can obtain, the more she is perceived as successful and, as such, enlisting the assistance of a consultant may be viewed (by self or others) as an act of surrendering control and thus personal and organizational failure. Under these conditions, it might be assumed that for the consultee, maintenance of a semblance of control is more important than increasing her professional effectiveness. In this situation, the consultee may be willing to resist consultation and maintain control even if it results in poorer performance (Block, 1981).

Consider Case 8.1, the issue of extinguishing "book throwing behavior." The consultee, feeling as if the consultant was demeaning and attempting to illustrate how much more competent he was, gained a sense of control by inappropriately employing the consultant's recommendations for extinction and behavioral shaping. The disastrous results not only justified her inability to rapidly resolve the problem, since the consultant was also unable to resolve the problem, but she was also able to dismiss the consultant, take back control of her class, and suggest to the world, "I'll simply have to do it myself!"

The more the consultant can enlist the consultee's participation and thus ownership in the creation of the intervention plan, the more control the consultee will feel. With this increased sense of control, resistance will be reduced. The challenge for the consultant is to create a condition in which the consultee not only feels in control but is, in fact, a coequal partner controlling the nature and direction of the consultation. This is not always easy.

The effective consultant, while being interested in demonstrating her value and effectiveness, will not compete for control over the recognition for the operation and success of the consult. Instead, it is crucial to allow the consultee to feel actively contributing to and directing the process and outcome while at the same time feeling as if he can share the work, the burden, and the responsibility for possible failure.

Feeling Vulnerable

Engaging in consultation, like any helping encounter, requires the consultee to disclose, to share, to reveal their professional (and perhaps personal) experience. In the process of such sharing, the consultee exposes her competencies and incompetencies, her strengths and weaknesses. Sharing with the consultant about her professional practices that have proven unsuccessful increases the consultee's vulnerability to the recognition of imperfection and failures. In fact, the consultee may even be concerned that she will be blamed for the problem (Alderman & Gimpel, 1996).

This sense of vulnerability can often be compounded by the very fact that consultation often involves learning new behaviors. As a natural outcome of the learning process, the consultee will experience an increase in feelings of incompetence as he learns these new behaviors. This possible demonstration of reduced competence may increase the consultee's sense of vulnerability, especially if the consultee is unclear about the nature of the consultation or the role and function of the consultant and anticipates that the consultant may evaluate him, personally or professionally.

Besides possibly experiencing a sense of personal vulnerability as a result of disclosing and demonstrating one's level of incompetence, many consultees experience vulnerability within the organization should they enlist the support of a consultant. The climates of many organizations are not conducive to asking for help. For example, Gutkin, Clark, and Ajchenbaum (1985) reported that teachers working in closed organizational climates, characterized by administrators who were below average in consideration and structure, typically were less open to engaging in consultation. Further, organizations that tend to be quite competitive and in which asking for help may be viewed as a sign of weakness, and something which may be used by others as a way of advancing over the individual seeking help, would certainly inhibit a consultee's interest and willingness to engage in consultation.

Engaging in consultation can at some level place the consultee at risk and vulnerable to others who seek to get ahead. It would not be completely out of the question for a new teacher to be concerned about how her tenure may be impacted if she enlists the counselor's support. And it is not just teachers who can feel this sense of vulnerability, as highlighted by the following case illustration (Case Illustration 8.2).

Case Illustration 8.2
Consultee Vulnerability

Ms. Anita Wilson, assistant vice principal, called the counselor seeking some assistance. Rather than stop in at the counselor's office or invite the counselor to hers, she merely called and left the following message:

> *"This is Anita Wilson, and I would like to discuss the possibility of you working with me on some in-service training I am preparing. The principal asked me to develop an in-service for the teachers around the issues of cultural diversity, sexual harassment, and racial tension. I would like to discuss with you the ways you may be of assistance to me. Please give me a call at home rather than here at school. My phone number is 555-5555."*

The manner in which Ms. Wilson contacted the counselor-consultant (via phone) and the request to call her at home rather than simply stopping into her office suggests that there may be a little more behind this request than initially suggested. It appears that Ms. Wilson would like to keep the meeting with the counselor-consultant somewhat private. Perhaps this desire was based in some political or organizational reality or may be truly a matter of her self-induced vulnerability. Regardless, the consultant who ignores such signs of vulnerability may also proceed in insensitive ways that increase that sense of vulnerability and result in increased consultee resistance.

Until a consultant can change the norms and values of a consultee and the system in which she is functioning, she must remain sensitive to the consultee's experience of personal and organizational vulnerability. To reduce this sense of vulnerability in the consultee, the consultant should (a) remain descriptive and nonjudgmental in her communications with the consultee, (b) demonstrate respect for the consultee, (c) exhibit a belief in the value of discussing success and failures as a way of growing, and (d) highlight the confidential nature of the relationship.

Anxiety About Problem Finding/Problem Solving

The process of consultation will undoubtedly gather data reflecting the current situation, the ecosystems in which the concern occurs, and the consultee's approach to resolution. Clearly for some, this dynamic can be perceived as forcing acceptance of some less than desirable conditions. Piersel and Gutkin (1983) suggest that the consultee's anxiety about the possibility of uncovering consultee short comings or other problems may be a source of resistance. The resistance may be the consultee's defense against having to confront reality and make difficult choices regarding change.

A very subtle twist on this source of resistance comes in the form of the consultee who is eager to identify problems but may be less than enthusiastic, and thus resistant, to finding solutions. Piersel and Gutkin (1983) note that another source of consultee resistance might result from what the consultee "benefits," or experiences of secondary gain from having a problem. While experiencing the problematic realities of a problem, the consultee may also be experiencing some personal benefit by the existence of the problem and as such may feel anxious that such an issue will be resolved.

Consider the situation in which a company "rewards" an efficient, effective teacher by placing most of the "problem students" in her class or by increasing her adjunctive work assignments. In this setting, the teacher who has a problem may find that she is given increased support and reduced adjunctive work. Thus, finding a solution to the "problem" could prove costly to this teacher.

Resistance—A Reaction to Consultant Style

As noted by Wickerstrom and Witt (1993), consultants experiencing consultee resistance would do well to reflect upon their approach and style of consultation. The importance of the potential impact of the consultant's personal characteristics on the process and outcome of the consultation has been noted by others (e.g., Brown et al., 2006; Dougherty, 2000).

Specific consultant thoughts, feelings, and actions can contribute to resistance or blockage experienced in consultation. Specifically, consultants who restrict consultee freedom, exhibit abrasive characteristics, and loose professional objectivity may stimulate consultee resistance.

Restricting Consultee Freedom

According to the theory of psychological reactance (Brehm, 1966; Brehm, 1976), individuals are more likely to resist attempts by another to change them whenever they perceive their freedom to be reduced or eliminated. As noted above, a consultant who attempts to impose control over the consultee or employ power to coerce the consultee to embrace the recommendations may threaten consultee freedom and thus elicit resistance.

A straightforward directive aimed at reducing consultee resistance is to *ask* the consultee to do something, rather than *tell* or *direct* them to do something. In addition to this simple step, a consultant can increase the consultee's perception of freedom and control by developing a collaborative relationship that (1) emphasizes the consultee's freedom to accept or reject consultant recommendations, (2) encourages consultee participation, and (3) deemphasizes consultant contribution. It is important to highlight the "we" nature of the relationship as a means to reduce reactance (Knotek, 2006).

Abrasive Personal Characteristics

The consultant's personal characteristics can impact the degree of consultant persuasiveness (Burkhouse, 2012) and thus influence the degree to which resistance will be experienced within the consultee-consultant relationship.

As with other forms of helping, consultants who fail to exhibit essential helping attitudes and skills and thus appear nonauthentic and uncaring, or lack adequate communication skills, will increase the possibility of consultee resistance. But other factors such as the consultant's manner of self-presentation, including being inappropriately dressed, using unprofessional or inappropriate language, or manifesting distracting and distasteful personal habits will elevate the possibility of resistance. But perhaps it is the consultant's use and/or misuse of power within the consultation relationship that contributes the most to the resistance encountered.

The consultant who can find the appropriate balance between expert and referent power may be able to reduce the amount of resistance encountered. Without evidence of a consultant's professional preparedness, experience, competence, and intelligence (i.e., factors of expert power), consultee engagement may be less than desired. But expertise is not all that is needed to reduce resistance. Consultants also need to be seen as approachable and able to empathize with the consultee. Communicating a sense of equity and collaboration facilitates such a perception of approachability. It would appear that by adequately blending expert and referent power (Wilson, Erchul, & Raven, 2008) the consultant will elicit both perceptions of competence and willingness to help and, as such, reduced resistance.

Resistance—A Reaction to a Poor Cost/Payoff Ratio

Consultation, as viewed from a social-psychological perspective, is first and foremost a social interaction, a helping relationship (Parsons, 1996). As a social interaction, success and failure can depend in large part on the dynamics of the social encounter (Tingstrom, Little, & Stewart, 1990). Specifically, consultee resistance may indicate that the consultation process is experienced as aversive, and more costly than the benefits experienced.

Costs and payoffs can be the direct result of being in an interaction with the consultant (i.e., endogenous costs/payoffs) or be experienced outside of the relationship and interaction but as a result of the consultative interaction (i.e., exogenous costs/payoffs). Table 8.1 provides a number of examples of such costs and payoffs.

TABLE 8.1 **Illustrations of Endogenous and Exogenous Costs and Payoffs**

	COSTS	PAYOFFS
Endogenous (experienced as a direct result of the engaging in the consultation relationship)	• Anxiety about disclosing difficulties handling the situation • Time and energy expended during sessions with consultant	• The opportunity to feel supported • Release of tension by venting to the consultant • Receiving affirmation for strategies employed
Exogenous (experienced as a result of engaging in consultation but coming from a source outside the actual interactive relationship)	• The need to engage in data collection or application of new strategies • The need to give up time for preparation, lunch, or other "free" time to meet with consultant	• Problem resolved and student less distracting in class • Principal impressed with consultee's new approach • Successfully employing techniques learned to other students

It would appear that any time engaging in a consultation that is costlier physically, socially, or psychologically than it is rewarding, the consultee will find the interaction aversive and tend to resist it. The effective consultant will attempt to maximize payoffs within the consultation while at the same time reduce the costs associated with and experienced in consultation. Rewards include any aspect of the relationship that is enjoyable or satisfying. Resolving the presenting complaint would certainly be a payoff but so is the experience of feeling heard and supported by the consultant. Then there are the physical, social, and psychological costs that could accompany the engagement in consultation. It was previously noted that for some, consultation is anxiety provoking, is costly in terms of time and energy, and may even be seen in a negative light within the organization. These potential costs need to be reduced to lower the resistance. The important point is that the payoffs or rewards need to outweigh these costs for the relationship to be maintained rather than resisted (see Exercise 8.2).

Exercise 8.2 Reducing the Aversive Nature of Consultation

Directions: This exercise is best accomplished by working in a small group or a dyad (with a supervisor, mentor, or colleague) to allow for brainstorming. Below you are presented with a brief description of characteristics surrounding a consultation. After reading the description, complete the following:

1. Identify three possible costs that could occur within the relationship (endogenous) and three costs that may be incurred as a result of the encounter (exogenous). Similarly, identify three exogenous and three endogenous rewards.
2. Be specific and concrete, and generate strategies aimed at reducing each of the determined costs.
3. Create strategies for adding as many additional payoffs as you (or the group) can produce.

Scenario 1: Because of recent school redistricting, Mr. Adams, a teacher with 33 years of experience at the middle school, has been assigned to teach third grade. Mr. Adams is one year away from retirement age, even though he hopes to continue teaching for at least five years past this point. Mr. Adams has been experiencing a lot of frustration and stress because of the "immaturity" of his class. He approaches you informally at lunch one day and states, "Boy, kids are different today. I don't know where they get the energy. Sometimes an old guy like me can feel pretty worn out at the end of the day. You have any magic tricks you could share with me?"

Scenario 2: Hector Henriques is a new teacher hired to work in the 6th grade math and science department. Hector contacts you and asks you to reassign two students from his fifth period math class. Hector, the first Hispanic American to work in the school district, stated that he observed some racial and ethnic slurs written in notes being passed by these two boys, and he is afraid that he will "loose his cool" with them if he catches them again. Hector made it very clear to you that he has a very hot temper, and he wants these students out. Further, Hector suggests that he is aware that there are people within the school who would like to see him fail, and that he "hopes that you are not one of them."

Recognizing the Manifestations of Resistance

The first step in working with resistance is recognition. That is, the consultant must be aware of resistance when it is present. Too often consultants get lost in the task of problem solving and fail to register or record the interpersonal cues that are conveyed by the consultee and that suggest that the consultee is not embracing this process. A consultant needs to remain sensitive not only to the progress of the problem solving but also to the health and well-being of the relationship.

As the process unfolds, it is vital for the consultant to ask directly about the consultee's level of comfort, or feelings of apprehension or concern. This inquiry into the consultee's experience with the consultative process is not only a useful form of evaluation but is also a valuable means of involving and empowering the consultee throughout the consultation.

Often the resistance is less than obvious. It is important for the consultant to be aware of the verbal and nonverbal cues that provide evidence of the consultee's experience in the consultation. Is the consultee attentive? Is the consultee enthusiastic and participative? Is the consultee demonstrating a sense of ownership or is she exhibiting signs of discomfort?

The ways a consultee can manifest discomfort and resistance are many and varied. Some of the forms are quite obvious as in the situation where the consultee directly, explicitly, and perhaps even quite dramatically says no to the process. But most often resistance is less obvious, less direct, and therefore less easy to assess.

The Push Away

Sometimes a consultant may find that a consultee, who initially approached consultation enthusiastically, begins to see reasons within the dynamics of the relationship to "push the consultant away" and terminate the relationship. The consultee using this form of resistance will find an opportunity to become angry at the consultant. The consultee may blame the consultant for having imposed an overwhelming amount of work on the consultee. The consultee may complain that doing what the consultant requests disrupts the normal flow of his work. Whatever the form of blaming, accusing, and fault finding takes, these are manifestations of the consultee's desire to resist consultation by pushing the consultant away.

Yes, But...

A somewhat subtler form of resistance and one that can prove incredibly frustrating for a consultant is that which comes in the form of "agreement...but." The consultee, employing a "yes, but" kind of resistance will demonstrate a willingness and even enthusiasm for the process and direction of the consultation. However, this excitement, this desire, is quickly followed by a point of objection and concern that undermines the previous work. This form of resistance is especially noticeable when the prescriptive modality is employed using directives from the consultant.

Passive Aggression

Passive aggression refers to an indirect form of resistance expressed through such maneuvers as forgetfulness, procrastination, repetitive mistakes, and inefficiencies. Consider the resistance exhibited by the consultee in the illustrations below. The consultee had met with the consultant previously and was scheduled for a follow-up meeting at which time they would discuss the data the consultee was to have collected. Rather than outright refusal, the passive-aggressive consultee will feign eagerness to perform only to have been blocked by events beyond his control. Consider the following consultee responses and how you may feel as the consultant.

Consultee A: "I'm sorry about missing our meeting. I know it's the third time (is it a charm?), but I just have so much on my mind that I forgot. Oh, I know I was supposed to do something or prepare something for today, but it slipped my mind. I need to start writing things down."

Consultee B: "Hi, how goes it? Before you begin, I know I promised to gather that baseline data, and actually, I started, but there has been so much other stuff going on I just didn't get a chance to do it this week. I promise you, I'll complete it next time! So, anything else I can do?"

Consultee C: "I gathered the data you asked for, but I can't seem to find the file. It's here somewhere! I think I can remember what I wrote because it was only five items, you know. I counted how many times he was late following morning break. Oh, I'm sorry. Was I supposed to record how many times he was late following both morning and afternoon breaks?"

This response style not only actively blocks progress but can serve as a significant source of frustration and irritation to the consultant. The danger is that the consultant may, in fact, be seduced into venting her frustration and anger, giving the consultee justification for terminating the specific process, if not the entire relationship.

Requesting Counseling

An interesting form of resistance identified by Caplan (1970) was that involving the consultee's request for personal counseling. It is interesting in that as a mental health consultant, one might be quickly pulled into believing this is a profitable direction for the consultation to go. But the fact is that engaging in counseling is effectively terminating the consultation.

A request for counseling directs the focus away from the consultation. Such a request attempts to change the nature of the relationship. No longer is the focus on the client; it is now on the consultee. No longer is the target a work-related issue; it is now on the consultee's personal problem. Thus, no longer is the relationship one of coequal problem solving; it is now a helper-helpee encounter.

While the consultee may ask the consultant for counseling directly, often the consultant is seduced into this role shift by the consultee's expression of negative affect around their work performance (Randolph & Graun, 1988). In these situations, the consultant must remember that consultation is not counseling. The consultant, in these cases, should provide the consultee with "supportive refocus" (Randolph, 1985). The consultant, while showing a level of empathic support, needs to draw the consultee and the relationship back to focus on the client, the consultee's skills, and the knowledge and objectivity with working with the client.

Quick Sell/Quick Buy

In discussing the process of entering a consultative contract, Meyers, Parsons, and Martin (1979) warned that "even when no reservations or concerns are raised, the consultant should raise typical concerns to be sure there are no problems" (p. 66). While it can be quite gratifying for the consultant to have the consultee immediately embrace his orientation and consultation delivery model, the reality is that often too rapid of an agreement and blind acceptance of the consultant's recommendation may be one way the consultee can avoid involvement in the process. The consultee who actively nods agreement and provides verbal affirmation for the suggestions ("Oh, yes, absolutely," etc.) may be dismissing the consultant and the consultation process. Quite often, the rapid "that's great, you bet, no problem" response reflects either a lack of understanding or an intentional decision not to follow through even though providing wholehearted verbal support.

The consultant confronting such a situation would be wise to encourage discussion of reservations, objections, or concerns experienced by the consultee. When the consultee fails to identify his concerns, the consultant, while not attempting to create problems, should be willing to raise common concerns often aired by other consultees.

Working With, Not Defeating, Consultee Resistance

Resistance should be viewed as something to subdue or push away. The effective consultant who understands consultee resistance can utilize that understanding to develop a productive, collaborative relationship with the consultee. Once resistance has been identified, it is essential for the consultant to (1) invite the consultee to "own the resistance," (2) reframe the resistance as a source of valuable information, and (3) recognize and remove the source(s) of resistance.

The Invitation

The invitation stage is intricately tied to the identification stage in that the consultant is acknowledging resistance as a natural, regular part of any change process. Once consultee resistance has been experienced, a consultant may be tempted to attack or directly confront the consultee and the resistance. While such a tendency may be understandable given the consultant's frustration, such a strategy would most likely be ill fated. Block (1981) suggests that a consultant take on somewhat of a Zen quality to working with resistance. The school counselor-consultant will acknowledge the consultee's resistance, affirm the consultee's right to that resistance, and join them in their desire to overcome that resistance. The consultant seeking harmonious resolution of resistance will directly encourage the consultee to express her concerns, reminding her about the collaborative contract and the consultee's right to reject the suggestion. The goal of this step is to move the consultee from the indirect expression of concerns (i.e., resistance) to direct expression of concerns, which now can be addressed.

The consultant needs to assist the consultee to accept her concerns as valid and to reframe her apprehension and concerns so they are viewed as important data to the process of the consultation. Exercise 8.3 is provided to assist you in practicing this reframing process.

Exercise 8.3 Working With Resistance

Directions: Because resistance is experienced at different levels of awareness by various consultants and because the manner in which a consultant identifies, invites, and reframes varies from consultant to consultant, completing exercise 8.3 is best performed with another or in a small group. Additional cues will be identified, and alternative ways of inviting and reframing can be experienced by working within a group. The task involves reading the consultative interaction to follow and responding to each:

- Identify the specific point in the exchange when you became aware of the resistance.
- Identify what it was that specifically cued you to the resistance.
- Identify how you would feel as the consultant up to that point. This awareness of your reaction may be useful as diagnostic cues.
- After recognizing the presence of resistance, write out the specific response which you would employ to "identify" and "invite" the consultee to embrace this resistance. Be sure to engage nonjudgmental, descriptive, empathic counseling, and here-and-now responses.
- After reading the entire exchange, identify how you would respond to the consultee's implicit concerns to reframe the consultation experience in a more positive and hopeful light.

Consultant: Hi, Marie, it is very nice to meet you. I understand through Dr. Ruiz [the principal] that you wish to speak with me regarding your third-grade student, Max.

Consultee: Yes. I am grateful you had time to see me. Max has been a real problem. I was hoping you would talk with him.

Consultant: Well, that could be a possibility, but I find that it is much more efficient if I work along with the teacher to develop some problem-solving ideas. After all, you are the expert when it comes to Max and the work that he is failing to produce. So, perhaps you could help me understand what it is that Max is doing, or not doing, that concerns you, as well as some of the things you have tried up to this point.

Consultee: Oh, I thought you were going to just take him out of my class and do counseling with him.

Consultant: Marie, if after discussing the situation, we feel that is the best strategy, it certainly will be considered. Maybe we could start by you telling me what you think is up with Max and the kinds of things you have tried.

Consultee: OK, but I only have a 30-minute free period now, so will we have to do this another time?

Consultant: I'm OK with at least starting on this if you are, and 30 minutes is quite a bit of time.

Consultee: Well, what is it exactly that I should tell you?

Consultant: Marie, there isn't anything in particular that you should tell me, but anything that could help me get a feel for what it is about Max that is concerning you would be useful. Further, it might help both of us to understand the kinds of things you have found that worked and those things that haven't been as successful.

Consultee: Did Dr. Ruiz seem to be concerned that I needed help?

Consultant: No, she appeared impressed with your concern for Max and your willingness to seek assistance.

Consultee: Assistance! That's putting it mildly. You know, maybe I ought to be talking with you about me. I think I'm losing it.

Consultant: I know it can feel overwhelming at times, but I feel confident that if you could help me understand a little about the situation with Max, you and I could begin to work out some things that could help.

Consultee: You know, I guess you are right. Maybe working together will help but right now I have to prepare for class. I'll give you a call and set up an appointment so we can meet again.

Exercise 8.3 Working With Resistance

Ameliorating the Source of Resistance

Once the concerns and basis of resistance are identified and owned, a focus for the consultation relationship should turn to the reduction of these concerns. For example, it is possible that the goals and methods to be employed along with the consultant's approach to the problem may simply be inappropriate, and the consultee's resistance serves as a directive that an adjustment is needed.

When adjusting the direction or dynamic is not the source of the resistance, the consultant needs to employ appropriate helping skills and attitudes, and present her experience with this resistance in genuine, nonjudgmental, nonaggressive, and empathic language. This is most effective when done in the here-and-now experience rather than reporting or describing something that has passed and about which our memories may be clouded. Consider the exchanges listed in Case Illustration 8.3

Case Illustration 8.3
Identifying the Source of Consultee Resistance

Each of the following demonstrates one way in which a consultant attempted to unearth the possible existence and source of a consultee's resistance.

Situation 1: The "Yes, But" Form of Resistance

Consultant: I am a bit confused. For the last 10 minutes, I have been making suggestions, and you seem to initially agree and support them. You have been nodding and saying, "Yes, that's a good idea." However, each time we can begin discussing how to implement the idea you seem to offer a "but" as to why it won't work. Perhaps I'm missing something that may be very important to the formulation of strategies that we both can support.

Situation 2: The Passive-Aggressive (Forgetting) Form of Resistance

Consultant: I know you said that you were sorry that you forgot about implementing the task we agreed upon. I appreciate that you were apologetic for the fact that this was the third time in a row that you have now forgotten to do the task. As you told me you were sorry, you appeared to be annoyed or angry at something. Could we talk a little about how you have been feeling about working together around this issue?

Situation 3: The Quick Sell/Quick Buy Form of Resistance

Consultant: You certainly appear supportive. But it seems that everything I suggest is equally as acceptable to you. It may be useful if you could help me see what the possible costs or downsides to each of the suggestions may be. That way we could tailor the idea that fits best with your thoughts and style.

Reducing the Risk of Resistance

It is essential for the effective consultant to develop the knowledge and skill needed to recognize and identify consultee resistance, and to invite the consultee into a reframing of her concerns in light of a favorable view of consultation. However, establishing conditions which reduce the risk of resistance may prove even more beneficial to successful consultation.

Establishing a working relationship that is genuinely collaborative is the best way to prevent or at least reduce the risk of resistance (Caplan & Caplan, 1993; Friend & Cook, 1992; Parsons, 1996). The unique characteristics of a collaborative consulting relationship, including the creation of a coequal and mutual balance of power and ownership, stimulate a sense of freedom and control and thus reduce the need for reactance and resistance.

Summary

- Resistance is any behavior that thwarts the probability of a successful process or outcome and reflects the consultee's failure to participate constructively in the process of consultation.
- The source of that threat can lie within (1) the actual demands encountered as a result of the consultation, (2) the consultee's personal issues and concerns, (3) the consultant's style, or (4) the nature of the consulting relationship and dynamic established.
- It is important to understand that sometimes consultee resistance may, in fact, be a reasonable response to unrealistic and costly demands.
- Consultee resistance can be a protective response to what is to be too risky or too dangerous.
- Resistance is often an indirect way for the consultee to express discomfort with the consultant or the consultation process.
- The counselor-consultant who is experiencing consultee resistance as a result of adverse expectations the cost-payoff benefit will need to clarify and (re)establish specific elements of a collaborative consultation contract.
- Resistance often reflects the consultee's concern about losing control or, at a minimum, being perceived as without control and the consultee will resist a sense of being forced to engage, a response termed *reactance*.
- The first step in working with resistance is recognition of the presence of resistance.
- Resistance can be presented directly with a straightforward rejection, a "no," or it can be subtler and more indirect as would be the case with a push away, a "yes, but" response, a passive-aggressive engagement, and even a rapid, unquestionable acceptance of the consultant's suggestions.
- Establishing a working relationship that is genuinely collaborative is the best way to prevent or at least reduce the risk of resistance.

Additional Resources

Print

Cowan, E. W., & Presubry, J. H. (2000). Meeting client resistance and reactance with reverence. *Journal of Counseling and Development, 78*(4), 411–429.

Crawford, M. T., McConnell, A. R., Lewis, A. C., & Sherman, S. J. (2002). Reactance, compliance and anticipated regret. *Journal of Experimental Social Psychology, 38*(1), 56–64.

Wynne, C. P. (2002). The explanatory value of psychological reactance and cognitive dissonance theory in mandated consultation in schools. *Dissertation Abstracts International Section A: Humanities & Social Sciences, Vol 63*(1-A), 89.

Web-Based

Alsher, A. (2016). 9 effective tactics for managing resistance to change: Do what works. Retrieved from https://www.imaworldwide.com/blog/9-effective-tactics-for-managing-resistance-to-change-do-what-works

Nguyen, S. (2010). 6 steps to manage resistance to change. Retrieved from https://workplacepsychology.net/2010/05/13/6-steps-to-manage-resistance-to-change/

Prosci. (2018). Five tips for managing resistance. Retrieved from https://www.prosci.com/change-management/thought-leadership-library/managing-resistance-to-change

Yilmaz, D., & Kılıçoğlu, D. (2013). Resistance to change and ways of reducing resistance in educational organizations. *European Journal of Research on Education*. Retrieved from http://iassr2.org/rs/010103.pdf

References

Alderman, G. L., & Gimpel, G. A. (1996). The interaction between type of behavior problem and type of consultant: Teachers preferences for professional assistance. *Journal of Educational and Psychological Consultation, 7*, 305–313.

Block, P. (1981). *Flawless consulting*. San Diego, CA: Pfeiffer & Company.

Boohene, R., & Williams, A. A. (2012). Resistance to organizational change: A case study of Oti Yeboah Complex Limited. *International Business and Management, 4*(1), 135–145.

Brehm, J. W. (1966). *A theory of psychological reactance*. New York, NY: Academic Press.

Brehm, S. S. (1976). *The application for social psychology to clinical practice*. New York, NY: Wiley.

Brown, D., Pryzwansky, W. B., & Schulte, A. C. (2006). *Psychological consultation and collaboration*. (6th ed). Boston, MA: Allyn & Bacon.

Burkhouse, K. L. S. (2012). *Core competencies for training effective school consultants* (Doctoral dissertation, University of Maryland). Retrieved from https://drum.lib.umd.edu/bitstream/handle/1903/13156/Burkhouse_umd_0117E_13385.pdf;sequence=1

Butler, T. S., Weaver, A. D., Doggett, R. A., & Watson, T. S. (2002). Countering teacher resistance in behavioral consultation: Recommendations for the school-based consultant. *Behavior Analyst Today, 3*(3), 282–288.

Caplan, G. (1970). *The theory and practice of mental health consultation*. New York, NY: Basic Books.

Caplan, G., & Caplan, R. B. (1993). *Mental health consultation and collaboration*. Long Grove, IL: Waveland Press.

Cautilli, J. D., Riley-Tillman, T. C., Axelrod, S., & Hineline, P. N. (2005). Current behavioral models of client and consultee resistance: A critical review. *International Journal of Behavioral Consultation and Therapy, 1*(2), 147–154.

Dougherty, A. M. (2000). *Psychological consultation and collaboration: A casebook*. Belmont, CA: Wadsworth/Thomson.

Dougherty, A. M., Dougherty, L. P., & Purcell, D. (1991). The sources and management of resistance to consultation. *School Counselor, 38*, 178–185.

Friend, M., & Bauwens, J. (1988). Managing resistance: An essential consulting skill for learning disabilities teachers. *Journal of Learning Disabilities, 21*(9), 556–561.

Friend, M., & Cook, L. (1992). *Interactions: Collaboration skills for school professionals*. New York, NY: Longman.

Gonzalez, J. E., Nelson, J. R., Gutkin, T. B., & Shwery, C. S. (2004). Teacher resistance to school-based consultation with school psychologists: A survey of teacher perceptions. *Journal of Emotional and Behavioral Disorders, 12*(2), 30–37.

Gutkin, T. B., Clark, J. H., & Ajchenbaum, M. (1985). Impact of organizational variables on the delivery of school-based consultation services: A comparative case study approach. *School Psychology Review, 14*, 230–235.

Knoff, H. M. (2013). Changing resistant consultees: Functional assessment leading to strategic intervention. *Journal of Educational & Psychological Consultation, 23*(4), 307–317.

Knotek, S. (2006). Administrative crisis consultation after 9.11: A university's systems response. *Consulting Psychology Journal: Practice & Research, 58*(3), 162–173.

Kurpius, D. J., Fuqua, D. R., & Rozecki, T. (1993). The consulting process: A multidimensional model. *Journal of Counseling and Development, 71*, 601–606.

Meyers, J., Parsons, R. D., & Martin, R. (1979). *Mental health consultation in schools*. San Francisco, CA: Jossey-Bass.

Nugent, P. (2013). Reactance theory. In *Psychology Dictionary*. Retrieved from https://psychologydictionary.org/reactance-theory/

Parsons, R. D. (1996). *The skilled consultant*. Needham Heights, MA: Allyn and Bacon.

Parsons, R. D., & Meyers, J. (1984). *Developing consultation skills*. San Francisco, CA: Jossey-Bass.

Piersel, W. C., & Gutkin, T. B. (1983). Resistance to school-based behavioral consultation: A behavioral analysis of the problem. *Psychology in the Schools, 20*, 311–320.

Randolph, D. L. (1985). *Microconsulting: Basic psychological consultation skills for helping professionals.* Johnson City, TN: Institute of Social Sciences and Arts.

Randolph, D. L., Graun, K. (1988). Resistance to consultation: a synthesis for counselor-consultants. *Journal of Counseling & Development, 67*(3), 182–185.

Robbins, S. P., & Judge, T. A. (2009). *Organizational behavior.* Upper Saddle River, NJ: Prentice Hall.

Slonski-Fowler, K. E., & Truscott, S. D. (2004). General education teachers' perceptions of the prereferral intervention team process. *Journal of Educational and Psychological Consultation, 15,* 1–39.

Spratt, J., Shucksmith, J., Philip, K., & Watson, C. (2006). Interprofessional support of mental well-being in schools: A Bourdieuan perspective. *Journal of Interprofessional Care, 20,* 391–402.

Sterling-Turner, H. E., Watson, T. S., Wildmon, M., Watkins, C., & Little, E. (2001). Investigating the relationship between training type and treatment integrity. *School Psychology Quarterly, 16*(1), 56–67.

Thornberg, R. (2014). Consultation barriers between teachers and external consultants: A grounded theory of change resistance in school consultation. *Journal of Educational and Psychological Consultation, 24*(3), 183–210.

Tingstrom, D. H., Little, S. G., & Stewart, K. J. (1990). School consultation from a social psychological perspective: A review. *Psychology in the Schools, 27,* 41–50.

Wickerstrom, K. F., & Witt, J. C. (1993). Resistance within school-based consultation. In J. E. Zins, T. R. Kratochwill, & S. N. Elliot (Eds.), *Handbook of consultation services for children* (pp. 159–178). San Francisco, CA: Jossey-Bass.

Wilson, K.E., Erchul, W.P., & Raven, B.H. (2008). The likelihood of using social power strategies by school psychologists when consulting with teachers. *Journal of Educational & Psychological Consultation.* 2008, 18 (2), p101–123.

Wynne, C. P. (2002). *The explanatory value of psychological reactance and cognitive dissonance theory in mandated consultation in schools* (Doctoral dissertation). Retrieved from https://fordham.bepress.com/dissertations/AAI3040405

CHAPTER 9

Counselor as Consultant: Ethical Considerations

I know Mrs. Lane is dying to know more about Jasmine's home situation, and actually, some of this information may help us to work more effectively with Jasmine, but I don't know if....

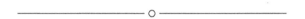

The hesitancy expressed by the school counselor, the consultant in our opening scenario, reveals the ethical challenges encountered by a school counselor working from a consultation frame of service. Issues of confidentiality, informed consent, professional competence, and boundaries are not new to those in school counseling. However, these issues, along with all of those issues involved in the practice and delivery of counseling services within the school, take on an added dimension when viewed from the triadic relationship found in consultation.

This chapter presents a number of the unique ethical challenges for the school counselor functioning in the role of consultant. It should be noted that the discussion that follows and the concerns raised are not intended to be the definitive, all-inclusive statements on the issue of ethics in consultation practice. As such, it is essential that the school counselor-as-consultant remain vigilant in her professional development and also engage with others in professional dialogue as a way of checking and shaping practice decisions.

After completing this chapter, the reader should be able to describe the unique challenges confronting the school counselor as a consultant when attempting to

1. competently practice,
2. establish and maintain confidentiality,
3. gain informed consent,
4. maintain professional boundaries,
5. employ efficient and effective treatment procedures, and
6. employ influence and power within the consultation relationship.

Engaging in Consultation: An Ethical Directive

The need for and benefits of employing a consultative form of service delivery within the schools have been the themes woven throughout the previous sections. The realities of working within an ecosystem, addressing heavy caseloads, and then attempting to provide preventive services to support the need and value of consultation as a mode of service delivery include ethical considerations, just as any mode of counseling does.

Beyond the practical value of consultation as a model of school counselor service delivery, the need to engage in this mode is a reflection of the guiding ethical principles of the American School Counseling Association (ASCA) (2016). As noted in the preamble to the ASCA Ethical Standards for School Counselors, school counselors are called to be advocates, leaders, collaborators, and consultants who create systemic change. More specifically, the code (ASCA, 2016) calls for counselors to (a) "collaborate with administration, teachers, staff and decision makers around school-improvement goals" (A.3.a); (b) "provide leadership to create systemic change to enhance the school" (B.2.d); and (c) "collaborate with appropriate officials to remove barriers that impede the effectiveness of the school" (B.2.e).

Unique Ethical Challenges

The triadic nature of consultation, the possibility of multiple clients, and the issues surrounding advocacy and innovation offer many unique ethical challenges for the consultant. Further, the unique nature of consultation and the consultation relationship often makes the resolution of these ethical concerns somewhat more complicated than might be the case in the more traditional, direct-service model of helping. Consider Case illustration 9.1.

Case Illustration 9.1
Challenges When Consulting With a First-Grade Teacher

Bob, the first-grade teacher, caught Pat, the school counselor, in the faculty room and asked to see her about one of his students, Alice. According to Bob, Alice is quite an active child and appears to be either unable or unwilling to follow the classroom rules. Bob told Pat that he is a bit concerned about speaking with her since he was a first-year teacher and worried that others might perceive his seeking assistance as a sign of incompetence. As they began to discuss the situation, Bob revealed that his approach to classroom management included the use of a particular "time out" procedure that he had developed. According to Bob, anytime Alice misbehaved, he would have her stand in the back of the room facing a blank wall. Bob noted that even if he had her stand for an hour, it failed to change her behavior, and he is at his wit's end.

As is suggested by the brief scenario, school counselors working from a consultation mode of service delivery can face numerous ethical issues in their delivery of services. While the teacher in our illustration is making what appears to be a straightforward request for assistance, his disclosure regarding the use of his particular time-out procedure presents some ethical issues for the counselor-as-consultant.

In responding to the request and the information ascertained, the school counselor-consultant needs to address questions such as: Who is the client? What is the responsibility of the consultant to the child's welfare and safety? What is the consultant's ethical responsibility regarding the use of Bob's unique form of time-out? What are the limits of confidentiality? What values and possible value conflicts may exist between the consultant, the consultee, and the system (i.e., the principal), and how will these impact the consultant's response?

In observing all the ethical guidelines offered by the American Counseling Association (ACA) (2014) and the American School Counseling Association (ASCA, 2016), the school counselor-as-consultant needs to pay particular heed to those directives addressing competence, cultural sensitivity, informed consent, confidentiality, power, and treatment efficacy.

Consultant Competence

While being called to provide consultation services, the ethical school counselor is aware of the directive to operate within her professional level of competence. Both the American Counseling Association and the American School Counselors Association point to the ethical mandate to be qualified to perform one's duties. "Counselors practice only within the boundaries of their competence, based on their education, training, supervised experience, state and national professional credentials, and appropriate professional experience" (ACA, 2014, Principle C.2.a), whereas the American School Counselor Association highlights the need for school counselors to "have unique qualifications and skills to address pre-K–12 students' academic, career and social/emotional development needs" (ASCA, 2016, Preamble).

Beyond this mandate of general competence, those engaging in consultation as a specialized service are also directed to take "reasonable steps to ensure that they have the appropriate resources and competencies when providing consultation services" (ACA, 2014, Principle D.2.a.). The challenge is that when it comes to school consultation services, the specific cognates and skills deemed essential to ethical practice are not universally defined.

Consultant Cultural Sensitivity

The school counselor operating from a consultation frame of reference understands that her services are provided within the unique cultural context of that school and as such must be sensitive to the culture and values of the system, the consultee, and the client. For a school counselor-consultant to view individual concerns or a personal problem as separate from social and cultural context is to misunderstand them (Parsons & Kahn, 2006). According to Sue & Sue (2013), the ethical and culturally sensitive school counselor needs to (a) understand his own culture and worldview and its influence on the consultation process, (b) value engaging with alternative worldviews in the delivery of service and, (c) develop and engage services that are reflective of a cultural sensitivity.

Awareness of One's Own Culture and Its Influence

In addition to being sensitive to the unique value and culture of those with whom they consult, school counselors must also be aware of their worldview and the impact that such a worldview may have on their consultative interactions. Counselors are directed to "be aware of—and avoid imposing—their own values, attitudes, beliefs, and behaviors"(ACA, 2014, A.4.b.).

While an ethical mandate, this increased awareness of one's worldview is also a practical directive if one is to be an effective consultant. The effective and culturally sensitive consultant is aware of how his cultural background and experiences, attitudes, and values influence his definitions of normality and abnormality and his approach to the process of helping. He understands and accepts that his worldview is but one (of many) valid and valuable sets of assumptions, values, and perspectives from which a person may function. As such, the ethical and competent consultant is open, via collaborative exchange, to craft interventions that reflect the culture of the client, consultee, and system.

Awareness of the Narrowness of a Single "Mainstream" Perspective

The ethical and culturally sensitive consultant is aware of the limitedness and narrowness of any one single cultural perspective, even if, and perhaps especially when, that perspective represents the cultural mainstream. The ethical and skilled consultant is aware that the "truth" is culture colored and as such accepts the relative and nonabsolute nature of any one cultural view. With this awareness, he will avoid functioning from an ethnocentric perspective and "pursue additional training and supervision in areas where they are at risk of imposing their values" (ASCA, 2016, A.6.e.).

Employ Culturally Sensitive Approaches to Service Delivery

Although it may be argued that there are few human universals, the one universal is that variation exists. People, although similar, are also distinctly different. The culture in which we operate and develop affects our values, our goals, and our behaviors, and as such will also influence the decisions we make or should make within the consulting context.

The ethical and skilled consultant continues to assess goals and consulting strategies to ensure that these are relevant and appropriate to the culture in which the consulting occurs and in line with the values of the consultant, consultee, and system. In addition, the ethical counselor-as-consultant employs culturally inclusive language in all forms of communication (ASCA, 2014, B.2.p) and approaches problem definitions and goals with an appreciation of cultural context. For example, the assessment of desirable behavior in one cultural context may be diagnosed as undesirable in another. This point is not lost on the culturally sensitive consultant.

The consultant must be aware and accepting of the fact that there can be wide variation of cultural definitions, both normal and abnormal. As such, the consultant, in attempting to define what is dysfunctional, needs to be sensitive to the culture of the system in which he is working and how that culture defines *acceptable*, *desirable*, or *functional*. As the professional help provider, the school counselor-as-consultant may have assumptions about what constitutes conflict and problems as well as what defines solutions and health. However, the ethical consultant will be mindful that these definitions are culturally impacted and as such will place his goals and concerns within the context of the client, consultee, and systems culture (see Case Illustration 9.2).

Case Illustration 9.2
Double Meanings

Ms. Toby, the school counselor at Friendship Elementary School, was approached by Ms. Anderson about a new student in her third-grade class. It seemed that Duke was having difficulty connecting with the other students and was often alone at lunch and recess. Duke had moved to the United States about two months ago, having been born and residing in England until that time. Ms. Anderson told Ms. Toby that the students reported that it was hard to talk to and play with Duke because they didn't "do things the same way." Ms. Anderson did not understand these issues "because after all, they speak the same language."

Having worked with other students who had transferred into the school from other countries, Ms. Toby realized that language and cultural norms could in fact be an issue, even if the primary language is seemingly the same. Ms. Anderson and Ms. Toby agreed that it would be helpful to observe Duke during lunch and recess. Ms. Toby completed the observations by the next day and observed the following:

Lunch — Duke brought his lunch to school; it included a thermos of hot soup and crackers. When his peers questioned him about why he had a thermos and "weird" crackers they had never seen before, he appeared agitated and replied, "Don't know!" One of his classmates then asked, "Why are you always so mad?" to which Duke yelled, "I am NOT MAD!"

Recess — Duke ran up to a group of students who said they were playing football and said, "I played this all the time in England. I can help you win!" At that point he proceeded to dribble the ball down the field while the other students shouted, "What are you doing?"

Ms. Toby set up a follow-up meeting with Ms. Anderson where they talked about the difference in language and culture between where Duke had lived and Friendship Elementary. Although English is the language being spoken in both cases, the meaning of many words is different. Ms. Toby knew from her work with other students from England that "mad" was being interpreted as "crazy" by Duke, and indeed, he was not crazy; however, he was "cross," which is how he expressed his feeling of anger. Additionally, in England, football is played like soccer, not American football.

The culturally sensitive counselor knew Duke needed to learn the language and cultural norms of his new setting, and his teacher and classmates needed to learn to celebrate diversity and new perspectives. Perhaps if introduced to the class during a "Celebrate Your Culture" day, the soup and "weird" crackers, new vocabulary, and different ways to play games would broaden the perspectives of the young students and enhance their tolerance and acceptance for all individuals.

Informed Consent

The ethical consultant must demonstrate respect for the rights of the consultee to be fully informed. The American Counseling Association Code of Ethics (ASCA, 2014) is clear on this matter, stating: "When providing formal consultation services, counselors have an obligation to review, in writing and verbally, the rights and responsibilities of both counselors and consultees. It is important to use clear and understandable language to inform all parties involved about the purpose of the services to be provided, relevant costs, potential risks, and benefits, and the limits of confidentiality" (ACA, 2014, Principle D.2.b.).

The goal of informed consent is to promote cooperation and participation of the client and consultee in the consultation process. To facilitate such full engagement, the ethical consultant will provide the consultee and client information that can assist them to decide if they wish to enter, continue, or terminate the consultation relationship.

When working with the consultee, it is essential that the consultant assist the consultee to understand both what consultation is and is not. Consider the example of a father meeting with the school counselor to discuss ways to support his child, who is having difficulty in advanced biology class. The father, acting from the role of consultee, was seeking to engage the counselor in a prescriptive mode of consultation. As the discussion unfolded, the father turned the conversation away from the development of strategies that may help his son in advanced biology to complaining about his relationship with his wife and the lack of "spark" in their relationship. The father began to ask the counselor for marital advice, a request that not only felt outside of the school counselor's area of competency but also was clearly outside the boundaries for a consultation relationship. Having informed the father about the nature of consultation along with the roles to be played may have helped the counselor to have avoided this request for personal counseling.

In addition to defining what consultation is and is not, the consultant should inform the consultee about the nature and responsibilities of collaborative consultation. The consultee needs to understand the role the consultant is to play, the role the consultee is to play, and the anticipated nature and character of the relationship as it unfolds through the various stages of the consultation process. Further, it is important for the consultant to highlight the possible impacts (both positive and negative) of engaging in consultation. In Exercise 9.1, we invite you to think about providing informed consent.

Exercise 9.1 Providing Informed Consent

Directions: Establishing a consultee's informed consent is neither as simple nor as straight forward as one might believe. Below you are asked to identify (a) factors that could impact the establishment of informed consents, (b) strategies that could be used to address those factors, and (c) ways to implement those strategies. Examples are provided. You may also find it helpful to discuss this exercise with a practicing school counselor.

Factor Impacting Informed Consent	Strategy	Implementation Needs
• Consultee is unfamiliar with a consultation mode of service, having only engaged in "direct" service	• Written description in a brochure or on the counselor webpage • The establishment of a detailed contract	• Publication access • Webpage access
• Consultee who is an English Learner (EL)	• Translator for written material • Interpreter for spoken information	• Budget for translator and/or interpreter
Other		

Informed consent is not a process that occurs only at the beginning of a consult. The consultant needs to continually update the consultee on the process and progress of the consultation, the anticipated steps to be taken next, and the unfolding consequences of each action. This ongoing process of being informed allows the consultee to fully engage in the process of consultation from the perspective of understanding. The same mandate for achieving informed consent, or in the case of children, informed assent, applies to the client (Parekh, 2007). The student-as-client needs to be told that the approach employed will involve coordination of information, and efforts on the part of the counselor-consultant and the consultee. Also, the client needs to be assisted to understand the benefit of this triadic approach and helped to understand the limits to which personal information will be shared.

Confidentiality

In seeking help, both the client and the consultee should be able to expect a relationship that is trusting, honest, and safe. The American School Counseling Association is clear on this issue. In the preamble to its ethical standards, it states that all students have the right to "privacy that should be honored to the greatest extent possible, while balancing other competing interests (e.g., best interests of students, safety of others, parental rights) and adhering to laws, policies and ethical standards pertaining to confidentiality and disclosure in the school setting" (ASCA, 2016). The same concern for client privacy extends to the data exchanged during the consultation. The American Counseling Association code of ethics states: "Information shared in a consulting relationship is discussed for professional purposes only. Written and oral reports present only data germane to the purposes of the consultation, and every effort is made to protect client identity and to avoid undue invasion of privacy" (ACA, 2014, B.7.a.).

This ethical mandate, when placed within a school setting, can take on legal implications. It is crucial for the school counselor-as-consultant to know when rules governing the release of information and parents' rights come to play in the sharing of information in a collaborative relationship (ASCA, 2016, A.2.d).

While the ethical mandate to protect client privacy is clear, the reality of its implementation can sometimes be complicated. The triadic nature of consultation requires an exchange of information between the consultee and the consultant. Thus, maintaining client confidentiality is somewhat dependent upon the consultee's willingness to respect that privacy. As such, the school counselor-as-consultant must accept the limits to her ability to maintain total privacy and protect confidentiality.

In addition to committing to the maintenance of confidentiality of the data shared during the consultation, the consultant must ethically inform the consultee of conditions in which this confidentiality would need to be broken. One condition that would require disclosure is when there is evidence of clear and imminent danger. Unlike a situation found in a one-to-one counseling relationship, the threat referred to need not be restricted to the client. Confidentiality may need to be broken when there is a clear and imminent danger to the client, the consultee, and even the system.

When the consultant is uncertain whether confidentiality should be maintained, she should consult with colleagues or even her professional association's legal resources. As with all ethical decisions, when contemplating disclosing or maintaining confidence, one should employ an ethical decision-making model. Table 9.2 outlines the American School Counselor Association's steps to be taken when making ethical decisions (Stone, 2013).

TABLE 9.2 **Steps: A Model for Ethical Decision-Making**

The STEPS model for school settings is outlined below. A full description of the nine steps can be found in Stone (2013).

STEP	TARGET
1	Define the problem emotionally and intellectually
2	Apply the ASCA Ethical Standards for School Counselors and the law
3	Consider the students' chronological and developmental levels
4	Consider the setting, parental rights, and minors' rights
5	Apply the moral principles (beneficence, autonomy, nonmaleficence, loyalty, and justice)
6	Determine potential courses of action and their consequences
7	Evaluate the selected action
8	Consult
9	Implement the course of action

Exercise 9.2 will help to highlight some of the difficulties in maintaining confidentiality in consultation relationships.

Directions: For each of the scenarios, identify the specific factors that would make maintaining confidentiality difficult. With a colleague, mentor, or supervisor, discuss steps that could be taken to address these challenges.

- *Situation 1:* As the school counselor, you have been invited to provide organizational consulting to a large high school. The principal of the school has two specific agendas: (1) he wants you to identify the teachers' needs for in-service training, and (2) he wants you to determine which teachers may have drinking and drug problems, sexual hang-ups, and problem marriages.
- *Situation 2:* You have been requested by the school's instructional support teacher (IST) to work with her team. Apparently, their work has become increasingly less professional (e.g., poor record keeping, incomplete goal monitoring), with evidence of much interpersonal conflict among the six members. Through interviewing the team members, you find out that two have been pursuing other employment and have no interest in IST work. On more than one occasion, they came to meetings unprepared and left early. They ask that the consultant give them some time to settle their employment situation rather than tell the principal.
- *Situation 3:* You are a school counselor in an urban elementary school. You have been invited to work with a fifth-grade boy because of what the consultee describes as "irritating, disrespectful behavior in class." In gathering additional information from the consultee (his science teacher), the consultee states, "I need you to do something immediately! I have had kids like this before. In fact, I lost my last job because a kid like him got me so mad, I literally pushed him out of class. Hey, this is confidential, nobody knows about that. You are *not* allowed to tell anybody. But I'm telling you, you got to get this kid to straighten up. He is *really* getting to me!"

Exercise 9.2 Maintaining Confidentiality?

Establishing and Maintaining Professional Boundaries

Working in the school invites counselors and teachers to develop close, personal relationships. However, as with all helping relationships, once a counselor engages with a teacher or an administrator in a triadic consultation relationship, the counselor is responsible for ensuring that the relationship is one marked by appropriate professional behavior. The ethical consultant will remember that the purpose of the consultee-consultant relationship is to assist the consultee with a work-related need rather than helping the consultee address his personal needs (ASCA, 2016, A.5.c).

Two specific conditions can threaten the ability to maintain professional boundaries. First, professional boundaries and objectivity may be compromised when the consultant and the consultee are engaged in relationships outside of the consultation. Such dual relationships can impair the consultant's level of objectivity and professional judgment and thus need to be avoided whenever possible.

While this principle is clear, the reality for those working within a school is that it is most often impossible to avoid consulting with a consultee (e.g., a teacher) with whom other professional and personal relationships have been formed. It is not unusual to find colleagues sharing living arrangements, playing on community sports teams, or even co-coaching at school. In these situations, the counselor-as-consultant must be sensitive to threats to professional objectivity that may exist and also share these concerns with the consultee. When the consultant and consultee share a personal relationship as well as a professional one, it is essential to commit to keeping all case discussion and work confined to "formal" consultative interactions. Case Illustration 9.3 provides an example of this type of boundary issue.

A second potential threat to the professional boundaries occurs when the consultee attempts to engage the consultant in personal counseling. Consultation is a process that focuses on work-related issues and not the consultee's personal, psychological needs and concerns. This focus on the work-related nature of the consultation contract must be articulated and agreed on. When engaging with the consultee, the consultant needs to make clear that the relationship and the process to be employed is not counseling for the consultee, and, as such, personal, nonwork-related issues will not be addressed. When the consultee's personal problems are interfering with her job performance, the consultant should refer the consultee for individual counseling. Under these conditions, the consultant should not offer to provide that counseling.

Assisting the consultee to understand these boundaries, as well as maintaining the integrity of the boundaries, is an ethical responsibility of the consultant.

Power

In the previous discussion of the issue of entry and the development and maintenance of a collaborative relationship, an emphasis was given to the value of the use of expert and referent power to influence the nature of the relationship. As should be evident, the role of the consultant is by its nature a role of potential power and influence.

Case Illustration 9.3
I Thought I Was Your Friend. . .

Taylor and Molly both started to work at Marlin Middle School two years ago. They went through the new teacher induction program together, sat on many of the same committees, and quickly became the go-to person for each other. When they first started, they both taught subject area classes; however, this year, after Taylor finished her degree in school counseling, she was asked to fill the vacancy in the school counseling department. Taylor and Molly were both excited that they would still be working together.

At the end of the first week of school, Molly went to Taylor's counseling office to see how things were going and to ask for help with one of her new students, Rex. Molly was already frustrated with the new, unruly student and wondered what Taylor knew about him. Taylor went over the same information that had been given to all of Rex's teachers, and Molly grew a bit indignant. "I know all that already! I want to know what's going on with his family. There must be something strange happening. You know I just want to help him." When Taylor explained she had revealed all she was able to, Molly huffed out of the office exclaiming, "I thought I was your friend!"

Taylor was upset and realized that it would have been a good idea to have taken some preventative measures concerning boundaries as she transitioned into her new role. She asked the principal if she could have some time at the next faculty meeting to go over confidentiality and what it looks like in a school. She knew that, as a teacher, she always wanted to know more information when it came to supporting a student who was having difficulty, and now that she was on the other side of the consultation, she understood that there were issues that would be unethical to discuss.

The reality is that all consultants, by the definition of having expertise and being requested to assist their consultees to reach a previously unachieved goal, have power and are in the business of influencing. It is not the reality of power nor its use that is at issue; it is the potential for misuse or abuse that needs to be considered.

Sadly, our professional literature is filled with stories of counselor misuse of power. The issue of boundaries and boundary violation continues to be a focus of litigation and ethics hearings. This danger of the misuse of power is not limited to direct, one-on-one counseling situations, and can extend to the consultation and to the relationship between consultant and consultee.

The focus of this text has been on promoting the value of employing a collaborative style when engaging in school consultation. This emphasis not only reflects the practical value of collaboration but is also congruent with the ethical principles governing a school counselor's responsibilities (see ASCA, 2016, B.1.a, B.2.a., B.2.e, B.2.f, B.2.q).

The establishment and maintenance of the collaborative nature of the consultation relationship will by definition protect the consultee from the potential of the consultant's abusive use of power. A collaborative relationship, by definition, is voluntary and mutual.

A collaborative relationship is one in which the consultee has the right to accept or reject the consultant's suggestions and recommendations at any time. The development of a truly collaborative, informed, and voluntary relationship may be the best means to ensure that power is not abused.

The Ethics of Treatment

The ethical consultant is, according to the American School Counseling Association, one who "provides effective, responsive interventions to address student needs" (ASCA, 2016, A.1.h). More specifically, the ethical counselor employs "techniques/procedures/ modalities that are grounded in theory and/or have an empirical or scientific foundation" (ACA, 2014, C.7.a).

A first step in the provision of such ethical service is for the school counselor to have both knowledge of and skill in best practice techniques. Although there is an ever-increasing empirical database across multiple disciplines that can be used to assess the relative efficacy of different approaches and methods for consulting, no one set of operating procedures has been identified. The ethical school counselor-as-consultant needs to be alert to update his professional knowledge and skill, as well as to keep abreast of the ever-increasing research supporting specific intervention strategies.

Beyond the continuing development of knowledge and skill, the school counselor-as-consultant needs to monitor and evaluate the effectiveness of her services. The employment of outcome and process assessment methods is not only a good idea; it is one promoted as an ethical mandate. According to the American Counseling Association, counselors need to "continually monitor their effectiveness as professionals and take steps to improve when necessary" (ACA, 2014, C.2.d.). The use of data in the process of monitoring effectiveness is also promoted in the American School Counseling Association's Ethical Standards, which states that school counselors "collect process, perception and outcome data and analyze the data to determine the progress and effectiveness of the school counseling program" (ASCA, 2016, A.3.e.). The directive is clear that when engaging in school consultation, the ethical consultant will employ those techniques that are recognized as best practice and engage in both formative and summative evaluation methods to ensure effectiveness.

Summary

- The ASCA Ethical Standards for School Counselors (2016) charges school counselors to be advocates, leaders, collaborators, and consultants who create systemic change.
- There is an ethical mandate to be qualified to perform one's duties: "Counselors practice only within the boundaries of their competence, based on their education, training, supervised experience, state and national professional credentials, and appropriate professional experience" (ACA, 2014, C.2.a).
- The ethical school counselor needs to (a) understand his own cultural and worldview, and its influence on the consultation process; (b) value engaging with alternative worldviews in the delivery of service; and (c) develop and engage services that are reflective

of cultural sensitivity.

- The American Counseling Code of Ethics (2014) is clear on informed consent, stating: "When providing formal consultation services, counselors have an obligation to review, in writing and verbally, the rights and responsibilities of both counselors and consultees. It is important to use clear and understandable language to inform all parties involved about the purpose of the services to be provided, relevant costs, potential risks, and benefits, and the limits of confidentiality" (ACA, 2014, Principle D.2.b.).

- School Counselors are ethically mandated to protect client privacy, yet the reality of its implementation can sometimes be complicated. The triadic nature of consultation requires an exchange of information between the consultee and the consultant.

- The consultant must ethically inform the consultee of conditions in which this confidentiality would need to be broken, including when there is a clear and imminent danger to the client, the consultee, or the system.

- The ethical consultant will remember the purpose of the consultee-consultant relationship is to assist the consultee with a work-related need rather than helping the consultee in addressing his personal needs.

- Consultants have power by the very fact that they possess the expertise and have been requested to share that expertise in helping a consultee reach previously unachieved goals.

- The development of a truly collaborative, informed, and voluntary relationship may be the best means to ensure that power is not abused.

- The ethical counselor employs "techniques/procedures/modalities that are grounded in theory and/or have an empirical or scientific foundation" (ACA, 2014, C.7.a.).

Additional Resources

Print

Brown, D., Pryzwansky, W. B., & Schulte, A. C. (2011). *Psychological consultation and collaboration: Introduction to theory and practice* (7th ed). New York, NY: Pearson.

Herlihy, B., & Corey, G. (2014). *Boundary issues in counseling: Multiple roles and responsibilities.* Alexandria, VA: American Counseling Association.

Lowman, R. L., & Cooper, S. E. (2017). *The ethical practice of consulting psychology.* Washington, DC: American Psychological Association.

Parsons, R. D., & Dickinson, K. L. (2016). *Ethical practice in the human services: From knowing to being.* Thousand Oaks, CA: SAGE.

Parsons, R. D., & Zhang, N. (2014). *Becoming a skilled counselor.* Thousand Oaks, CA: SAGE.

Web-Based

Ingraham, C. L. (2016). Education consultants for multicultural practice of consultee-centered consultation. *Journal of Educational and Psychological Consultation, 27*(1), 72–95. Retrieved from https://doi.org/10.1080/10474412.2016.1174936

Sander, J. B., Hernández Finch, M. E., Pierson, E. E., Bishop, J. A., German, R. L., & Wilmoth, C. E. (2016). School-based consultation: Training challenges, solutions and building cultural competence. *Journal of Educational and Psychological Consultation, 26*(3), 220–240, Retrieved from DOI: 10.1080/10474412.2015.1042976

Websites

American Counseling Association Code of Ethics, 2014. https://www.counseling.org/Resources/aca-code-of-ethics.pdf

American School Counselor Association 2016 Ethical Standards for School Counselors. https://www.schoolcounselor.org/asca/media/asca/Ethics/EthicalStandards2016.pdf

Family Educational Rights and Privacy Act (FERPA). https://www2.ed.gov/policy/gen/guid/fpco/ferpa/index.html

Health Insurance Portability and Accountability Act (HIPAA). https://www.hhs.gov/hipaa/index.html

Office of Civil Rights (OCR)/Department of Education. https://www2.ed.gov/about/offices/list/ocr/index.html

For more information about school districts' obligations to English-learner students and limited English-proficient parents, additional OCR guidance is available at http://www2.ed.gov/about/offices/list/ocr/ellresources.html

References

American Counseling Association. (2014). *ACA code of ethics*. Retrieved from http://www.counseling.org/resources/aca-code-of-ethics.pdf.

American School Counselor Association. (ASCS). (2012). *ASCA school counselor competencies*. Retrieved from https://www.schoolcounselor.org/asca/media/asca/home/SCCompetencies.pdf

American School Counselor Association. (ASCA). (2016). *ASCA ethical standards for school counselors*. Retrieved from https://www.schoolcounselor.org/asca/media/asca/Ethics/EthicalStandards2016.pdf

Parekh, S. A. (2007). Child consent and the law: An insight and discussion into the law relating to consent and competence. *Health and Development, 33*(1), 78–82.

Parsons, R. D., & Kahn, W. J. (2006). *The school counselor as consultant*. Belmont, CA: Thomson Brooks/Cole.

Stone, C. (2013). *School counseling principles: Ethics and law* (3rd ed.). Alexandria, VA: American School Counselor Association.

Sue, D. W., & Sue, D. (2013). *Counseling the culturally diverse: Theory & practice* (6th ed.). New York, NY: John Wiley.

Section III

Consultation: Moving Beyond
Intervention to Prevention

CHAPTER 10

Level III Prevention: Client-Focused Consultation: Intervention with a Twist

It certainly was helpful being able to sit with Dr. Jameson and get a better feel for what may be going on with Jasmine in his music class. His perspective and observations of Jasmine provide a unique angle, something that I wouldn't typically get by talking with Jasmine. I think that with both of us gathering additional information, we will be able to come up with a plan that helps Jasmine and may even give us some ideas about what else could be done to prevent this kind of thing from happening again.

———————————— ○ ————————————

The inclusion of Dr. Jameson, as the consultee, into the planning of services for the client, Jasmine, broadens not only the counselor-consultant's perspective on what may be going on with Jasmine, but also increases the number and types of strategies that can now be used to remedy this situation. Expanding our approach to engage other responsible parties and targeting extrapersonal factors will not only increase the effectiveness of our service to the student but will offer the opportunity to engage in preventive programming.

This is true for our model counselor-consultant. Her inclusion of Dr. Jameson, the consultee, into the mix not only broadens her perspective on what may be going on with Jasmine but also it increases the number and types of strategies she (they) can now use to remedy this situation.

The current chapter addresses the process of client-focused consultation. As described, client-focused consultation is a process that allows for direct service to the student-client while at the same time engaging others in a consultative mode. After completing this chapter, the reader should be able to

1. describe the differences between a restricted direct-service model and a consultation approach that allows for direct contact;
2. expand the goals of service to include those addressing student need, the tasks the student is assigned, and the environment in which the student functions; and

3. describe the application of a multimodal behavioral model as applied to a student-centered form of consultation.

Beyond Direct Service

The school counselor engaging in individual counseling with a student would meet with the student and employ a variety of techniques or approaches to evaluate or assess the student's problems or concerns. Once these are identified, the counselor and student typically set goals and then begin to implement a plan of action to move toward the achievement of these goals. Quite often, this entire process is carried out behind the closed door of the counselor's office, without input from, or to, the teacher or teachers who share a concern for that student.

Such an approach, while potentially useful, is missing the opportunity to expand on the efficacy of service and the chance of engaging in prevention programming. Many counselors step out of their office not only to observe the student but also to engage with others (e.g., teacher, administrators) in an attempt to gather information from a new perspective. This extension of the problem defining, goal setting, and intervention planning process to include the input from the classroom teacher not only increases the utility and validity of the data gathered but also allows both the teacher and the counselor-consultant to benefit from their unique perspectives and skills. The result of this "joining forces" is the development of a better plan for the student and the possibility of changes to the classroom that will positively impact all of the students.

The inclusion of the teacher-as-consultee in this process of problem identification, goals setting, and plan development is based on the following rationales:

1. The teacher-consultee knows the client, and it may be difficult, if not impossible, to understand the client and their concerns as well in the brief, focused, counselor-student encounter.
2. "Problems" are to some degree contextually defined and thus are best understood within the context in which they occur. The teacher-consultee can provide information regarding the uniqueness of the classroom along with its unique task demands and social environment.
3. Intervention plans will prove more effective if they can be applied both within the counselor's office and within the actual classroom or environment of concern. Such spread of intervention will be more accepted if the teacher-consultee was involved in its development.
4. The student's current level of functioning is assumed to be a result of the client interacting with a particular task and in a specific environment. Understanding and intervening with the task and the environment is best achieved with consultee involvement.

The counselor-consultant seeking to modify the behavior, attitudes, and feelings of a student or students may gather needed information directly (e.g., interviewing, testing, observations) or more indirectly through dialogue with the consultee (i.e., teacher, parent, administrator). In either case, the focus of problem identification, goal setting, and intervention planning processes is on the student, a client. When engaging from a consultation perspective, the process involves the mutual involvement of consultee and consultant and extends the focus on to extrapersonal factors contributing to both the problem and its resolution.

Focusing on the One While Impacting the Many

Client-focused consultation (Caplan & Caplan, 1993, 1999; Parsons, 1996) involves the full collaboration of consultant and consultee in problem identification, goal setting, and intervention processes. Such consultative collaboration provides a number of potential benefits. First, by incorporating varied perspectives (i.e., counselor-consultant and teacher or administrator-consultee) on data collection and interpretation, the potential bias intrinsic to either view is checked, and the validity of data collected may be increased. Second, by gathering data on the specific elements of the task and environment in which the client is operating (e.g., the classroom), the possibility of achieving an assessment-intervention linkage has been increased. Finally, the collaborative exchange can serve an educative and thus preventive function for the consultee, expanding her knowledge of the influencing effects of task and environmental demands.

Through their collaborative efforts, not only will the counselor-consultant gain better insight into the student's functioning but the consultee will be assisted to use the experience with this case to improve her abilities to reduce the possibility of similar situations occurring in the future.

From this consultation frame of reference, not only are the diagnostic and intervention planning processes expanded to include consultee collaboration, but the approach has been developed to ensure both remedial and prevention effects. This expanded approach is based upon the assumption that behavior is a function of the interaction between the unique characteristics of the client, the task the client is asked to accomplish, and the environment in which this occurs (i.e., behavior = f(client-task-environment)).

Consider for example the case of Bennie, a 13-year-old Caucasian male who has just recently been diagnosed as having an attention deficit disorder without hyperactivity (ADD). The identification of his ADD has helped Bennie to understand why he is and has been inattentive in school, is prone to accidents, and has trouble remembering what his mother has asked him to do. Bennie's behavior is affected by his neurological state. However, the degree to which this behavior is manifested and problematic can be influenced by the nature of the task or the characteristics of the environment in which Bennie is asked to function. For example, it is fair to assume that Bennie may have greater difficulty staying attentive to a task that has low motivational value and is repetitive than he would to one that is of high interest. Similarly, one may expect that Bennie would have more difficulty attending to a teacher's direction if he is sitting next to an active gerbil cage than if he was sitting in the front of the class, near the teacher. The behavior of concern, which in the case of Bennie may be his turning around, playing with his pencils, et cetera, is a product of Bennie's unique makeup, which is interacting with the characteristics of a task he is assigned and the social and physical context in which he is asked to perform.

The result of employing a client-task-environment model to assess the problem is that it results in the identification of multiple points of intervention. The application of various interventions, some implemented by the counselor-consultant and others delivered by the consultee, not only facilitates change in this student-client but can be used as preventive as well. The analysis of the task demands and environmental pressures, and the way they can impact this client, helps the consultee to begin to consider modification of these variables as a way of avoiding similar problems with other clients in the future. Efforts to intervene with one student can result in the application of positive, preventive steps that, in turn, may impact many, thus increasing the breadth of impact.

Engaging Others: Problem Identification and Intervention Planning

If we remember our operational model of behavior as being a function of the interaction of the person, the task, and the environment, then we can begin to understand the unique value and expertise that the consultee can bring to the identification and analysis of the problem and then the introduction of interventions.

Specifically, the teacher-consultee can help provide valuable information about the unique demands of the classroom tasks as well as the characteristics of the physical and social environment. This is not to negate the possible psychosocial factors that directly impact the student and inhibit her performance. The suggestion here is that when such elements are present, they can be mollified or exacerbated by the characteristics of the task and the conditions in which the work is performed.

For example, consider the case of Liz, a fifth-grade student. Liz's teacher reported that within the last month, Liz's academic performance has deteriorated. Liz's teacher noted that Liz appears very stressed and is having difficulty concentrating. Further, Liz, while previously being an almost model student when it came to homework, now either fails to hand in any homework or if something is handed in, it is only partially complete. Upon further investigation, the counselor finds out that Liz's parents are currently in a very heated divorce process. Liz is spending every other night with either her father or her mother, in two different locations. In this situation, the source of Liz's work difficulty may be her physical and emotional exhaustion, which are the results of her current living situation and the stress of her parent's very hostile divorce process.

Now, consider Ana. Ana's English teacher reported that Ana has also shown a dramatic decline in the quality of her homework assignments. The teacher said that in the past, Ana's homework assignments were creative, descriptive, and quite elaborate, but that recently they have become very brief, without full description, and often are handed in without being complete.

In interviewing the teacher (consultee), the consultant discovered that this change in Ana's performance appeared to correlate with a change in the requirements of the task. Whereas in the past the teacher allowed the students to employ word processing or block printing to produce their assignments, she now requires them to use cursive writing. Further investigation revealed that, as a result of a mild neuromuscular issue, cursive writing proved difficult for Ana. The requirement to employ cursive interfered with her ability and interest to elaborate and to be sufficiently descriptive in her writing. In this case, it was most likely that the unique demands of the task itself, rather than any personal problem, was the primary contributor to Ana's poor work performance.

Assessing Task Demands

Thus, while the difficulty a client exhibits may be the result of some unique personal problem, it is also possible that the specific demands of the task with which the client is having difficulty may be augmenting the effects of the personal problem or perhaps may even be the primary source of the work-related problem. It is important to include an assessment of the task demands as part of an expanded diagnostic or problem-identification process.

By analyzing the task that appears to be involved with the client's problem and reviewing the specific demands that such a task places upon the person attempting to complete it, the consultant and consultee can identify those areas mastered by the client, as well as those areas causing the most difficulty. Perhaps the client is having a problem because he lacks the necessary prerequisite skills. This could indeed be the case of a student who has been "misplaced" in an advanced mathematics class without having had the training in the prerequisites. The frustration experienced by the student, along with the potentially disruptive behavioral manifestations of that frustration, can best be understood and remedied by the realization of this lack of prerequisite skill acquisition.

But in addition to possibly lacking the skills required to complete a particular unit or task successfully, perhaps there is something unique in the task demands that interacts with the client's own current psycho-social-emotional resources in such a way as to produce or elicit an interfering response. Consider the case of Keith, found in Exercise 10.1.

Directions: In this exercise, you will be given a brief statement of the problem, provided by Keith's teacher, Dr. Hagerstown, along with some background information on Keith. For Part I, you are asked to read the referral information. Your assignment is to identify the particular tasks causing Keith some problem. More specifically, you are to identify five factors involved in performing the task, which you will use in Part II. In Part II, you are asked to identify five personal issues or experiences that may interact with these components of the task to inhibit Keith's performance. Through discussion of your response with a colleague, mentor, or supervisor, you will begin to see the value of task analyses to the diagnostic process.

Part I

Problem statement

Dr. Hagerstown, Keith's creative writing teacher, has noted that "Keith's performance in class has become simply unacceptable. I am not sure what happened. He has been an excellent student up to this point, and he is certainly a compliant youth, but he is simply not producing the creative work which is required and expected of one so talented. Since the beginning of the second marking period (November 8th), his essays have been short and not descriptive, his journal writing has been sporadic, and his verbal contribution during our class creative roundtable is simply sterile! Keith is simply not putting himself into his work."

Exercise 10.1 The Case of Keith—Focusing on the Task

Classroom (environmental) information:

Dr. Hagerstown runs his class like a college seminar. Students are assigned a theme at the beginning of each marking period. Their assignments (all of which will vary in form and genre) reflect aspects of that theme. The topic for this marking period has been Family/ Community/Belonging: Essential to our Human Existence.

Students orally present their creations to their study group for peer feedback before correcting and submitting to the class as a whole. Students' presentations to the class are somewhat formal, with the presenter standing at a podium. Following each presentation, the student will answer questions about the process they employed in producing this work.

While other teachers have noted a drop in Keith's overall performance, most have attributed it to "senioritis." Further, his math, science, physical education, and art teachers feel Keith is performing at expected levels.

Background information on Keith:

Keith has always considered himself to be a proficient writer, especially when he has a structured outline for a topic. Keith's parents recently (at the end of October) told him they were divorcing, a shock to Keith, who now resides with his mother during the week and his father on the weekends.

Part II

In column A, identify five separate task demands. In column B, provide five unique personal characteristics or experiences that may be negatively interacting with the task demand to reduce Keith's performance.

Column A	Column B
Task analyses (sample):	Personal Characteristics
Knowledge and comfort with theme	Parents currently in divorce process

1) _____   _____

2) _____   _____

3) _____   _____

4) _____   _____

5) _____   _____

Assessing the Environment

Studies have shown that the physical and social environment in which one learns and performs can affect academic success (e.g., Chen & Duh, 2008; Dascalu et al., 2015; Millwood, Power, & Tindal, 2008). In a school setting, it is important to consider the following when referring to the environment.

Physical Environment

There are numerous studies (see Dunn and Honigsfeld, 2013) providing evidence that support the notion that the social-physical environment can impact both learning and performance. This research suggests that an individual's performance can be significantly affected by variables such as the amount of light, noise, temperature, formality, and mobility found within the learning environment (Dunn, & Griggs, 2007).

Sociocultural Climate

The sociocultural climate of an environment can also impact learning and performance. Research (e.g., Park, 2001; Park, 2000) reported on the cultural preferences of those from Hispanic, Native American, Asian American, and African American cultures regarding learning in groups or alone. Some stated that group learning interfered with learning and performance. When attempting to understand and intervene with a student having academic difficulty, it is important for the counselor-consultant to view the presenting concern in the context of the physical and sociocultural environment in which it occurs. This approach provides an expanded framework for problem identification as well as added directions for intervention and prevention that can be collaboratively pursued by consultant and consultee. Let's return to the case of Keith (see exercise 10.2).

Directions: As with exercise 10.1, your task is to review the data provided. The additional data highlight some unique factors of the physical-social-psychological environment found in Dr. Hagerstown's classroom. After reading the five pieces of information supplied, identify two possible ways these unique environmental factors could negatively impact Keith's performance.

Discussing your conclusions with a colleague, mentor, or supervisor will help you to expand your awareness of the possible interactions between environment and client.

Classroom observation: In observing Keith in his creative writing class, you collected the following data:

- The classroom is arranged in major sections. There appears to be an area for small peer groups and one for large class discussion (20 students).
- The classroom is very bright and cheery and has many decorations, both commercial and student-created. According to the teacher, the decorations reflect the theme of the marking period and therefore change four times throughout the year. Presently, the decorations correspond with the Family/Community/Belonging unit.

Exercise 10.2 Keith—An Environmental Analysis

- When students are working in their small groups, they review each other's written work, rough notes, and any graphics or pictures that accompany the work.
- Keith's peer group (five students) includes himself and four females. There are eight other boys in class besides Keith.
- Keith's group meets in the rear-left corner of the room, and Keith is in a seat facing the back of the larger section of the room.
- You understand from one of the students that the girl directly facing Keith (in his small group) is his ex-girlfriend.

Possible Impacts:

Example:

1. The pictures placed around the room show happy families, both commercial products and snapshots of the students' families (e.g., on vacation, at home). The pictures are very upsetting to Keith, and he has trouble focusing on his work, being pulled to fantasize about his "one-time, happy family."

2: _____

_____

3: _____

_____

Assessing the Client

Our discussion of the client has been placed last to emphasize the extrapersonal focus of the consultation model employed. However, this is not to suggest a linear approach to assessment, that is, that one first assesses the task, then the environment, and then the client. Clearly, in assessing each of the previous focal points for diagnosis (i.e., task and environment), consideration has been given to the client. Thus, assessing the client has already begun.

As with all assessments, our focus and data collection will be guided by the operative model we are employing. There are many models for overseeing assessment and treatment formulation. One, the multimodal behavioral approach (Lazarus, 1989), has been demonstrated to have meaningful benefits across entire school populations (Silverstone et al., 2017).

The multimodal approach posits that a person's functioning or dysfunctioning manifests across seven areas, or modalities. These seven areas are behavior, affect sensations, images, cognition, interpersonal relationships, and drugs (or biological functions).

B: Behavior. In assessing the student's challenge, it is important to begin to identify how it is that the student "acts." Are there behavioral excesses (e.g., client drinks too much, interrupts too often) or deficits (e.g., doesn't initiate conversation, fails to do homework), that are interfering with his academic performance? What behaviors does he exhibit or does he fail to employ that appear to contribute to the current problem?

Consider Keith's situation. Dr. Hagerstown suggested that Keith's performance has dropped off drastically. He describes the problem behaviors as:

1. writing short essays,
2. not being descriptive in his journal writing, and
3. not being personal in his classroom discussions.

In looking at the client's behavior, we must also consider what events (antecedents) lead up to his acting a certain way and, similarly, what the results (consequences) of his actions are. Frequently, one's behavior is heavily influenced (if not caused) by these antecedents and consequences. For example, if every time Keith attempted to enter into the classroom discussion he began to cry and feel sick to his stomach, it may be hypothesized that lack of participation is a way of avoiding these painful consequences. Such an understanding not only clarifies the nature of the problem but also may help the consultant and consultee identify other means of gaining Keith's participation in a way that results in less harmful consequences.

A: Affect. Feelings are important aspects of the human experience and thus need to be identified, especially as they are tied to a presenting complaint. However, recognizing feelings is not sufficient. The consultant and consultee need to be attentive to both those feelings that are reported and those that are never or rarely noted. The consultee and the consultant will need to consider the degree to which the client's feelings appear appropriate to the situation as well as the degree or intensity with which the feelings are experienced. Questions such as "Are these emotions overdone and the client too sensitive?" or "Are the client's feelings being blunted, somewhat insensitive, or underdone?" need to be considered. Also, the consultant and consultee need to consider the degree of control (too much, too little) the client exhibits in the expression of his feelings.

Perhaps the "sterility" of expression exhibited by Keith is a reflection of his grieving of the ending of his parent's marriage. It may be appropriate following such a loss, but is it proportional to the actual loss? Does Keith experience the loss in ways other than sadness? Does he feel depressed, hopeless? Does he find any pleasure in the activities he enjoyed before the divorce? Discovering the answers to these types of questions not only clarifies the depth and breadth of the problem but begins to identify goals and outcomes desired.

S: Sensation. When considering the client sensations, we are concerned about their five major senses and the degree to which they are accurately receiving the signals around them. Also, we need to identify the degree to which the client targets body sensations (e.g., sick to the stomach, dizziness, headaches) as part of the problem. For example, when Keith speaks of being upset, does he also mean that he feels sick to his stomach, or has headaches or muscle tensions?

The sensations the client reports may be valuable for two reasons. First, as with the other modalities, identifying sensations associated with the concern more clearly defines the nature of the problem and how it is experienced. Second, the identification of such sensations may even provide us with an early diagnostic warning system, as when a person experiences a muscular tension (in the neck) before becoming very angry. Such an early warning system could be useful in developing strategies for early intervention.

I: Imagery. As used here, imagery involves the various mental pictures that seem to influence our life. For example, the student who "sees" himself as being laughed at may tend to withdraw from volunteering an answer in class. Or, the person who may "see" himself as fat, even after losing weight, may still act and feel fat. Having a better understanding of the way the client sees himself and his world is useful information. It not only reflects part of the client's concern but it can also suggest an important goal to be achieved. Questions such as "What bothersome dreams or memories do you have?," "How do you view yourself?," and "How do you view your future?" may begin to reveal such imagery. Again, consider Keith.

As noted, Keith has withdrawn from active participation in the classroom discussion. In fact, he reports feeling sick to his stomach when he attempts to participate (sensation). In an interview with Keith, the consultant learns that he "sees himself starting to talk about his family and losing control in class. He sees the others in the class as being disgusted by his emotional outburst. He especially envisions his ex-girlfriend making fun of him. Further, Keith reports that he can hardly get the image of his mom crying out of his mind. This is especially difficult to do when surrounded by all the "happy family" pictures hung on the wall of the classroom.

These images play an essential role in the overall problem Keith is experiencing. Helping Keith remove or reshape these images would be a useful goal for the consultation.

C: Cognition. The C in Lazarus' BASIC ID stands for cognition. Cognitions are thoughts, beliefs, or ways of making meaning out of one's experience. Often, the way we interpret our experience is inaccurate. We need to learn to identify when our thinking is distorted and thus learn to correct it.

The effective consultant needs to unearth the client's cognitive patterns as a part of their overall experience of the problem. Seeking the answers to questions such as "What does this mean to the client?" and "What assumptions about herself and her world is she making?" will provide a clearer picture of the client's cognitive orientation.

For example, while the loss that Keith is experiencing is one that is both undesirable and disappointing, it is not unbearable nor does it provide evidence of his failure. In reviewing Keith's journal, it becomes clear to Dr. Hagerstown that Keith blames himself for his parent's divorce; in fact, in one section he wrote "If I had been more like the son my dad wanted, he would never have left my mom! It is all my fault!" Concluding that his parent's divorce is his fault is certainly a distortion of reality. Such a distortion both exaggerates the importance of his role in the marriage and leads to an inordinate amount of guilt tied to a decision over which he had no control. Further, correcting such a distorted interpretation would prove to be a beneficial and helpful goal and relieve much of what is most likely debilitating guilt.

I: Interpersonal relationships. In assessing the interpersonal modality, the goal is to identify how this component may reflect the problem encountered or in some way contribute to it. In the case of Keith, we come to understand that he becomes overly withdrawn when emotionally upset. This tendency to withdraw from friends and family can undoubtedly increase the experience of anxiety and concern over the demise of his intact family by removing him from other possible sources of support. Further, his social withdrawal in class has created a situation in which his grades are declining, and this, in turn, has compounded his feelings of guilt. Thus, a useful goal for this consultation would be to assist Keith to learn to use appropriate disclosure and reliance on friends and families as a way of adjusting to the emotional crises he is experiencing.

D: Drugs (biology). While the D does complete the acronym, it may be a bit misleading. Lazarus is not focusing only on drugs. He is suggesting that we consider the nonpsychological aspects of a person's experience. We need to consider the client's diet, general health, well-being, and general physiology (hormones, nervous system, etc.).

The consultant and consultee are most likely not trained to intervene with organic conditions, but they need to increase their awareness of the effect of substances (such as chemicals, food additives, or even natural substances such as caffeine) and physiology (e.g., hormones) in creating problems in our life. In the case of Keith, the consultant and consultee need to consider whether Keith's reaction may be associated with his lack of sleep or change in eating (which may result from the disruption of the family patterns at home). Does Keith's emotional response pattern have any possible connection with any medicine he may be taking or has stopped taking? Again, seeking the answers to such questions not only gives the consultant and consultee a complete picture of the depth and breadth of the problem but also begins to provide clarity about the goals to be achieved.

While the purist may wish to define a client's problem in terms of each of these seven modalities, what is being suggested here is that the BASIC ID model is a useful template or guide for systematically assessing the client's situation. Whether the consultant or consultee employ seven or fewer modalities, such a model enables them to more specifically and more concretely define the nature and scope of the client's concern as the first step to formulating useful and achievable goals and outcomes.

Exercise 10.3 will help to demonstrate the use and value of problem defining using the model of the BASIC ID.

Directions: After reading the case information below, use the BASIC ID to identify the various components or modalities involved in Keith's experience.

In an interview with Keith, the consultant discovered the following information. Since the beginning of the second marking period, Keith has found himself daydreaming a lot in class. He sometimes sees himself on a small boat, like a dingy, and the big ship is going off in the sunset. He doesn't feel very energetic in creative writing (and says he seems and feels okay in other classes).

Keith admitted that he is not spending much time on his creative writing assignments. He seems to get distracted with thoughts about his mom and his dad, thinking that "I can't make it without them!" When he thinks like this, he finds it hard to concentrate on the various writing tasks. In fact, sitting down to write seems to make this daydreaming and thinking happen. As such, he merely avoids the tasks.

Keith also noted that he has split up with his girlfriend (Elana), who is in the same creative writing class. As a result, he just doesn't feel like he can talk to anyone.

Keith shared that he is losing weight and has some difficulty getting to sleep. He finds himself feeling sad and nervous, like sometimes his body is tingling.

Exercise 10.3 Keith—Assessing the Client Using BASIC ID

Analysis of the Client:

B — BEHAVIOR: _____
_____
_____

A — AFFECT: _____
_____
_____

S — SENSATION: _____
_____
_____

I — IMAGERY: _____
_____
_____

C — COGNITION: _____
_____
_____

I — INTERPERSONAL: _____
_____
_____

D — DRUGS (diet, etc.): _____
_____
_____

Goals Setting and Intervention Strategies

The analysis of the client, task, and environment will most likely lead to the generation of a wide variety of goals. When identifying goals, it is useful for the consultant and consultee not only to identify those goals that result in immediate and long-term change for the client but to expand the focus of change beyond that for the client. It is helpful to establish goals that provide for prevention. Goals that reflect a desired change in the consultee; the program (classroom norms, curriculum, structure); or the broader systemic factors existing within the school, family, or community invite just such prevention programming.

While the identification of numerous desired and desirable goals is worth pursuing, it can also be overwhelming. After identifying the targets, the consultant needs to facilitate the narrowing of the focus and the prioritization of goals and strategies. In selecting both the goals and the nature of the intervention plan or solutions to be employed, the consultant should consider the following general guidelines.

The Breadth of Impact

One of the first points to be considered when selecting an intervention is the breadth of impact. The consultant and consultee should attempt to choose goals and strategies that provide the broadest impact, given the effort. Solution strategies that impact a variety of client modalities, and task and environmental elements, may have a higher chance of being successful and thus should be first considered for implementation. Further, since the goal of the consultation is twofold (i.e., remedial and preventive), the consultant needs to consider the remedial and preventive value of each intervention in hopes of identifying the intervention with the broadest (i.e., both corrective and preventive) impact possible.

In our case illustration, it becomes clear that expanding the subject matter of the pictures decorating the classroom will not only help Keith but will also provide other students living in single-parent conditions a point of personal preference. This single intervention would therefore impact not only Keith but all students "distracted" by the exclusion of their family experience in the models presented.

Address the Goals of Priority

Strategies or solutions that achieve goals of greatest satisfaction will most likely be those embraced and accepted. These are the issues that the client and the consultee would be most motivated to do something about and thus be less resistant to the intervention process.

The desire to once again be able to elaborate upon Keith's writing appears to be a significant goal for Dr. Hagerstown and Keith. Any suggestion that would help accomplish this goal should be acceptable to both the consultee (Dr. Hagerstown) and the client (Keith). Perhaps, the degree of disclosure will increase if Dr. Hagerstown could assure Keith that his writing would not have to be presented to the entire class until he was ready. With such an assurance and sense of control, Keith may be willing to risk some vulnerability and personal disclosure with Dr. Hagerstown, thus enriching his written work.

Achieving Success

When identifying goals for initial attention, it is helpful to select one that has a high chance of achievement. This affords the consultee and the client the opportunity to experience success and can contribute to their motivation to continue in the process. When the target goal is clearly something that will take time and resources, it might be important to attempt to break down the larger goal into more manageable subparts that can be addressed one at a time, starting with the step that appears to have the most likelihood of success.

Again, while it is desirable to have Keith expand on his formal writing projects, what might be needed is to assist Keith first in feeling comfortable with elaborating on his journal writing. For example, one point of problem definition was that Keith experienced some intrusive and upsetting images that interfered with his attending and concentrating on his class work. Understanding that these images, while being responses to his fears surrounding the divorce of his parents, are also responses to the visual stimulation found around the classroom (i.e., pictures of happy, intact families).

In this situation, the professional counselor may attempt to employ strategies such as rational emotive imagery training (Wilde, 1996a; Wilde, 1996b) to assist Keith to reduce the debilitating effect of his imagery. As a collaborating consultant, this professional counselor would not only employ such imagery training techniques but help the consultee to reconsider the posters and pictures that decorate the classroom. Through a collaborative dialogue, the consultee may choose to reduce the emphasis on dual-parent family photos and include additional images of happy, single-parent families.

Reduce the Costs

While the breadth of impact of the solutions we select is an important consideration, it needs to be tempered by the cost to the consultee of implementing such a solution. As noted throughout the text, consultation implies change, and change by its very nature is costly. For the solutions to have a chance of succeeding, they must be implemented and maintained. As such, it is vital to select solution strategies that cause the least strain, or costs, on the consultee or the system's resources. For example, if a consultant can choose between an intervention that requires the consultee to learn new skills and acquire some additional resources (e.g., materials, supplies) versus an intervention for which the consultee has the ability and resources needed, it is generally more useful to consider the latter as least costly and thus more attractive.

Putting It All Together: A Case Illustration and Exercise

There are many considerations to include when working with a consultee in a client-student-focused consultation. Next, you will find a comprehensive case. Following the case data, you will find an exercise to guide your reflection on the case and your application of all that you have learned.

A Case Illustration and Exercise
Case Information

The School and Community

Nestled snuggly along the Hudson River, Richfield Borough heaved its last sigh when the smokestacks of its manufacturing plants puffed their final smoke fumes. Businesses failed and the community struggled. However, townspeople believed firmly that education offered opportunities to its youth and unfailingly supported the public schools.

When farmers realized that their best cash crop was the land itself, they sold their land rights to developers. The area's landscape changed as the New York suburban sprawl overtook the pastureland. Developers could barely keep pace with housing demands and Richfield Borough and Richfield Township schools began to flourish again.

To accommodate growth, the local school board approved the construction of several new elementary schools and one magnificent high school. The middle school moved to the old high school building, where the dark, dingy halls enveloped students and teachers like an old, wet, wool coat. No one seemed to mind this too much as long as everyone was accommodated. The local community, unswervingly proud of its children, continues to support the academic, musical, and athletic efforts of its schools.

Among the ninety-six new students to enter Richfield Township Middle School this fall is Samantha M. Samantha missed the new student orientation and picnic because she arrived, records in hand, just two days prior to school's opening. Her quick placement in Mrs. Morgan's homeroom makes thirty students, an uncomfortably large number of students for the fifty-nine-year-old teacher.

On the first day of school, shortly after the homeroom bell rings, a confused Samantha and an angry Mrs. Morgan arrive at the counselor's office. Barely out of Samantha's earshot, Mrs. Morgan hisses, "There's something dreadfully wrong with that girl. Her pants are ripped. Her T-shirt is filthy. And she keeps muttering that she doesn't understand her schedule."

With that last comment, she adds, in a high-pitched Southern drawl, "This isn't like Texas. Well, I've tried explaining the schedule to her, but she doesn't get it. It's your turn. I've got twenty-nine other children to worry about."

"Come in, Samantha," you offer gingerly, recognizing the fair-skinned girl.

"What's wrong with her?" queries Samantha. Then, as if glad to have your undivided attention, she says abruptly, "I don't understand my schedule. It's not like how it was in Texas."

"Can you tell me how it was in Texas?" you ask.

Samantha

Born and raised in Texas, Samantha's parents divorced when Samantha was two years old. Immediately following the split, her father left the military and moved to Richfield Township, New York, to join his parents. His eventual remarriage resulted in spending less time with Samantha. With the birth of his two children, his infrequent visits became even fewer.

Samantha speaks little of her mother other than to mention that she was poor. Choosing to remain single, mother and daughter survived on little more than the minimum wage earned through waitressing and the occasional support checks that arrived from Samantha's father. Samantha has not eaten nutritionally well and has not had very good health care, resulting in frequent, painful intestinal bouts, which are exasperated by stress.

Longing to learn more about her father, stepmother, and stepsiblings, Samantha, at age thirteen, asked to move in with her father. All parties agreed that this offered an important opportunity to further Samantha's personal development. Samantha and her one suitcase arrive at her father's doorstep in Richfield Township. She reports that she often daydreams about her father spending time with her and praising her, which is what encouraged her to ask for the move. She is sure she will have a wonderful relationship with her father and will spend lots of time with him alone, since they missed so much time together as she was growing up.

The Consultee: Mrs. Morgan

Tiny, bespectacled Mrs. Morgan has taught English to seventh and eighth graders for thirty-seven years at Richfield Township Middle School. Years after their high school graduation, students return to thank Mrs. Morgan for her dedication to teaching English grammar and composition writing. They often attribute their high school and college success to her class.

History (Samantha's Second Week)

Mrs. Morgan comes to your office at the end of the second week of school and says that she thinks Samantha needs help, and more help than she can give. Her complaints include Samantha still not getting to class on time, not handing in homework, not paying attention, and never participating. She assigned a buddy to Samantha so that Samantha would stop asking Mrs. Morgan so many questions—way too many for an eighth grader! Mrs. Morgan also reports that Samantha does not seem to be making friends very easily. Mrs. Morgan emphatically states, "There must be something terribly wrong with that girl, and I don't want to be blamed for her failing!"

Exercise: Applying What We Know

Directions: As a review to this point, consider the information you have learned and complete the following tasks.

1. Name the participants in this consultation triad.
2. Explain how you might employ each of the following modes in this case:

   Provisional
   Prescriptive
   Collaborative
   Mediational
3. Explain which mode would be the most appropriate in this case (which consultation mode would be the most helpful) at this point in time.
4. Explain which mode would be the most feasible at this time (which consultation mode is likely to have the most success to start).
5. Think of the factors in BASIC ID. Use the factors to record what you know about Samantha and then think about what else you like to learn. Discuss your thoughts and perspective with a colleague or supervisor.
6. What other factors might be relevant for this case?

   a. Are there cultural considerations? If so, what are they?
   b. Could the consultee (teacher) use support? If so, what and from whom?

7. How will you proceed?

   a. What interventions and preventions might you employ that will support Samantha?
   b. What interventions and preventions would be helpful for Mrs. Morgan?
   c. What changes in the system would be beneficial?

Summary

- All consultation could be said to be client-targeted or, in the case of school counselors, student-targeted. However, not all consultation involves direct student assessment and intervention.
- In the client-focused form of consultation, diagnostic and intervention efforts center on the client as he interacts with a specific task within a specific environment.
- In client-focused consultation, the counselor-consultant is free to interact directly with the student, and gather diagnostic information and implement intervention strategies indirectly, using the consultee as the conduit for such activities.
- Client- or student-focused consultation involves the full collaboration of consultant and consultee in problem identification, goal setting, and intervention processes, thus expanding the perspectives and resources brought to defining and resolving the problem.
- The collaborative exchange can serve an educative and thus preventive function for the consultee, increasing her knowledge of the influencing effects of task and environmental demands.

Additional Resources

Print

Alberto, P. A., & Troutman, A. C. (2012). *Applied behavior analysis for teachers* (9th ed.). Upper Saddle River, NJ: Pearson Educated.

Brigman, G., Mullis, F., Webb, L., & White, J. (2005). *School counselor consultation: Developing skills for working effectively with parents, teachers, and other school personnel.* Hoboken, NJ: John Wiley & Sons.

Lazarus, A. A., & MacKenzie, K. R. (1997). *Brief but comprehensive psychotherapy: The multimodal way.* New York, NY: Springer Publishing.

Rossett, A. (1999). *First things fast: A handbook for performance analysis.* San Francisco, CA: Jossey-Bass/Pfeiffer.

Web-Based

Institute for Learning Styles Research. *Overview of the seven perceptual styles.* Retrieved from https://www.learning-styles.org/styles/aural.html

Lazarus, A. A. (n.d.) *Multimodal therapy: A primer.* Zur Institute. Retrieved from https://www.zurinstitute.com/multimodaltherapy.html

Mariani, L. (2007). Learning styles across cultures. *Perspectives, 34*(2). Retrieved from http://www.learner-autonomy.org/ld/wp-content/uploads/2011/10/Learning-Styles-Contextual-Influence.pdf

References

Caplan, G., & Caplan, R. (1993). *Mental health consultation and collaboration.* San Francisco, CA: Jossey-Bass.

Caplan, G., & Caplan, R. B. (1999). *Mental health consultation and collaboration,* Long Grove, IL: Waveland Press.

Chen, C. M., & Duh, L. J. (2008). Personalized web-based tutoring system based on fuzzy item response theory. *Expert Systems with Applications, 34*(4), 2298–2315.

Dascalu, M.I., Bodea, C.N., Moldoveanu, A., Mohora, A., Lytras, M., & de Pablos, P. O. (2015). A recommender agent based on learning styles for better virtual collaborative learning experiences. *Computers in Human Behavior, 45,* 243–253.

Dunn, R., & Griggs, S. A. (2007). *Synthesis of the Dunn and Dunn learning-style model research: Who, what, when, where, and so what?* Jamaica, NY: Center for the Study of Learning and Teaching Styles, St. John's University.

Dunn, R., & Honigsfeld, A. (2013). Learning styles: What we know and what we need. *Educational Forum, 77*(2), 225–232.

Johnson, D. W., & Johnson, F. P. (1987). *Joining together: Group theory and group skills* (3rd ed.). Englewood Cliffs, NJ: Prentice Hall.

Lazarus, A. (1989). *The practice of multimodal therapy.* Baltimore: Johns Hopkins University Press.

Millwood, R., Powell, S., & Tindal, I. (2008). Personalised learning and the multiversity experience. *Interactive Learning Environments, 16*(1), 63–81.

Park, C. C. (2000). Learning style preferences of Southeast Asian Students. *Urban Education, 35*(3), 245–268.

Park, C. C. (2001). Learning style preferences of Armenian, African, Hispanic, Hmong, Korean, Mexican and Anglo students in American secondary schools. *Learning Environments Research, 4*(2), 175–191.

Parsons, R. D. (1996). *The skilled consultant.* Boston, MA: Allyn and Bacon.

Silverstone, P. H., Bercov, M., Suen, V. Y. M., Allen, A., Cribben, I., Goodrick, J., Henry, S., Pryce, C., Langstraat, P., Rittenbach, K., Chakraborty, S., Engles, R. C., & McCabe, C. (2017). Long-term results from the empowering a multimodal pathway toward healthy youth program, a multimodal school-based approach, show marked reductions in suicidality, depression, and anxiety in 6,227 students in grades 6–12 (aged 11–18).; *Frontiers in Psychiatry, 8.*

Wilde, J. (1996a). The efficacy of short-term rational-emotive education with fourth-grade students. *Elementary School Guidance and Counseling, 31,* 131–138.

Wilde, J. (1996b). *Treating anger, anxiety, and depression in children and adolescents: A cognitive-behavioral perspective.* Muncie, IN: Accelerated Development.

CHAPTER 11

Level II Prevention:
Consultee-Focused Consultation

Dr. Jameson is undoubtedly concerned about Jasmine. In fact, I'm worried that he may be a bit overly concerned, and too involved with her. My observations suggest that Jasmine can use some assistance, but he seems to be catastrophizing the situation. Somewhere along the process, I will need to confront this and see if I can help him regain some professional distance and objectivity about what's going on.

––––––––––––––––– ○ –––––––––––––––––

The title of the chapter and the nature of the consultation to be discussed focuses on the role and function of the consultee. However, it is important to remember that the goal of consultee-focused consultation, as with all consultation, is to assist the student with her school-based performance. In consultee-focused consultation, the counselor-consultant attempts to increase the work-related functioning of the student by targeting changes in the professional functioning of the consultee.

Consultee-focused consultation employs many of the same observational and interpersonal skills previously discussed, but it will also rely heavily on consultee self-monitoring techniques, direct and indirect consultant confrontation, and educational programming. Consultee-focused consultation will most likely result in the consultee gaining personal insight. However, it must be emphasized that consultee-focused consultation is not intended to serve as individual counseling or psychotherapy for the consultee. The primary goal is to increase the consultee's professional knowledge and skills. The consultant engaged in consultee-focused consultation must be alert not to cross the boundary between consultee-focused consultation and personal consultee counseling. The knowledge and skills required for maintaining such a balance are the focus of the current chapter. After completing this chapter, the reader should be able to

1. describe the nature and value of consultee-focused consultation;
2. identify when the consultee's level of professional knowledge, skill, or objectivity is pivotal to the creation, maintenance, and eventual amelioration of a student problem;

3. employ appropriate confrontational skills as the base for intervention at the consultee-focused level of consultation; and

4. describe techniques employed in consultee-focused consultation, including didactic information-giving and theme interference reduction strategies.

The Consultee: A Significant Extrapersonal Variable

Much attention has been given to the fact that a student's behavior is the result of the interaction between student characteristics, the task demands, and the environment within which the task is being performed. An essential factor operating within the student's situation and one having a potential impact on the current problem and its resolution is the consultee's professional style and interpersonal mannerisms.

It is possible that it is the consultee's response to the student that, if not causing the current student-related problem, is exacerbating the situation. Consider the case of Tanisha, a bright, achieving, 17-year-old who has been referred to the counselor's office by her social studies teacher, Ms. Bias. Ms. Bias reported that Tanisha has been "giving her attitude" since day one of this academic year. Ms. Bias reported that Tanisha has this look of "disdain" each time she is called upon in class and that when confronted about her attitude, simply explains "it's not [her] problem!" Tanisha is doing all her work and continues to be an A student in all her classes except for social studies, where her level of performance and participation is significantly less than that reported in other classes. When interviewed, Ms. Bias stated that she was confused by Tanisha's behavior. "I have tried everything with this girl. I know she is applying to Ivy League schools, and I remind her that her attitude is not going to serve her well in those environments. Further, when she hands in less than acceptable work, I have tried to motivate her by writing reminders like "Ivy League?" and "Valedictorian?" on the top.

The counselor-consultant interviewed Tanisha and found her to be a highly achieving and self-motivated individual. Tanisha shared with the counselor that since her mom's death three years ago, keeping up her school work has been difficult. Tanisha's father works multiple jobs, and as such Tanisha helps out by assuming some responsibility for the care of her three younger siblings. When asked about her reaction to Ms. Bias, Tanisha explained that she doesn't appreciate Ms. Bias's demeaning tone of voice and her constant referral to Tanisha as "her little star." Tanisha continued that she felt Ms. Bias's comments of "Ivy League?" and "Valedictorian?" were sarcastic. Tanisha explained that while she was taught to respect her teachers, and as such would not say or do anything offensive in Ms. Bias's class, she didn't feel the need to "act nice and friendly" to someone so uncaring.

As the counselor-consultant reflected upon the situation, it became clear that while intended as praise and motivators, "my little star" and "Ivy League?" were being received as sarcastic, devaluing, and demeaning commentary. Helping Tanisha to reframe Ms. Bias's comments as originating from good intent would be one target for intervention. However, with the possibility that others may also misinterpret Ms. Bias's comments, a broader, more preventive approach would be to increase Ms. Bias's awareness of the impact of her commentary. The consultant wondered aloud with Ms. Bias that "maybe Tanisha was interpreting Ms. Bias' best intentions as sarcastic and demeaning." This reframing question helped Ms. Bias to increase her understanding of Tanisha's concerns and consequently began to reduce her own "attempts using prods as motivators." More importantly, with this new understanding, Ms. Bias started to speak with Tanisha about both her own college experiences and the pressure she felt being the first female in her family to go on to higher education. This openness and personal sharing helped Tanisha to appreciate that Ms. Bias was genuinely trying to help, and served as a basis for the development of a better relationship and the reduction of the inadvertent antagonism that had developed.

It indeed would have been possible and appropriate to focus on merely helping Tanisha become less sensitive to Ms. Bias's comments. However, given the broader desire of achieving prevention, a more efficient target and focus for consultation is to increase the consultee's (Ms. Bias) understanding of her behavior. With this new awareness, Ms. Bias could make the needed adjustments in her approach, which not only helped reduce the negativity between her and Tanisha but also reduced the possibility that this scenario would be replayed with another student in the future. This preventive piece has become increasingly important as the student population becomes more diverse in culture, language, and learning needs.

In this example, the focus of the consultation was on expanding the consultee's level of understanding. Once accomplished, the consultee had the needed skills and professional level of objectivity to adjust her style to more effectively "motivate" her student. There are times, however, when increasing the consultee's level of understanding and knowledge are not sufficient. The consultant working in a consultee-focused consultation will encounter situations in which the focus will go beyond increasing consultee knowledge to increasing consultee skill and professionalism. Each of these targets for consultee consultation (i.e., knowledge, skill, and objectivity) present unique opportunities and challenges for the consultant, and therefore each is discussed in further detail.

Increasing Knowledge

It is not unusual to discover that the steps employed by a consultee to remediate a situation are based on faulty information and as such not only fail to improve the situation but in fact exacerbate it. Thus, for example, when Ms. Bias assumed Tanisha was becoming less involved because of her lack of motivation, she began to increase her use of "motivating comments" such as "Ivy League?" and "Valedictorian?" However, as we soon found out, these interventions did not achieve the intended outcome; in fact, they stimulated further withdrawal and reluctance to participate.

In such situations, it is not the lack of good will nor even professionalism that serves as the base for consultee involvement with the student's problematic behavior. Instead, it is merely the consultee's lack of a clear understanding about the nature of the situation. To further clarify this point, consider the case of Mrs. H.

Mrs. H. has been a teacher for the past 38 years. Her health, particularly her hearing and eyesight, is not as good as it used to be, and her speech is sometimes slurred. She is terrified of losing her job through forced retirement and is very defensive about any suggestion that she may no longer be fit to teach. She has sent two boys to the school counselor's office, writing "Please counsel these two disrespectful, disruptive hoodlums!"

After the consultant spoke with Ms. H. about her concerns, they both decided that it would be helpful if the consultant talked to the two boys. In speaking with them, the counselor, contrary to the comments from Mrs. H., found neither of the youths disrespectful nor having any history of acting out in class. In fact, the direct opposite has been the case with the two in question. In reviewing the records, the counselor finds that the boys have excellent academic histories and are very interested in pursuing careers in education. Further, it appears that their talking to each other during Mrs. H.'s class was the result of their need to clarify Mrs. H.'s lectures. They stated that they have difficulty understanding her sometimes, and they check with each other to validate what they heard was accurate. Further, it appears that what Mrs. H. interprets as "disrespectful" is the fact that these two often ask questions of Mrs. H. which may appear off topic. Through observations of the class interaction, the consultant soon realized that the questions asked were a result of the boys misinterpreting what Mrs. H. said, a misinterpretation created by Mrs. H.'s tendency to sometimes slur her words. It was clear, through the observation, that the boys were not intending to disrupt or embarrass Mrs. H. but were only seeking clarification.

The consultant working with this case could certainly assist the boys (the students) to develop more effective styles of coping with this environment. However, a better approach, regarding both immediate remediation and potential prevention, would be to focus the consultant's efforts on providing Mrs. H. further understanding of the nature of and motivation for the boys' behaviors.

In this situation, a fuller understanding of the dynamics of the classroom and the real motivation behind the boys talking with each other and asking questions may assist Mrs. H. to reduce her negative perception of them. Further, her increased understanding of the nature of the situation may result in her adapting her style by, for example, employing lecture outlines and printed handouts. Such a change in her teaching approach would not only reduce the boys' need to interrupt with questions or to dialogue with one another but would also prevent other students from needing to engage in similar actions.

The negative impact of a consultee's lack of knowledge or understanding may occur in situations where the students now assigned to that consultee have learning needs for which the consultee is ill-prepared to address. This would certainly be the case for a teacher who, as a result of the implementation of least restrictive environment mandates, now has students enrolled within his class who have special needs for which he has been ill-prepared to address. Exercise 11.1 provides an example of such a situation, highlighting the impact that a consultee's limited knowledge can have on a student's work-related problem.

Directions: Read the following case scenario. For Part I of this exercise, develop two hypotheses regarding the possible point of connection between the consultee's level of understanding and the referral problem. Further, identify ways you as the consultant could develop the data required to support either of your hypothesized connections and engage the consultee in this validation process. You may find this exercise more effective if performed with another, such as a classmate, a colleague, or a supervisor.

Case Presentation

Referral: Manny was referred to your office by his fifth-grade teacher, Ms. Ellison. Ms. Ellison reported that Manny, a new student to your school, is "constantly getting out of his seat, not giving enough personal space to other children, and always asking to go to the bathroom." Ms. Ellison reported that Manny has been doing this "since day one, and it is only getting worse each day." Further, she noted that she cannot tolerate it anymore and is truly "beginning to dislike this boy!"

Classroom observations:

In observing the classroom, you note that Ms. Ellison, a third-year teacher, is highly energetic and enthusiastic in class. She scurries around the room, speaks loudly and employs a lot of animation in her communication patterns. Ms. Ellison's is an activities-driven classroom. She has her class set up in learning stations that are very stimulating, both visually and auditorily, and she has the children moving around the classroom, going from one learning center to another. The class is very active, stimulating, and energetic. It is clear that there is much opportunity for students to be engaged in the learning process.

Additional information:

In looking at Manny's records, you find that he had been diagnosed with a sensory integration disorder when he was younger. In Manny's previous school setting, he was placed in a classroom that had fewer students and was co-taught by a general education teacher and a special education teacher.

Part I: Connecting Ms. Ellison's lack of information to Timothy's behavior.

Hypothesis 1:
Hypothesis 2:

Part II: Supporting your hypothesis.

1. What type of data would you attempt to gather to support either of your hypotheses?
2. What or who might be useful resources?
3. How would you engage Ms. Ellison in this process?

Exercise 11.1 Sensory Overload

As suggested by the example in Exercise 11.1, inclusion could certainly create problems for both the regular classroom teacher and the child with special needs enrolled within that class, when that teacher lacks the understanding of what to expect and how to respond to the child's special needs. In situations where the consultee is responding to people and processes without the proper understanding and knowledge, the consultant needs to serve as a source for information dissemination and education.

Identifying the Problem

Interview and observational skills will prove invaluable tools in diagnosing the lack of consultee knowledge. In discussing the student, the consultant serving as content expert needs to be sensitive to the consultee's accuracy of understanding of the student's functioning and the interpretation of such student's behavior as compared to normative developmental or job-related behavior.

For example, consider the situation with Sister Patrice, an eighth-grade teacher at a local parochial school. Sr. Patrice had over 12 years of teaching experience, but before this year all of her experience was with first graders. Sister contacted the consultant, extremely upset over the inappropriate and quite possibly aggressive physical behavior of one of her male students. Sister described Jorge as "always touching someone, and he is old enough to know better!" She thought it was important for the consultant to work with Jorge since this behavior could get him in deep trouble. After observing Jorge's behavior in the playground, it became apparent that what Sister saw as hostility was merely social interaction that was very much appropriate and acceptable in Jorge's Latino culture. Additionally, due to Jorge's friendly and kind manner, his peers had grown used to him patting them on the arm or giving a quick hug. While Sister may have identified an area where some instruction might be useful, it would be ineffective to approach it as if Jorge had a severe problem. What was needed was for Sister to become somewhat more familiar with the Latino culture's nonverbal behavior.

Sometimes it is not so much the consultee's comprehension of the student's behavior that is at issue. There are times when the consultee may need to develop a more accurate understanding of her response style as well as the degree to which that style is congruent with standards of professional practice. Consider for example Helena, a teacher in a community daycare center. Helena reported having an unusually difficult time managing one particular four-year-old child. Helena was acutely aware of what typical four-year-old children like to do, and she was even knowledgeable about the use of reinforcement as a means of shaping behavior. She just could not understand why she was unable to manage Theo, the four-year-old in question.

The center was part of a university research project and as such was equipped with a one-way mirror and a video recorder. The consultant asked the consultee, Helen, if he could tape the children at play so that together they could attempt to understand what might be going on with Theo. As they observed the tape, Helen almost embarrassingly exclaimed, "Wow, look at me. I look so serious. I don't seem to be enjoying myself, and it has been 45 minutes, and I have yet to provide any child with a word of praise!" It became apparent to both the consultant and the consultee that even though she was quite knowledgeable about child development and classroom management techniques, Helen was somewhat less aware of her teaching style. As they continued to view the tape, Helen quickly identified that Theo's behavior was entirely normative and that his limit testing appeared to be an attempt to gain her attention.

In assessing the existence of a consultee's lack of knowledge or understanding, the consultant will attempt to answer three separate questions (Meyers, Parsons, & Martin, 1979). First, does the consultee possess accurate self-knowledge in regards to his behaviors?

To answer this first question, the consultant needs to observe the consultee in interaction with the student systematically. The consultant needs to have the consultee estimate his behaviors and compare them against the data collected. The feedback provided must be objective and nonevaluative. In the previous case involving Theo and the preschool teacher Helena, data obtained from the videotape provided objective and nonevaluative information highlighting the quite apparent incongruency between the way Helen thought she behaved and how, in fact, she did behave.

Assuming that the consultee demonstrates an accurate awareness of his response style, the consultant proceeds to the second question: Are the consultee's observed and self-defined behaviors congruent with the consultee's attitudes about how he should professionally function? In this case, the consultant is attempting to identify whether the consultee is doing what he desires to do. The final question to be addressed is whether what the consultee is doing and wishes to do is congruent with what is known to be the accepted form of professional practice. Discrepancies along any point of the questioning need to be confronted and accurate information needs to be provided as the potential remedial steps to increasing consultee knowledge and understanding.

Interventions

In the situation where the consultee lacks understanding, the intervention of choice is to provide the consultee with the information needed. As noted, the consultee may need specific information about the student, about the developmental or theoretical principles operating, or even information about his response style. Providing the consultee information may allow him to more accurately understand the student's responses and perhaps open him up to a variety of options that were not apparent previously.

Interventions employed, while tailored to the specific needs of the consultee, in general involve two steps. The first step is to help the consultee realize that he needs more information. The second step would be for the consultant to serve as an informational resource and to develop an educational program for the consultee collaboratively. While obvious, this form of feedback and didactic instruction requires the consultant to be both directive and confrontational. Because of the possible resistance encountered, it is essential for the consultant to be sure to have developed a collaborative relationship with the consultee before implementing such consultee-focused consultation. Further, the consultant needs to remind the consultee of the confidential, nonevaluative nature of the relationship.

The goal of the intervention would be to provide the consultee with nonevaluative feedback about his current level of knowledge and the degree of congruence that knowledge has with that of current research or expert opinion. Further, the input needs to highlight the impact that this lack of information has had on the consultee's choices of response in working with the student and how these choices have contributed to (if not caused) the student's current work problem. Once the need has been identified and embraced by the consultee, the second phase of intervention would be to provide an educational program for the consultee.

Developing an effective intervention means first establishing concrete goals and learning objectives. Identification of the targets will help give shape to the specific form of information dissemination and education needed. It is essential that the consultant establish these goals in collaboration with the consultee and that the consultee expresses clear ownership of both the goals and the process to be employed. Table 11.1 provides helpful suggestions for the creation of effective goals.

TABLE 11.1 **Developing Effective Goals**

For goals to be effective in guiding interactions and providing criteria for their achievement, they should be established with the following characteristics in evidence.

FACTOR IN CREATING THE GOAL OR OBJECT	WHAT IS NEEDED
S — Specific	Did you include the who, what, where, and when, as appropriate?
M — Measurable	How will you know you achieved your goal? Can you measure it? How?
A — Achievable	Is the goal reasonably attainable and within the time frame you will supply?
R — Relevant	Is the goal helpful to the client/consultee? Does it work with the system?
T — Time-Bound	What is the time frame in which the goal is to be completed?

Consultee Skill Development

It is not usual to find a consultee who is very accurate in her self-observation and is also aware that her behavior is not prescribed as professional practice. However, this same consultee may be having a great deal of trouble eliciting the type of response or behavior she desires, simply because she lacks the necessary skills.

Consider the case of a teacher who understands the limited effectiveness of the use of mild reprimands and other types of punishment as forms of classroom management and embraces the value of employing positive reinforcement within his classroom. However, this same teacher finds that his typical style is to ignore the desired behaviors, being happy that the student is doing what is expected, and to reprimand the child when not performing. While understanding the inefficiency of his classroom management style, the consultee in question is having difficulty shedding the old habit. In this situation, it is skill development rather than information acquisition that is needed. This consultee needs assistance in increasing the habit strength and skill in using positive reinforcement within his classroom.

Program Development

When the goal involves increasing the consultee's skill, practice is essential. One or two in-service or professional development programs do not typically accomplish skill development; instead, it requires a system of practice and corrective feedback. Because of the need to be systematic in such skill training, the consultant should attempt to connect the consultee to any of the training programs, or mechanisms (in-services, workshops, etc.), currently available. Connecting the consultee to the system's natural device for training will ensure ongoing support for the consultee.

In the absence of such a "natural" mechanism, the consultant along with the consultee will need to develop an individualized program of training and skill development. Consultants engaging in consultee skill development need to employ a social learning theory approach (Codding, Feinberg, Dunn McKenney, Waldron, & Conroy, 2005 Trivette, Dunst, Hamby, & O'Herin, 2009). The consultant needs to not only teach the consultee the specific steps for implementing the intervention but also the consultant needs to model the application of these steps and provide the consultee with practice opportunities, followed by consultant feedback.

Regaining Objectivity and Professional Perspective

There are situations in which the consultee, while both knowledgeable and skilled at efficiently managing the student and the student's work-related behavior, is currently ineffective. Often, such ineffectiveness is the result of the consultee's loss of professional objectivity or the fact that his own emotional needs and particular psychosocial history are interfering with the performance of his professional duties. For example, while Dr. Jameson, in our sample case, can provide the student with support and assistance, his best professional insights may be somewhat compromised by his involvement with her and the resulting loss of professional objectivity. It is even possible that the student's current behaviors are in direct response to Dr. Jameson's loss of objectivity and over-involvement.

Working in the arena of loss of objectivity can genuinely tax the consultant's ability to maintain a collaborative relationship. The consultant will most certainly have to confront the consultee's loss of objectivity. It is important that the intervention attempt to keep the focus on the consultee's current level of professional functioning with the student while avoiding any in-depth discussion of the personal issues or experiences that may have contributed to this loss of objectivity.

Categorizing Loss of Objectivity

Gerald Caplan provides one model for understanding the different sources of loss of objectivity and the depth of impact (Caplan & Caplan, 1993). Caplan & Caplan (1993) suggest that in most cases loss of objectivity can be classified into five, overlapping categories: (1) direct personal involvement, (2) simple identification, (3) theme interference, (4) transference, and (5) characterological distortions.

Direct Personal Involvement

While it is less than optimal, it would not be unusual to find a teacher who has both a professional and personal relationship with a student. This would happen in the situation where a teacher is also a student's aunt or next-door neighbor, a good friend of the student's mother, or possibly a coach of a recreational sport team. In this situation, the personal relationship the consultee has with the student outside of the school environment could interfere with the consultee's objectivity and ability to respond professionally to the student within the school. This would be the case where a teacher fails to "discipline" a student because the student is the daughter of a person that teacher is dating.

The consultee whose objectivity is compromised because of a personal relationship with the student may be aware of this distortion in her professional judgment and behavior. However, even with such an awareness, the consultee may be unwilling to publicly admit this distortion of her professionalism because of her sense of guilt or shame. The consultant will need to foster a conscious awareness and acceptance of this distortion of professional objectivity before providing any strategies for assisting the consultee in separating her personal needs from those of her professional duties and responsibilities.

Interventions employed with this and all of the various forms of loss of objectivity will involve confrontation. The goal of this confrontation will be to assist the consultee to not only regain her professional relationship with the student but to discover ways to replace the satisfaction of her personal needs with appropriate appreciation found in professional goal attainment. Thus, the consultee who is unable to reprimand the daughter of a friend may benefit from reframing this reprimand not as punishment but as an attempt to help this student perform and achieve to her potential.

Simple Identification

The second form of loss of objectivity occurs when the consultee "relates" or identifies with the student or one of the other significant individuals within the student's situation. Often, this process of simple identification is easy to recognize in that the point of connection or similarity may be quite apparent. For example, the consultee and student may share physical similarities, ethnic backgrounds, unique behavior (e.g., tics, stutters), or common social experiences (e.g., recently divorced, moved out of the house, have an overbearing parent). The consultee's description of the student or student's current situation will often highlight these points of similarities. Further, it is not unusual for the consultee to refer to the student in very positive and sympathetic terms, speaking as if it were from personal experience. This was the case of Ms. Z.

Ms. Z. is a young, highly achieving, African American woman who expressed concern over the social harassment and bullying experienced by one of her fifth-grade students, Aisha. Ms. Z. reported that the children were being cruel, taunting Aisha in the playground and actively rejecting her from all social interaction. The consultant observed Aisha and her classmates in the playground and at lunch and reported back to Ms. Z. The following dialogue ensued:

Ms. Z. (very excited): Well, didn't I tell...they are cruel.

Mr. L.: I know how much concern you are feeling, so I observed Aisha in both the playground and at lunch, and...

Ms. Z. (interrupting): ... do you believe how they treat her?

Mr. L: Well, actually that is what I wanted to share. During the time I was observing I noticed some teasing...

Ms. Z. (interrupting): Some? I bet you have never been on the receiving end of a cruel comment!

On further reflection and with supportive interaction, Mr. L. was able to have Ms. Z disclose her own experience of being one of a very few African American children in her elementary school and of the painful rejection and bullying she experienced. Further, in this dialogue, Ms. Z. was able to consider that perhaps her own experience was making her somewhat overreactive to typical fifth-grade teasing when it came to Aisha. Mr. L. reframed this "overreaction," viewing it as being sensitive to the possible impact cruel comments can have on all children. The result was that Ms. Z. inquired about the possibility of providing a guidance lesson on teasing and bullying to her class, stating that all the children could benefit from such a lesson.

As with all forms of loss of objectivity, the consultant in this case needed to confront the consultee about her possible distortion and loss of professional objectivity. Using skills of confrontation, both direct and indirect forms (to be discussed later within this chapter), the consultant attempted to raise the consultee's level of consciousness around the emotional identification she felt regarding this particular student and student situation. Further, the consultant helped the consultee to recognize the ways such identification may be distorting her professional judgment and behavior.

Theme Interference

The consultee experiencing theme interference appears blocked in her response to the work situation and may appear unaccountably sensitive to some facet or aspect of the work situation (Caplan & Caplan, 1993). According to Caplan & Caplan (1993), what happens is that a conflict related to the consultee's personal experience has not been satisfactorily resolved and now persists as an emotionally toned cognitive constellation, called a "theme." A theme is some distorted or dysfunctional and rigid thinking that links two separate thoughts or interpretations without empirical bases. Caplan (1970) noted that a consultee expressing theme interference operates from a rigid, syllogistic form of thinking. A consultee displaying theme interference behaves from the belief that if event A occurred, then B had to follow. Consider the case of Terell.

Terell, having taught for six years at the middle school, was now reassigned to teach eleventh-grade social studies. While being knowledgeable about content and pedagogy, Terell was experiencing a great deal of difficulty in managing his classroom, something that he had never previously experienced. In discussing the matter with the counselor-consultant, Terrell emphasized that he hates having to discipline the students, he hates being mean, "a real ogre!"

It appears that Terell is making an inevitable link between one thought, "I need to manage my classroom," with a second thought, "You have to be mean to discipline high school students, and therefore nobody will like you." Assuming this is the case for our consultee, then finding himself in this position of now teaching high school stimulates the inevitable conclusions regarding the fact that everyone will dislike him. This conclusion is both unpleasant and unacceptable and thus blocks his utilization of effective classroom management techniques. The result is a classroom that is on the verge of being out of control.

The rigid, almost syllogistic thinking found in theme interference leads the consultee to jump to conclusions about the students. In Terell's case, the conclusion is that students would dislike him. As such, the consultee's reaction, that of failing to discipline the students, would be in response to this anticipated student response rather than any reality.

Unresolved themes can lead the consultee to not only draw invalid conclusions about a particular student (e.g., that student is outraged that I corrected him) but also may lead the consultee to respond in an automatic, nonfunctional way as an attempt to intervene with the perceived student problem. Exercise 11.2 is provided to clarify this point further.

Exercise 11.2 Theme Interference

Directions: Read the following case presentation, being especially sensitive to identify elements of the student's situation that appear to have an unusual emotional tone or charge for the consultee. Next, identify those consultee responses that appear to be an artifact of the theme as opposed to reflecting an objective response to the student's need.

Case: Ms. Roberts is a sixth-grade teacher. She is a recent college graduate, and this is her first professional teaching assignment. Ms. Roberts has invited the consultant to help her with one particular child in her class, Alee. According to Ms. Roberts, Alee needs to be watched very closely. Ms. Roberts stated that Alee is a child "just waiting to explode." Ms. Roberts is unable to point to anything specific that Alee is doing or not doing, but she wants the consultant (the school counselor) to begin to counsel Alee.

From her position as the teacher, Ms. Roberts will keep "tight control on Alee, giving her a lot of structure and be sure to check up on her daily." Ms. Roberts continued: "I have made time in my day where I can meet with Alee and let her know I'm available if she needs to talk, but I know she needs more than I can provide. She is a great kid, and it's a shame to see her throw it away and start to get out of control."

When the consultant questioned the need for the counseling and the extreme control, Ms. Roberts avoided the questions and instead turned the discussion to the fact that "Alee's mom is newly divorced and has since returned to work. Alee is obviously going to be one of those latchkey kids, and you know what happens to them! You sometimes have to wonder why people like that have kids."

Questions:

1. What possible theme(s) is operating to block Ms. Roberts's utilization of her skills as classroom manager?
2. Which responses appear tied more to Ms. Roberts's issues rather than student need?

When attempting to intervene with theme interference, the consultant can attempt to "unlink" the referral problem, or student behavior, from "category A" of the consultee's syllogistic thinking. Assisting the consultee to reexamine her perception of the student may help the consultee to understand that her perception of this particular student's situation was not accurate. Thus, in the case of the latchkey child, helping Ms. Roberts understand that Alee's mother works at a local elementary school and that her schedule parallels Alee's may help her to reframe her initial impressions regarding Alee as a latch-key child. Similarly, providing the consultee with additional data regarding the student or the student's situation may help the consultee to reframe the conclusion drawn from her syllogistic thinking. For example, providing Ms. Roberts information regarding Alee's after-school activities, such as her active involvement with Girl Scouts, peer tutoring, and church youth group, and the very loving and close-knit relationship that Alee has with both her father and her mother, may help her to reduce the feeling that Alee will inevitably become a problem child. This form of intervention may assist the consultee to give up on displacing her conflictual issues on the student since the student no longer is perceived as fitting the logic of the initial category.

Transference

Transference is the fourth form of loss of objectivity discussed by Caplan & Caplan (1993). The consultee who is acting out of transference will project onto the student a set of attitudes, expectations, and judgments that more accurately reflect the experience of the consultee (rather than the student's own experience) and that will distort the consultee's accurate and objective evaluation of the student and the student's life experiences. Under these conditions, the consultee will respond from their transferred feelings. This is different from simple identification, in which at least some of the conditions to which the consultee is reacting do exist for the student.

Consider the case of Bernard, a high school science teacher. Bernard approached the consultant seeking assistance with one of his students. Bernard explained that Elsie, the student with whom he had concerns, was new to the school. Elsie, according to Bernard, just moved to this area, having lived in Georgia. Bernard noted that Elsie appeared to be a bright and capable student. Even though it was hard for Bernard to pinpoint his concerns, he "felt that there was something just not right with Elsie" and he wanted the consultant to "check her out." After meeting with Elsie and having her assess her experience with the move and the new school, the consultant returned to Bernard. As he entered the second session with the consultee, Bernard met him at the door with a big smile and stated "What do you think, a religious fanatic?" Caught somewhat off guard, the consultant was unsure how to respond. In the silence that followed, Bernard continued by stating, "You got to watch these Bible Belt people. They'll jam it down your throat. You have a problem? Well, that's God's way of saying you are a sinner and dammed. I can hear her now, telling her parents we all need to "REPENT!"

The consultant reflected Bernard's feelings and asked if he or the other staff have noticed any such behavior. Bernard responded: "Oh, no, I was just having a little fun, you know. The Georgia thing, the southern Bible circuit. Just having a little fun."

In follow-up conversations with the student, Elsie, and the consultee, Bernard, it became clear that there was no truth to his concerns. Elsie was raised as a Roman Catholic and while attempting to live a good, value-based life, was not very active in her church. Further, it became apparent that Bernard had some unresolved issues regarding his faith stance and in particular his feelings of guilt surrounding some of his earlier choices in life. It appeared to the consultant that Bernard was allowing his fears of condemnation and sense of guilt to interfere with his assessment of Elsie. Further, his concern regarding her talking to her parents about the teachers need to repent appeared to be more a projection of his fear of being discovered as a "sinner."

In most settings, transference is inhibited by the very fact that the consultee and the student remain emotionally detached. In most situations, the consultee has separated his professional interactions from his private life, and thus the boundaries of the profession serve as a reality check to hold in place transferential distortions. The possibility of blurred boundaries can be a significant issue for teachers since they are responsible for maintaining close observations and connections with students, particularly those who are having the most difficulty functioning. In these situations, the characteristic of the student (e.g., new to the school) can encourage the consultee to provide emotional support or guidance. Along with this invitation to provide emotional support comes the call to engage at a psycho-emotional level with the student and thus become more vulnerable to the opportunities for transference.

Because transference typically reflects events or experience with significant personal relevance, working with a consultee around these transferential issues is extremely difficult if one is attempting to maintain a collaborative consultation relationship and avoid moving into a psychotherapeutic contract. Because of this delicate balance, it is often preferable for the consultant to employ less direct forms of confrontation to allow the consultee the opportunity to retain a sense of personal privacy while at the same time making the connections between his own experience and the current distortion of the student's reality. There may be times when the consultee is so defended from his awareness of the transferential issues that the best the consultant can hope for is to successfully refer the consultee for additional therapeutic support and individual counseling.

Characterological Distortions

There are times when the work-related problem experienced by the consultee is not a result of the dysfunctionality of the student but rather the enduring emotional problems of the consultee, herself. A consultee exhibiting exaggerated distortions of reality or enduring psychological disturbance is most often identified and responded to through normal administrative and supervisory channels. However, when that is not the case and the consultee's emotional issues are evident and negatively impacting the student, the counselor-consultant can attempt to raise the consultee's awareness of this emotional interference and help her find professional services so that she can regain the professional objectivity needed to perform her job. Beyond such direct intervention, the consultant should provide appropriate feedback regarding the work functioning of the consultee (not the personal, emotional history) to those with responsibility for her supervision and work assignments. This reporting to a supervisor represents one of those exceptions to confidentiality that occurs within the consultation relationship. The goal here would be to provide the consultee with the support needed for controlling her emotional needs within the work setting. The consultee needs help regaining professional distance from students who arouse these distortions, and the student(s) deserves protection from the further deterioration of the consultee's professional objectivity.

Confrontation: An Essential Intervention Skill

The specific forms and strategies for intervening with consultee-focused consultation will vary according to the unique needs of the consultee (i.e., knowledge, skill, objectivity), the depth and nature of the consultation relationship, and the unique knowledge and skill set of the consultant. However, central to all interventions with a consultee is the element of confrontation. As such, the remainder of the chapter will look at appropriate methods of direct and indirect confrontation.

Methods of Direct Confrontation

When attempting to understand the value and use of confrontation in consultation, the consultant must overcome the general tendency to equate the word *confrontation* with that of a destructive, aggressive, hostile act. Confrontation, when used within a helping context, does not take the form of lecturing, judging, or punishing. These are examples of the abuse of confrontation rather than the appropriate use of confrontation.

Within the context of a helping relationship, confrontation represents an invitation by one participant to have the other participant look at, discuss, clarify, or reconsider some event occurring within the helping exchange. It is an invitation to explore all the aspects of the relationship and the helping dynamic. Such an empathic invitation to self-exploration has been found to facilitate the other's self-exploration (Parsons & Zhang, 2014). For example, we have all had on occasion, while talking with a friend, to question a point they made about an issue for which we had contradictory information. Imagine the following dialogue between two teachers:

Ted: Geez, how will we ever get through this assignment for our accreditation visit, especially when we have to go on that training seminar this weekend!

Mary: I may be wrong, but I thought the memo said that the training seminar was next weekend.

The interaction, while not a hostile, attacking, or destructive exchange, is nonetheless confrontational. In fact, it reflects a particular type of confrontation called a didactic (informational) confrontation, a confrontation in which one member of the dialogue invited the other member to reconsider his position in light of this more accurate information. A consultant may find confrontation useful when she experiences the following situations:

1. A discrepancy between what the consultee says and how she behaves. For example, perhaps the consultee states that she is excited about trying the new techniques discussed in the consultation, yet week after week the consultee notes that she forgot to use the strategy.
2. A discrepancy between what the consultee "knows" to be true and the evidence or facts as the consultant knows them. This was the case with the previous example regarding the training weekend.
3. A disparity between the verbal and nonverbal expressions of consultee's emotions. This may be the case when a consultee states that he is okay with the recommendations of the consultant and yet demonstrates a frown and a worrisome look.
4. An inconsistency between two pieces of information the consultee verbally presents. This would happen in the situation where a consultee states that he understands and values the use of positive reinforcement and yet notes that his primary technique for controlling the class is through verbal reprimand.

While these are four situations in which a consultant should seek clarification of the inconsistencies, contradictions, or discrepancies, in reality, confrontation occurs anytime we call to question another's behavior, attitude, or feelings. Since confrontations are inevitable, the effective consultant will need to understand the elements that make a confrontation productive, facilitative, and relationship building rather than destructive and attacking. It is helpful for the counselor-consultant to consider each of the following as guidelines when engaging in a confrontation (Parsons & Zhang, 2014):

1. Describe, in nonevaluative, nonjudgmental terms, the points of confusion or points of apparent consultee inconsistency.
2. Use "I" language, since it is genuinely the consultant who is confused and seeking clarification.
3. Be empathic, mindful of the consultee's current situation. Are they physically and emotionally able to look at the issue and engage in a reflection and discussion?
4. Remember to express that the goal is to gain clarity rather than evaluate or find fault.

The consultant who, from a perspective of empathy with the consultee, can descriptively and tentatively point out areas of consultee misinformation or mixed and confusing messages can constructively move the consultation relationship to a higher level of accuracy, clarity, and collaboration. For example, the confrontation regarding the training seminar moved the interaction to more clear, accurate communication and agreement. However, that confrontation could have been less productive and much more destructive to the relationship if Mary had stated, "You are a nerd! You never read anything. The memo said the training seminar is NEXT weekend. WAKE UP!"

Even when we attempt to follow the "guidelines" to appropriate confrontation, our confrontation may be less than productive or effective. The real proof of effectiveness is not in the degree to which all the "correct" elements are present, but rather the degree to which the desired effect is attained. If the consultee attempts to discredit the statement or attempts to argue the point or tries to devalue the importance of the confrontation, he may be giving evidence that the confrontation was too much for him to accept. Remember that the purpose of the confrontation is to move the relationship to greater clarity and accuracy. When this happens, the consultee is likely to openly accept and consider the confrontation rather than deny or defend against it. So, the proof of the effectiveness of the confrontation is in the consultee's response! Exercise 11.3 will assist you in employing the previous guidelines while formulating your confrontation. As you formulate the confrontations, consider the possible impact your comment may have on the consultee.

Directions: Complete an appropriate confrontation with each of the following. As with other exercises, it is useful to compare your responses to those of a classmate, colleague, or supervisor. In writing a confrontation, be sure to

- consider the perspective of the consultee,
- use descriptive language,
- provide small steps of confrontation, and
- have your tone reflect your helping intentions.

1. Consultee (looking anxious): "I like what you are saying, and I am sure it will help."
   Consultant: _____

2. Consultee: "These students have a terrible attitude. I have to be on their backs every moment of the day."
   Consultant: _____

3. Consultee: "I'm going to develop a sense of teamwork in class, so I told them that they have to come to the class prepared next Friday—or else."
   Consultant: _____

4. Consultee: "NO! There is NOTHING wrong! Get off my back!"
   Consultant: _____

5. Consultee: "I know Alex called Alfred a name, but Alex is so frail, I just know the bullies in the class are always picking on him."
   Consultant: _____

Exercise 11.3 Effective Confrontation

Methods of Indirect Confrontation

Before employing direct confrontation, the consultant must determine the degree to which this relationship is established as an open, honest, trusting, helping exchange. The consultant needs to consider the extent to which the consultee has demonstrated openness to the consultant's inquiries and a willingness to be open to the consultant's ideas and feedback, and the degree to which the consultee has demonstrated a willingness to explore a variety of issues and topics. When the consultee appears to be somewhat closed and protected within the consulting relationship, indirect forms of confrontation may prove more productive.

Indirect methods of confrontation allow for the consultee to maintain her defenses and protective stance while at the same time becoming somewhat open to the new and potentially conflicting material. The goal is to provide the consultee with enough psychic safety to enable her to be receptive to the confrontation.

Two forms of indirect confrontation to be discussed are (1) modeling and (2) talking around the issue/use of parable.

Modeling

One indirect form of confrontation occurs when the consultant mirrors, or models, the consultee interacting with the student or the student's situation using professional strategies that are conflictual to that anticipated as necessary by the consultee. Consider the consultee presented in scenario 5 of exercise 11.3, assuming that Alex is not as helpless or as fragile as the consultee may perceive. A consultant could indirectly confront this consultee belief by interacting with Alex in a playful yet somewhat challenging way. The experience of having Alex "hold his own" with the consultant and possibly tease back would be an indirect confrontation with the consultee's perception that Alex needed to be protected from such interaction.

The use of modeling as an indirect form of confrontation does not force the consultee to admit something that may be uncomfortable, but it does provide the consultee with an experience that will "force" him to reconsider his perception and actions concerning the student.

Talking Around the Issue and the Use of Parable

Talking around the issue and the use of parable are additional forms of indirect confrontation. As is true for all indirect confrontation, these techniques when employed successfully will allow the consultee room to keep his ego in check while at the same time provide information that may create enough personal dissonance to motivate a change in the consultee's perception and behavior.

Talking around the issue is a technique in which the consultant describes similar situations in which she was involved. For example, rather than directly suggesting that the consultee has lost her objectivity, the consultant may directly share a story about a time when she misinterpreted a student's behavior because of having experienced a similar student in the past. Thus, the consultant working with the case of Tommie may note for the consultee, "You know, Tommie is very tiny. He reminds me of my next-door neighbor's child. Rob is small for his age, but he is really quick. All the kids like him on their team when they play tag since he is so fast and elusive. But, you know, he is quite a con. When he gets caught in tag, he often jokes with the bigger kids about picking on this little kid, referring to himself." Relaying this scenario is done with the intention that the consultee will recognize that she is projecting a need for a student who in fact does not have one.

A similar approach suggested and discussed by Gerald Caplan (1970) is the use of parables. In using a parable, the consultant "invents" an anecdote that is similar to that currently experienced by the consultee. Embedded within the parable are the messages of over-involvement and the role it played in creating the situation experienced by that consultee. The elements of a parable are characters and situations that are possible identification objects and behavior, and outcomes that convey a moral. The task for the consultant is to find a parable that, while portraying the essential features of the current case, is sufficiently different to allow the consultee's defenses to remain intact. As such, the consultee can "risk" accepting the morale of the parable and choose to apply it to his own experience or, if too threatening, privately refuse to embrace the morale without risking admonition from the consultant. From this perspective, the parable must balance being far enough removed from the current situation so as not to be threatening while at the same time having enough relevance and "realness" to prove instructional. Thus, for a consultant to share a story about Tina, who is pale and sickly looking and yet is always the instigator of problems in the classroom, may be too obvious and direct for Tommie's teacher. Perhaps, expanding on the story of the neighbor's child may afford enough distance to allow the consultee to dismiss it as irrelevant to the situation while at the same time providing a morale that may apply, that is, that that the child may be more competent and responsible than first appears.

The identification of the specific elements to include within a consultee-focused consultation is not always easy. What may at first appear to be simply a lack of clear information and understanding may actually be a situation in which the consultee lacks the skill to implement her knowledge or is blocked emotionally to do so. The accurate identification of the consultee's need is an essential step in the intervention process. A second crucial element to a consultee-focused consultation is the effective use of confrontation, both direct and indirect. To further illustrate and provide opportunity to practice these two processes, see Exercise 11.4.

Directions. For each of the following situations

1. identify the type or form of loss of objectivity exhibited by the consultee,
2. provide an example of a direct confrontation that could be used, and
3. describe an example of an indirect confrontation that might prove useful.

Situation A:

Mr. Hyatt is very concerned about Diego's home life. According to Mr. Hyatt, Diego appears to be uncared for; he is often "tired-looking," has only minimal lunches (a sandwich and a piece of fruit), and lacks personal hygiene ("He never combs his hair!"). Your observations and those of the social worker are that Diego has a good, yet modest, home life. Diego presents as both a happy and well-cared-for child. In discussion with Mr. Hyatt, you discover that as a child he was neglected, and at the age of 7 was placed in a foster home. You sense that Mr. Hyatt continues to have personal fears of abandonment.

Situation B:

Henry is in his first year of teaching. Henry is currently teaching 12th-grade English. He came to you because he is having problems controlling his seventh period class. In discussing the situation with you, Henry notes that he doesn't understand it, "the guys in my

Exercise 11.4 Confrontation in Consultation

7th period are really cool. I don't know why they treat me this way. I like them. I don't know what to do, after all. I don't want to come across like some monster."

Situation C:

Paul is distraught with the way the kids are teasing Jerome and rejecting him, just because he is "Orthodox." Paul lets you know in no uncertain terms that he "just knows" how horrible it is for Jerome. After all, he (Paul) "was also the only Jewish boy attending his public school." Your observations suggest that Jerome's interactions with his classmates are age appropriate and Jerome appears entirely accepted by his peers.

Putting It All Together: A Case Illustration and Exercise

With consultee-focused consultation there is a delicate shift to gathering information not only about the client but also about the consultee's knowledge, skill, and level of professional objectivity as these may contribute to the current problem situation. Using effective counseling skills such as active listening, affirmation of feeling, and clarification of content, the counselor-consultant can help the consultee feel heard and valued as a collaborator while gaining insight into the targets for intervention. We close the chapter with the following case illustration and exercise so that you may practice "putting it all together."

A Case Illustration and Exercise
Olivia

Case Information

Olivia, a freshman in high school, transferred to your school three weeks ago. Olivia's parents have called the school counselor, Dr. Kahn, to express their concern about Olivia's progress in her biology class.

Almost immediately into their discussion with the counselor, Olivia's parents quickly change their focus from Olivia's progress to complain about the biology teacher, Ms. Urth. They state that Ms. Urth is picking on Olivia because Olivia is new and is grading her quizzes and tests unfairly. They know Olivia understands the material because she was ahead in the curriculum before they moved; in fact, she was in advanced bio. They continued by stating that Olivia has always excelled in science and earned A's on her work instead of the C's that she is currently getting.

In talking with their neighbors, Olivia's parents discovered that Ms. Urth is planning on retiring at the end of the year and the "word on the street" is that she has checked out, no longer invested in her teaching. They would like Olivia moved to another biology class. When Dr. Kahn inquired if they had spoken to Ms. Urth about their concerns, they replied that they have been trying to get an appointment with her for the past two weeks but she has yet to return their calls.

Dr. Kahn offered to observe Olivia in class and gather more information from the teacher. The parents reluctantly agreed to wait a few days to meet once again but continued to insist on moving Olivia to another biology class. Dr. Kahn acknowledged the parents' concern for immediate action but again reiterated the value of gathering more data and even meeting with Olivia to gain her insight.

In the observation of the biology class, Dr. Kahn notices that Ms. Urth appears to be enjoying teaching the class. Most of the class appears to be engaged, although Olivia sits in the back and does not seem to be taking notes or participating. Rather, she appears to be staring at the boy next to her throughout the class.

Following the observation, Dr. Kahn met with Ms. Urth and shared Olivia's parents concern. Ms. Urth admitted that Olivia's parents had called and that she had not returned those calls. She stated that she felt it was way too soon to talk to them, as she hasn't had a chance to get to know Olivia, who, in her opinion, is way more interested in boys than in biology class. Dr. Kahn asked about Olivia's current C-level performance on her quiz and test grades. Ms. Urth responded that Olivia is doing fine and most of the class is getting C's. She added that she knows what she's doing because she's been doing it for 30 years. She then asked Dr. Kahn for his help in "getting these parents off my back!"

The invitation to Olivia to visit the counseling office as a new student check-in was met with great enthusiasm. Olivia tells Dr. Kahn that the new school is "Ok" and most of her teachers are "fine," with the exception of her biology teacher. Olivia explains that she already learned the material that is being covered, but since this school does not have an advanced biology class, she was enrolled in this regular bio class. "It could be an easy A for me," states Olivia, "but the quizzes and tests make no sense because they don't follow the book. The test material is only from what she teaches in class, and it's hard to focus on her. She bounces around and goes off on tangents. It's more interesting to focus on the guy next to me. He draws really cool pictures in his notebook. He should be an artist!"

Exercise: Applying What We Know

There are many factors impacting the success of the student in our case. In approaching this case, consider each of the following questions. The goal is to generate interventions that not only assist in this specific situation with Olivia but will serve a preventive value for this student and others. Identify what interventions can be implemented for Ms. Urth, considering the following:

a. Teaching and instructional style
b. Assessment style (tests, quizzes)
c. Professional responsibilities (communication with parents, students)

How might these help Olivia? How might these strategies broaden the breadth of the impact by helping other students or becoming preventive strategies?

1. Identify what interventions can be implemented for the parents. How might these also serve as prevention strategies?
2. Identify strategies that the school may wish to implement, considering the following:

a. Placing new students in classes
b. Leveled classes (appropriate instruction meeting individual needs)
c. Implementing guidelines for professional responsibilities (such as communication with parents)

Summary

- It is possible that the student's difficulty is a reflection of or reaction to the consultee's lack of professional knowledge, skill, or objectivity.

- Assessing a consultee's professional knowledge requires the consultant to determine the degree to which the consultee (1) is aware of his professional behavior, (2) desires to engage in that professional behavior, and (3) is aware of the professional standards for such action and practice.

- Intervention addressing knowledge and skill should be formulated collaboratively and employ effective teaching, modeling, and practice approaches.

- Consultee ineffectiveness often reflects a loss of professional objectivity as a result of (1) direct personal involvement, (2) simple identification, (3) transference, (4) theme interference, or (5) characterological distortions.

- Consultant intervention will range from increasing the consultee's awareness of a reduction in objectivity and its impact on the student, to getting the consultee professional support.

- Core to most interventions in a consultee-focused consultation is the effective use of direct and indirect confrontation.

Additional Resources
Print

Dougherty, A. (2013). *Casebook of psychological consultation and collaboration in school and community settings.* Belmont, CA: Brooks/Cole.

Lambert, N., Hylander, I., & Sandoval, J. H. (Eds.). (2015). *Consultee-centered consultation: Improving the quality of professional services in schools and community organizations.* New York, NY: Routledge.

Sandoval, J. H. (2014). *An introduction to consultee-centered consultation in the schools: A step-by-step guide to the process and skills.* New York, NY: Routledge/Taylor & Francis.

Web-Based

Cilliers, F., Rothmann, S., & Struwig, W. H. (2004). Transference and counter-transference in systems psycho-dynamic group process consultation: The consultant's experience. *South African Journal of Industrial Psychology, 30*(1), 72–81. Retrieved from https://www.researchgate.net/publication/47739463_Transference_and_counter-transference_in_systems_psychodynamic_group_process_consultation_The_consultant%27s_experience

Lai Yeung, S. W. C. (2014). The need for guidance and counselling training for teachers. *Proce-dia: Social and Behavioral Sciences, 113*(7), 36–43. Retrieved from https://ac.els-cdn.com/S1877042814000093/1-s2.0-S1877042814000093-main.pdf?_tid=d4ca7b75-6ba6-48d0-997e-b78f02e8f52a&acd-nat=1531440851_3207f3ef908c784d7a3b2daabe45e257

Newman, D. S., & Ingraham, C. L. (2017). Consultee-centered consultation: Contemporary perspectives and a frame-work for the future. *Journal of Education and Psychological Consultation, 27*(1), 1–12. Retrieved from https://www.tandfonline.com/doi/abs/10.1080/10474412.2016.1175307?journalCode=hepc20

Şahbaz, U. (2011). The effectiveness of in-service training for school counselors on the inclusion of students with disabilities. *Educational Research and Reviews, 6*(8), 580–585. Retrieved from ttp://www.academicjournals.org/article/article1379768710_Sahbaz.pdf

References

Caplan, G. (1970). *The theory and practice of mental health consultation.* New York, NY: Basic Books.

Caplan, G., & Caplan, R. (1993). *Mental health consultation and collaboration.* San Francisco, CA: Jossey-Bass.

Codding, R. S., Feinberg, A. B., Dunn, E. K., & Pace, G. M. (2005). Effects of immediate performance feedback on implementation of behavior support plans. *Journal of Applied Behavior Analysis, 38,* 205–220.

Meyers, J., Parsons, R. D., & Martin, R. (1979). *Mental health consultation in schools.* San Francisco, CA: Jossey-Bass.

Parsons, R. D., & Zhang, N. (2014). *Becoming a skilled counselor.* Thousand Oaks, CA: Sage Publications.

Trivette, C. M., Dunst, C. J., Hamby, D. W., & O'Herin, C. E. (2009). Characteristics and consequences of adult learning methods and strategies. *Winterberry Research Syntheses.* Asheville, NC: Winterberry Press.

CHAPTER 12

Level I Prevention: The System as Focus Point

Of course Jasmine is acting out. She is frustrated as hell. We knew when she transferred to our school that she had just been diagnosed with a learning disability. The fact that we don't have the necessary supportive service is just unacceptable. The school is responsible for her disruption, one that I feel is justified.

As discussed in Chapter 2, the school counselor and the students with whom she works are impacted by the ecology and system in which they operate. The reflection that opens this chapter highlights the fact that a school's resources and culture can have a significant impact on our students' performance. These same factors can also impact a counselor's ability to function effectively. It is possible that the student, being seen by a counselor, a student who is exhibiting difficulty in her academic achievement or in social interactions, may be a "symptom" of a broader, system dysfunction.

The current chapter will focus on both the particular demands and unique opportunities of systems-focused consultation.

After completing this chapter, the reader will be able to

1. describe the essential elements of a school as a social system,
2. explain how a faulty system can negatively affect the functioning of those within it, and
3. describe the levels of change that can be taken to facilitate system change.

The School as System

There are times when the absence of needed resources can give shape to a student's disruptive behavior or underachievement. It is evident that a crowded classroom where students are standing as a result of having too few desks invites disruption. Similarly, a school absent of bilingual teachers should expect underachievement if the majority of the incoming class are non–English-speaking students. The impact of the school as a system does not stop with such apparent failures.

There are times and circumstances when the policies, procedures, services, and even the culture of the school can serve as the source of student disruption and underachievement (see Ahn & Rodkin, 2014; Sundell, Castellano, & Overman, 2012). Without a full grasp of the system within which the counselor-consultant is operating, any attempt at remediating student difficulties may result in short-sighted, ineffectual, and incorrectly targeted interventions (Schein, 2003).

The Basics of Systems

According to one author (Kurpius, 1985, p. 368), a system is "an entity made up of interconnected parts, with recognizable relationships that are systematically arranged to serve a perceived purpose." So, what are these "interconnected parts?"

There are five basic elements of any system: (1) the identified population being served, (2) the specific needs of that population selected to be met, (3) the desired outcome or goals of the system's services, (4) the processes to be employed in achieving the desired outcome, and (5) the required resources or inputs necessary to engage these processes. As might be apparent, the specific characteristics and unique needs of the population that any one school hopes to serve will give form to the uniqueness of that school, as a system. Case Illustration 12.1 illustrates this uniqueness by contrasting two high school mission statements.

Case Illustration 12.1
Comparing System Elements

School X:

Mission: Our mission and focus is to prepare our Christian youth to develop their unique potential—academically, socially, and spiritually. The school emphasizes the development of self-discipline, value-driven behavior, and cooperation in order to prepare our students to become productive, ethical members of our diverse society.

School Y:

Mission: Our mission is to develop cadets, through emersion in a military culture, to be men of strong ethical character and skilled to become leaders of men. Cadets will be formed to exemplify our valuing of sound mind and body, and values such as duty, honor, loyalty, and courage.

Comparing System Elements of School X and School Y

System Element	School X	School Y
Population served	Christian men and women	Men
Need addressed (implied)	Spiritual growth	Leadership
Outcome/goals desired	Produce productive citizens in a diverse, challenging, and evolving world	Produce male citizen leaders who exhibit sense of duty, honor, loyalty, and courage
Processes employed	Fostering self-discipline, integrity, cooperation, and responsibility	Educate within an academic and military environment
Inputs, resources (implied)	Clergy, religious, and lay educators; culture of Christian values	Career military as educators; military culture

Regardless of the uniqueness of the population and needs served or the processes and resources employed, for any system to function effectively, these five elements need to operate in coordination. Changing any one of these components will impact the overall functioning of the system. Just consider the impact on such things as admissions processes, physical facilities, or performance criteria that may result from the decision of those at School Y (see Case Illustration 12.1) to admit female cadets. Or, how might the change in inputs, specifically the absence of clergy as teachers, impact School X?

The reality is that student needs, population characteristics, and school resources will change and, as such, for schools to remain viable and effective they need to be adaptable and respond to these changes.

Primary Prevention—Maintaining System "Openness"

The scenario that opened this chapter pointed to the simple fact that one student's under-achievement, elevated frustration, and resulting classroom disruption was a direct result of the school's failure to adapt to the changing needs of its consumer. Such failure to adapt is not unexpected given what is known about open and closed systems (Emery & de Guerre, 2007).

When created, systems, including our schools, employ resources to engage processes that were directly and explicitly informed by the needs of the specific population chosen to be served. Perhaps a school in an agrarian community would develop a schedule that included days off during hunting and harvesting seasons. Or another school, in response to its community's values, may create a curriculum that includes lessons in church history and religious practice and incorporates morning routines that involve prayer and spiritual service. In these situations, the system is responsive to the specific population's needs and values. Should each of these schools adapt their schedule, their curriculum, their daily procedures in response to a changing demographic and consumer need, they would be considered "open."

At their inception, all social systems are "open." They actively engage with consumers to identify needs, and they develop structures and processes that will address these consumer needs. Systems, however, do not always remain "open" (Emery & de Guerre, 2007).

Some systems, some schools, move from what was once flexible and responsive to the consumer it serves to become that which is no longer adaptive, adjusting, or servicing the needs of its consumer. The more a system is closed, the more rigid and codified their processes become.

As the system moves from employing processes that are seen as "a" way to meeting consumer needs to those that now are viewed as "the" way of operating, system creativity and innovation are discouraged and even punished. In these systems, "the" way becomes codified in manuals, policies and procedures documents, contracts, and charts. The comment most often heard is "This is how we do it!" In closed systems, the focus is on perpetuating and maintaining the status quo, even when there is evidence of a changing population or of changing population needs.

What happens to a school's ability to successfully meet its goals and objectives when the composition of the population it serves changes dramatically, and yet its curriculum, policies, and procedures remain the same? How would the changing needs of its consumer, as might be the case when a school begins to admit students with special learning challenges, impact the school's ability to function as it once did? Maintaining "the" way we do it in light of such a population change will prove ineffective.

With the inexorably changing demographics come new needs, new priorities, and new processes targeted to satisfying those needs. It is expected that the specific policies, procedures, and services employed by one school will differ from those of another, as a reflection of the unique needs of each school's consumer. It is also true that a school's programs (processes) should vary across time, as its own specific consumer population changes and the particular needs of these consumers change. When such openness to change and adaptive ability is absent, the school will miss its mark at addressing consumer needs, a reality that is often revealed by the actions of one student, now identified as "client."

System Intervention and Prevention Services

The counselor-as-consultant is in a unique position to inform, mobilize, and collaborate initiatives that will keep the system open, flexible, and responsive to student needs. It is a position recognized by the American School Counselor Association (2012) that directs counselors to act as system change agents, collaborating with "stakeholders such as parents and guardians, teachers, administrators and community leaders to create learning environments that promote educational equity and success for every student."

While the unique characteristics will shape the specifics of such intervention and prevention efforts, needs, and resources of the specific school, the nature of change can vary from a minor adjustment to the reformulation of the entire school and school culture.

The First Level of Intervention: Feedback

It is not unusual to find that the tension being experienced by students or teachers is the result of either misinformation or the lack of information needed to fully understand and accept a particular situation. This is dramatically illustrated at times of crisis events when information from official channels is lacking. At these times, those at risk may embrace rumor and innuendo to fill the void (Jones, Thompson, Dunkel-Schetter, & Cohen-Silver, 2017). The ill effects of poor communication and information sharing is not limited to times of crisis and threat. This was the case at one high school when student medical records suddenly disappeared from the central office files. Those teachers who needed access to those records to ensure accurate student accommodations were perplexed and angry. The tension was palpable, with rumors spreading among the faculty about the "disrespect" the administration was exhibiting by "not trusting" the faculty with such information.

When the principal was asked for an explanation, he embarrassingly informed the teachers that he forgot to tell them of the new Health Insurance Portability and Account-ability Act (HIPAA) (U.S. Department of Health and Human Services, 1996) regulations that required all student medical records to be private and secured. As a result of these regulations, the school nurse had moved all of the files to locked filing cabinets in the school infirmary. Teachers who required access to this information were on a "need to know" basis and would have to get prior parental consent. The teachers understood the requirement and respected the new procedures.

Healthy, productive systems employ feedback loops that serve to not only identify points of challenge but also give shape to new structures and patterns of behavior to adjust accordingly. Sometimes these data are collected in a formal process such as data assessment and strategic planning, but at other times they can merely emerge from the experience of those within the classroom. Thus, the counselor experiencing an increase in student anxiety sees this as data suggesting something out of balance or disruptive within the system. Sharing this information can result in a school-wide adjustment to some structure, policy, or procedure.

It is vital for the counselor-as-consultant to provide data on the nature of the problem and its likely causes. Providing information in a timely manner can make a significant difference in the lives of many, such as in the case of a teacher receiving a new student with special needs in her classroom. Often this first step is sufficient in and of itself to be remedial.

Take the example of Mrs. Jackson trying to conduct a learning activity when her newly admitted student, Braydon, kept yelling out and melting down every time the schedule bell rang. Mrs. Jackson knew Braydon would be receiving special education services; however, she had no idea what his interruptive behavior was about, and she and the rest of her class were very upset. Expressing her concern and dismay to the special education teacher and the school counselor, Mrs. Jackson learned of Braydon's auditory sensory issues. Braydon was extremely sensitive to loud noises such as the scheduling bell and thunder, and sudden or unexpected noises such as a fire drill bell. Had the information regarding Braydon's sensory needs been relayed prior to his arrival, preventive measures and strategies could have been put into place before he started attending Mrs. Jackson's class.

A Second Level of Intervention: Fine Tuning

While openness of communication and information exchange between all of the constituents involved in a situation is often the salve that remedies the problem at hand, other circumstances require some adjustment of procedures, policies, or approaches employed. This second level of intervention involves making changes to the existing structures and processes within the system.

Many schools have the policies, procedures, services, and curriculum in place that could and should support effective functioning and goal attainment. However, it is possible that these structures and processes may, for some reason, not be operating optimally. Under these conditions, the counselor-as-consultant collaboratively engages with those responsible for these processes and structures to bring all system processes up to running order. In the case with Braydon and his challenge in handling loud, sudden noises, the school counselor advocated for a change in the bell system. In addition, he had the forethought to make sure Mrs. Jackson knew about fire drills ahead of time so that she could alert Braydon to use his headphones to buffer the noise.

For an example with an impact of greater breadth, consider the following case (Case Illustration, 12.2.).

Case Illustration 12.2
Heightened Anxiety

Mr. Leno, an elementary school counselor, was very concerned about the significant increase in the number of students coming to his office with elevated levels of anxiety, evidence of stress, and even panic. While the students would most often identify an upcoming school-wide, state-wide, standardized test that they would be taking as the source of their upset, closer inspection revealed that it was the procedures being employed to "inform" the students and their parents about the test that was stimulating such anxiety.

In preparation for this newly implemented testing program, the school's principal held a series of school assemblies with the students gathering in the auditorium where, with the use of a power point presentation, the principal "drove home" the "importance" and "seriousness" of the test. The principal also told the students that the school could be negatively affected should they perform poorly. This same message was sent home in a letter to the parents. The intensity of the message sent, along with the "formal" method of delivery (from the stage), seemed to have been a major contributor to the students' high anxiety.

Mr. Leno spoke with the principal. He shared his understanding of the importance of the test but noted that the current levels of anxiety experienced by the students would impede their optimal performance. Recognizing the problem, the principal and Mr. Leno developed an alternative plan for disseminating information about the test.

First, it was decided that the teachers, within their homerooms, would encourage the students to do their best while at the same time downplaying the "potential dire consequences" of performing poorly. The teachers were also encouraged to answer the students' questions to correct any misinformation honestly. The second change in approach was for the principal to draft a letter to parents that once again explained the nature of the test, but with a shifted focus to valuing the test as a "good snapshot of all that we do." In the letter, the principal noted that many rumors were active and that misinformation had elevated the anxiety of the children. She explained that the teachers were addressing student concerns in homeroom and she invited the parents to a Q&A session.

While the culture of the school described in Case Illustration 12.2 was one that supported school-wide assemblies as a mode of distributing information, a simple adjustment to that culture, a fine tuning of the method of information dissemination, resulted in a reduction of overall student (and parent) anxiety.

When fine tuning a system, there are many possible targets for such fine tuning, and Exercise 12.1 invites you to consider such a form of system intervention.

Directions: For each of following brief scenarios, (1) identify the way in which the mode or method of communication is contributing to the manifested problem and (2) discuss how the communication processes can be "fine-tuned" to alleviate the problem. This exercise is best completed with another person or in a small group.

Scenario 1: Morning Announcements

At Marion elementary school, the announcements of activities and schedules for the day are presented immediately after the bell rings, signifying the beginning of school. A student reads the announcements over the public address system. Students have complained about missing meetings and sporting events because they "never heard the announcement" and teachers have noted the disruptive influence of some "readers."

Scenario 2: The Weekly Meeting

A small mental health clinic has weekly meetings with all clinical staff and supervisors. The original purpose of the meetings had been to staff cases, receive supervision, and discuss therapeutic procedures. However, because of organizational changes and the addition of many new clinical staff meetings, most of the weekly meetings go to providing information about administrative details around issues such as telephone usage, procedures for completing insurance forms, and reviewing staff schedules. The staff has complained about the lack of supervision and case staffing opportunities.

Exercise 12.1 Fine Tuning Communication Processes

The Third Level of Intervention: Opening a System to Change

In some situations, the issues encountered can be remedied by the provision of accurate information that allows for system adjustment, or perhaps a minor modification to an existing policy, procedure, or service. There are, however, some situations where student difficulties reflect the school's failure to address their unique needs and the changing times. Schools that over the course of time have failed to remain open, adaptable, and flexible, even in the face of the changing needs of their consumer, their students, need interventions that will result in the return to being more "open" and responsive.

Achieving school reform is a challenging endeavor, one made even more difficult by the natural resistance most often encountered in closed systems as they attempt to maintain the status quo (Fullan, 2007; McLaughlin, 2006). A classic model depicting the process of opening a system is that offered by Kurt Lewin (1958). Lewin (1958) suggested that change occurs in three phases: unfreezing the system, moving the system (change), and refreezing the system.

Unfreezing the System

The members of a school perceive a school's fundamental character and culture as a valid condition of the school, created and maintained by those currently operating within the school. As such, the first task that a counselor-as-consultant needs to address when attempting to change the culture of a system is to reduce system resistance by getting the system to accept both the diagnosis and the need for such a level of system intervention.

The counselor-as-consultant can reduce resistance and begin to "unfreeze" the system by assisting the members of the organization to see that while the way things "were done" was useful, the reality is that the environment (internal and/or external) has changed dramatically and these "ways" are no longer as helpful to providers or consumers. To achieve this heightened awareness requires that the counselor-as-consultant provide appropriate data. The goal is to sensitize the system to the need for change, the need to modify its current structure and processes to more successfully achieve its goals and fulfill its mission.

Quite often, the role of the counselor-as-consultant during this unfreezing stage of system change is to be somewhat countercultural. The process of asking questions and collecting data around issues that others within the system had taken for granted is the beginning of this counterculture response. It is as if the counselor-as-consultant is willing to both ask questions about the "emperor's new clothes," something people see and don't want to discuss, and report the data that suggest the clothes are nonexistent. While such data reporting will not automatically change the character or culture of the school, it is the beginning of the introduction of new observations, ideas, suggestions, or values not reflective of the operative culture. Being countercultural can be somewhat of a "risk" to the counselor who fails to approach the task with awareness and employment of those factors that facilitate the innovation of change (see Chapter 7), especially those increasing their sociopolitical power.

To stimulate the unfreezing, the data shared must be embraced by those who are formally and informally empowered to move the system. As such, the counselor-as-consultant needs to engage in collaborative dialogue with these opinion leaders. This process of encouraging shared ownership can be facilitated by the counselor who can connect the need for change with the "felt" need of those in power (Beer, Eisenstat, & Spector, 1990).

Moving the System

Once a general sense of dissatisfaction with the status quo has been established, the counselor-as-consultant can engage in moving the system to a new, more responsive position. The type of change will be situation-specific, reflecting the identified needs and available resources. These may involve the introduction of new expectations, job definitions, or skill applications at the level of the staff and faculty. It could mean the development of a new structure or set of operating procedures and policies. It also may take the form of the introduction of new programs, curriculum, and services.

Consider the middle school that had a sharp increase in referrals for arguments and conflicts between students in sixth and seventh grades. The school year had started with some very vocal seventh graders teasing the new sixth grade "babies" during lunch and in the hallways. The sixth graders, wanting to prove they were not "babies," started responding with sarcasm and a little shove now and then. It escalated to the point where there was yelling at lunch and pushing in the hallway.

The principal met with the school counselors to come up with a plan to decrease the behavior referrals. The school counselors added that it would be beneficial to not only address the inappropriate behavior but to institute preventive strategies that instructed the students on appropriate, prosocial behavior as well. The principal, who was under attack by parents and his faculty and staff about the apparent increase in unruly behavior, was very supportive of this suggestion.

The counselors-as-consultants designed a program that targeted (a) increasing an awareness and respect for diversity and (b) developing conflict resolution skills. The design for the program included faculty as group facilitators, with groups composed of both sixth- and seventh-grade students. The counselors-as-consultants suggested a change in the class schedule to accommodate a common meeting time for these groups. The suggestion was to develop an "opening period," which would be used for this group time and would also set a positive tone for the remainder of the day. The principal agreed it was worth the change in the school schedule to "get the students on the right track." See Case Illustration 12.3 for an example of how this issue and the resulting interventions fit into the MTSS framework.

Case Illustration 12.3
Implementing Interventions in a Multitiered Support System

The Phoenix Middle School drew from three elementary schools in a rural school district in the southeastern part of the United States. Due to increasing numbers of students in the middle school, eighth grade was moved to the high school. The middle school started a new school year with over 600 students in its sixth and seventh grades.

Not long after the start of school, discipline referrals starting pouring in to the principal's office, citing a large number of arguments and conflicts between the students in sixth and seventh grades. The principal surmised that the seventh-grade students, being the "oldest" in the school, felt very powerful and entitled to tease the sixth grade "babies" during lunch and in the hallways. The sixth graders, wanting to prove they were not "babies," started responding with sarcasm and a little shove now and then. It escalated to the point where there was yelling at lunch and pushing in the hallway.

The school utilized a MTSS framework for interventions, and the principal called his support team together, consisting of the three school counselors, the school psychologist, and the nurse. Realizing that students may be feeling unsafe and could possibly be getting hurt, the team developed a plan to address the concerns immediately.

For Tier 1, the team implemented a program for all students that targeted (a) increasing an awareness and respect for diversity and (b) developing conflict resolution skills. This was to commence as soon as faculty facilitators were given lesson material. This school-wide behavior support plan would use a research-based program focused on resiliency and tolerance, and would take place during an "opening period" time at the beginning of the day.

From the referrals, the team was able to discern those students who had been more involved with the inappropriate behavior, and thus, for Tier 2, the team set up small group counseling times involving these students. This would allow for more direct instruction on the conflict resolution skills and diversity awareness. The team also took note to check with teachers, staff, and parents regarding students who may be at greater risk of being teased, such as students with disabilities, students who are English learners, and new students, to see if they should be included in small group counseling as well.

Lastly, the counseling team took the names of the students who were the most involved with the poor behavior and on the verge of being suspended. For these students in Tier 3, they scheduled times for individual counseling, team meetings, and a daily check-in, check-out system, such as the one offered by Positive Behavioral Interventions & Support (PBIS, n.d.).

The principal and team knew it was vital to monitor and evaluate how the interventions and prevention strategies were working so they could either maintain the program or change the support plan.

Refreezing

The final step in the process is what Lewin (1958) termed refreezing. This refreezing involves institutionalizing and thus stabilizing these changes. Refreezing begins with public acceptance of the new structure and processes and continues through the inclusion of these changes into the formal documents of the system (e.g., including new organizational chart, job descriptions, procedures).

In the case of our example, the schedule change to accommodate an "open period" to get the middle school students "on the right track" should at a minimum be announced to all the parents as a way of institutionalizing the change. In addition, the experience of this one middle school might be used as the springboard to invite a change in district policy to incorporate such an approach district wide. The district could adopt a common meeting time at the beginning of the day to create and maintain a sense of community among all students, from kindergarten to senior year in high school.

Putting It All Together: A Case Illustration and Exercise

A system-focused approach to consultation is often initiated as a result of a counselor's observation of an unusual pattern of student concerns. Multiple presentations of similar issues may indicate a system element creating or maintaining these concerns and thus invites a system-wide intervention. A particular value of such a school-wide systems approach is that not only can it provide effective intervention for those students exhibiting difficulties but by affecting change within the system, it will also offer system-wide prevention service.

This was the experience of one high school counselor who found herself confronted by a significant increase in student conflict, conflict in the form of verbal and physical dispute. Exercise 12.2 invites you to review the nature of the initial referral and the data collection that revealed the systemic factors that were operating. The questions presented within the exercise will help you formulate your ideas about points of intervention and potential means of prevention.

A Case Illustration and Exercise

A High School in Need of Change

Directions: While many of the concepts and variables discussed within this chapter are present within the brief description of the case of the high school in need of change, your task is to focus upon the following questions and concerns:

1. Are there signs of this school moving from an open system to a closed one?
2. How did the external environment contribute to the current problem?
3. Where did unfreezing start? What stimulated the unfreezing?
4. Where is refreezing being evidenced?
5. What else do you feel could be done to move this system in the direction of increased adaptability and openness?

Case Description

The consultant was invited by the principal at a large, metropolitan high school to come in and work with one grade level of teachers that, according to the principal, was experiencing "extensive bickering and verbal accusations." Through discussion with the principal, the original focus of the problem was expanded to include all of the teachers in the school.

The principal stated, "I know that the problem is most notable in the ninth grade, but there is, and has been for some time now, increasing tension and antagonism among all the teachers across grades. In fact, I think there is a real significant, overall drop in teacher morale and motivation. I am also very frustrated by the reduction in the quality of their teaching."

By interviewing the teachers, the consultant became aware of the significant changes made to staff composition and responsibility. Because of their declining enrollment and school budget, the system had reduced its instructional staff by 20% and its support and clerical staff by 30%. This reduction forced a realignment of task assignments, with instructional staff required to not only cover more hours but also perform some duties that had previously been assigned to other teachers or the support personnel. In some cases, teachers and even counselors were assigned to cover classes outside of the boundary of their discipline. The increased workloads, the redefinition and blurring of instructional and staff lines, and the anticipation that things "might get worse" resulted in the identified "symptoms" of tension, hostility, and low morale. After gathering additional data regarding the internal environment of the system, including information on its mission, philosophy, and previous modes of operation, the consultant collected data regarding the external environment, providers, consumers, and their needs. What emerged from these data was that the current "symptoms" of those in the system, while directly attributable to the changes within the system, were a response to the system's inability to adapt to a changing external environment.

The history and current mission of this high school could be best described as providing a rigorous academic curriculum that prepares students for postsecondary educational success. Historically, well over 70% of this school's graduates went to college, receiving significant financial support from their affluent, upper-middle-class parents. The strong academic orientation that emphasized educational success leading to a professional career reflected the cultural norm and values of this school.

In reviewing the population demographics, it became evident that the community had changed significantly over the past decade. As manufacturing companies and businesses moved to suburban and rural locations or other countries, employment followed suit, leaving only unemployment and low wage jobs. Families and neighborhoods disintegrated into poverty, with desperation and pessimism replacing pride and the expectation for upward mobility. The previous culture that was imbued with strong family values, diligent work ethic, high regard for education, and opportunity for all was now ravaged by poverty, drugs, violence, and decay. Racial and ethnic minorities constituted the diverse demographic that attended this high school. While some students, such as those recently emigrated from Korea, still viewed academic success as the engine for upward mobility, far too many students placed education at the bottom of their priorities. With this high school clutching its historical mission, it daily confronted a culture that characterized the antithesis of that mission.

The most glaring challenge for the teachers was the delivery of academic processes (curriculum, support services) that were suitable for student achievement and motivation. With high rates of truancy and poor homework completion, many students were unable to meet even modest academic achievement. Moreover, with the mandate for full inclusion, students with special needs were sitting in classrooms lost, bewildered, and defeated. Teachers reported that custodial care was the best they could offer these students. As teacher turnover rates increased and more teachers exercised their sick and personal days, the principal was forced to reassign teachers and increase class sizes.

In reviewing their systems analysis data, it became apparent to the consultant and school principal that the difficulty currently experienced was not merely the result of some disgruntled and adversarial teachers. The principal encapsulated the problem best when he said, "Our problem is that we are too damn rigid and nonadaptable. Our kids are vastly different than they were, and yet we expect to teach and motivate them in the old ways that worked in the past." This rigid, inflexible school, with many of the symptoms of a system in entropy, was not responsive to its changing environment. If not addressed soon, it would cause the demise of the school. The most efficient approach (while at the same time perhaps the most difficult) was for the consultant to assist the system to open its boundaries and adjust its internal environment (i.e., structure and processes) to meet the needs of this changing consumer population.

The intent of the data feedback was not to force the system to change its original mission but rather to invite those within the system to consider the relationship between their current mission, the history of previous practice, and the needs of the consumers and providers. Using the data collected, the consultant and principal formed a task force of educators and interested parents with the following charge:

1. Identify the specific ways the mission of the organization is manifested in its structures and day to day processes.
2. Review the demographics and needs of its existing consumer population.
3. Identify those areas within the system's culture, as reflected in the structures and processes operating, that appear no longer useful or efficient given the changing external environment.
4. Identify those aspects of the organization's mission, philosophy, structures, and processes that remain useful even in light of the changing external environment.

This process of data feedback and analyses provided the school improvement task force with a clear understanding that maintaining the current approach would lead to further increases in academic failure and teacher dissatisfaction and, as such, lead to dismantling or take over by the government or private sector. This awareness helped the members accept the need for fundamental change and increased their willingness to undergo the draining process that such change would entail.

As a result of the data collected, the ad hoc task force was expanded into a strategic task force with the inclusion of representatives from the key consumer and provider groups. The charge for this task force was to begin to identify strategies for improving the school's efficiency and effectiveness. The consultant introduced an outline for determining how to move forward with the process, including:

1. the goals of the system,
2. the forces (internal and external) that would facilitate achievement of those goals,
3. the forces (internal and external) that would inhibit achievement of those goals, and
4. specific strategies for maximizing the facilitating forces and reducing the inhibiting forces.

With the realization that the current curriculum, teaching methodology, and student and teacher support services needed to be reevaluated and reconfigured, the task force took on its charge. Committing to the change based on empirical data on their "new" consumer population, and their needs, values, and culture, resulted in some significant structural and process changes. Class sizes were reduced and wrap-around services were contracted for students with special needs, needs both within and outside the classroom. Attendance policies were communicated and strictly enforced. Referent community leaders were enlisted to serve on specific task forces that addressed parental involvement in education, student motivation, and discipline, and the establishment of a realistic career counseling program. Teachers were teamed to work on specific subjects with specific students, with the authority and resources to tailor their curriculum and teaching methodology to the needs and abilities of those students. And finally, academic assessment and promotion were based on criterion-referenced testing instead of the norm-referenced assessment used previously.

The consultant in this case believed that he should not only assist the consultee by addressing the presenting problem (i.e., tension and low morale) but should do so in a way that would leave the consultee better able to cope in the future. With this preventive focus in mind, the consultant assisted the system to institute and formalize the school improvement task force. Moving the system from a long-range planning model to a more responsive, strategic planning focus would keep the system more open to the changing character of the internal and external environment and provide a structure and process that would facilitate ongoing adaptation to these changes.

Summary

- There are times and circumstances when the policies, procedures, services, and even the culture of the school can serve as the source of student disruption and underachievement, and thus require systems consultation.
- There are four basic elements of any system that need to be working in coordination for the system to be effective. These include (1) the identified population being served, (2) the specific needs of that population are selected to be met, (3) the desired outcome or goals of the system's services, and (4) the processes to be employed in achieving the goals.
- At their inception, all social systems are "open," actively engaging with consumers to identify needs and develop structures and processes that will address these consumer needs.

- Over time, some systems, some schools, move away from what was once flexible and responsive to the consumer they serve, becoming more closed, more rigid, codified in their processes, and less responsive to changing client needs.
- Intervention at the systems level can include (a) development of feedback loops and information sharing, (b) fine tuning and adjusting of existing structures and processes, and (c) reformulating the school's structures and processes.
- Opening a system to change requires the processes of (a) unfreezing the existing system, (b) moving and instituting desired changes, and (c) refreezing, thus institutionalizing the changes made.

Additional Resources
Print

Bogler, R. (2002). Changing schools in changing times: Implications for educational leadership. *International Journal of Educational Reform, 11*(3), 216–227.

Holman, P., Devane, T., & Cady, S. (Eds). (2007). *The change handbook: The definitive resource on today's best methods for engaging whole systems* (2nd edition), San Francisco, CA: Berrett-Koehler.

Johnson, S. (2002). *Who moved my cheese?* New York, NY: G. P. Putnam's Sons.

Johnson, S. (2002). *Who moved my cheese? For teens.* New York, NY: G. P. Putnam's Sons.

Johnson, S. (2003). *Who moved my cheese? For kids.* New York, NY: G. P. Putnam's Sons.

Leithwood, K. (Ed.). (2000) *Understanding schools as intelligent systems.* Stamford, CT: JAI Press.

Web-Based

Building School Capacity: Providing districts with systemic support for the process of change. www.ed.gov/pubs/turning/capacity.html

Center for School Change: Offers resources for educators, parents, business people concerned about student achievement and quality education. http://centerforschoolchange.org/

Organizational Development: Publishers clearinghouse for organizational development tools, all based on Systems Thinking resources. www.systemsthinkingpress.com

Positive Behavioral Interventions & Support (PBIS): Technical Assistance Center on PBIS supports schools, districts, and states to build systems capacity for implementing a multi-tiered approach to social, emotional and behavior support. www.pbis.org

School Change Collaborative: National association in support of school change. www.nwrel.org/scpd/natspec/coldev.html

References

Ahn, H. J., & Rodkin, R. C. (2014). Classroom-level predictors of the social status of aggression: Friendship centralization, friendship density, teacher-student attunement, and gender. *Journal of Educational Psychology, 106*(4), 1144–1155.

American School Counselor Association. (2012). *The ASCA National Model: A framework for school counseling programs* (3rd ed.). Alexandria, VA: Author.

Beer, M., Eisenstat, R. E., & Spector, B. (1990). *The critical path to corporate renewal.* Boston, MA: Harvard Business School Press.

Emery, M., & de Guerre, D. W. (2007). Evolutions of open systems theory: The two-stage model and unique designs for active adaptation. In P. Holman, T. Devane, & S. Cady (Eds), *The change handbook* (2nd edition). San Francisco, CA: Berrett-Koehler.

Fullan, M. (2007). *The new meaning of educational change* (4th ed.). New York, NY: Teachers College Press.

Jones, N. M., Thompson, R. R., Dunkel-Schetter, C., & Cohen-Silver, R. (2017). Distress and rumor exposure on social media during a campus lockdown. *Proceedings of the National Academy of Science of the United States of America, 114*(44), 1163–1166.

Kurpius, D. J. (1985). Consultation interventions: Successes, failures, and proposals. *Journal of Counseling Psychology, 13*(3), 368–389.

Lewin, K. (1958). Group decisions and social change. In E. E. Maccoby, T. M. Newcomb, & E. L. Hartley (Eds.), *Readings in Social Psychology.* New York, NY: Holt, Rinehart & Winston.

McLaughlin, M. W. (2006). Implementation research in education: Lessons learned lingering questions and new opportunities. In M. I. Honig (Ed.), *New directions in education policy implementation* (pp. 209–228). Albany, NY: State University of New York Press.

Positive Behavioral Interventions & Support (PBIS). (n.d.). Check In Check Out (CICO). Retrieved from http://www.pbisworld.com/tier-2/check-in-check-out-cico/

Schein, E. H. (2003). Five traps for consulting psychologists: Or, how I learned to take culture seriously. *Consulting Psychology Journal, 55*(2), 75–83.

Sundell, K., Castellano, M., & Overman, L. T. (2012). The role of school culture in improving student achievement in POS. *Techniques: Connecting Education and Careers, 87*(1), 28–31.

U.S. Department of Health and Human Services. (1996). *Health Insurance Portability and Accountability Act* (HIPAA). Retrieved from https://www.hhs.gov/hipaa/index.html

Section IV

Applying What We Know

CHAPTER 13

Consultation Illustrated: Reflections of One School Counselor

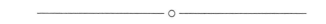

As the story is most often told, a young child interested in gaining directions asks a man: "How do I get to Carnegie Hall?" The man responded: "Practice, practice, practice!"

Perhaps the same prescription applies to each of us wondering how to ever feel comfortable and competent with consultation as a paradigm for school-based services. We need to practice, practice, practice! As a new paradigm or frame of reference for understanding presenting concerns and formulating approaches to working with those concerns, the model presented within this text may at first feel artificial and somewhat alien. With continued use, it will become a more natural, comfortable part of your professional identity.

In this chapter, we will revisit the case presented at the beginning of each chapter—the case of Jasmine and our school counselor-consultant, Ms. Thomas. Along with the client information, the case provides some insight into Ms. Thomas's thinking and decision-making. Interspersed throughout are questions and reflections that Ms. Thomas considered as she processed the information gathered. You will be able to observe how she draws conclusions about the data, which in turn guides her decisions and actions. It is this process of questioning, hypothesizing, and testing that should guide your practice of consultation.

Extended Case Illustration: Multilevels of Intervention and Prevention (With Counselor Reflections)

A Review of the Consultation Process

Before we begin applying what we have learned, it may be helpful to briefly review the stages of the consultation process. As you most likely remember, consultation, as with other forms of helping, is a process. It is a process in which the nature of the interaction and the specific focus of the task change over the course of the consultation. In Chapter 6, we detailed the stages of this process. Starting with the pre-entry stages in which specific processes and procedures are put into place to expedite efficient referral, the tone for a successful collaborative relationship is set. The second stage of entry is one in which permission to employ consultation as a mode of service delivery and a specific "contract" of the consultee has been established. The third stage in this developing process of consultation

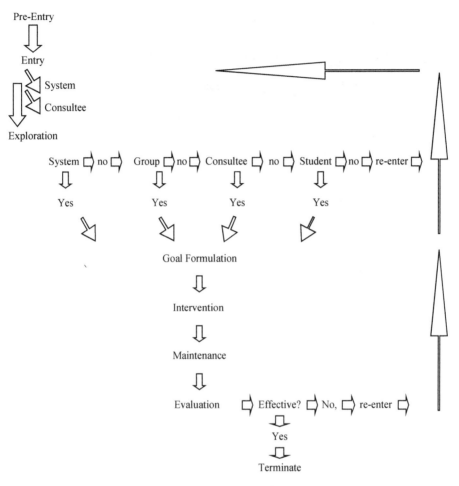

FIGURE 13.1   Stages of Consultation

is exploration, in which consultant and consultee come to a consensual agreement about the nature of the problem. Once the area of concern has been articulated and agreed upon, the consultation moves to goal formulation and intervention planning. From this point, the consultation proceeds through a maintenance stage, then to evaluation and termination.

While the stages were presented as discrete components occurring in linear sequence, consultation, in practice, is a dynamic process. The consultant may at times experience the stages as occurring in neat, linear order, while at other times she may experience the consultation process as cycling in and out of various stages almost simultaneously. Figure 13.1 depicts an integrated view of the stages of consultation. The graphic highlights the stages of consultation and will serve as a reference point for the cases that follow. Further, Table 13.1 provides a listing of the types of tasks to be accomplished at each stage.

The uniqueness of the model is that it provides for a system of consultation services that focuses on prevention and intervention and that emphasizes the extra-personal factors involved in the client-related problem. Thus, while continuing to target the student as the client, the focus for any one consultation could be the student

TABLE 13.1 **The Specific Considerations and Tasks for Each Stage of Consultation**

STAGE	GENERAL FOCUS	TASKS
Pre-entry	Creating systemic norms that encourage, facilitate, and reinforce consultee referral for consultation.	1. Identify what is envisioned, desired, and sanctioned by the highest-level administrator to whom you will be responsible (when negotiating the formal contract). 2. Identify culture, frame of reference, and points of resistance. 3. Create optimal conditions for consultee referral.
Entry	Establishing the consultative relationship concerning roles, functions, and expectations.	1. Explain the collaborative, expanded, integrated model of consultation to surface mixed feelings and concerns, and to educate as to the rationale and value of such an approach. 2. Remedial and Preventive Focus: Present a contract that addresses immediate felt needs while at the same time providing freedom to operate in a more preventive manner. 3. Role Definition: Describe the specific roles to be played (i.e., consultant and consultee) and the nature of the relationship (i.e., collaborative)
Exploration	Identifying and defining the consultee's presenting problem. The operational definition of the consultee's concern should consider the ABCs of the client, the requirements of the client's task, and the specific environmental factors influencing the problem. The consultant needs to look beyond the consultee's original conceptualization of the problem and solution to test whether other, more indirect and thus more preventive, approaches could be employed.	When attempting to identify the possible level of focus, the consultant needs to consider a number of factors such as: (1) the level of immediate crises (system, consultee, or client); (2) the nature of the system's culture, structure, processes, and history; and (3) the consultee's expectations and openness to the collaborative exchange.
Goal Setting	Operationalize the desired goal(s) to be achieved. The model employed assumes that the client's behavior is a function of the interaction between the unique characteristics of the client's ABCs, the task requested, and the environment in which the client is to function. Thus, all attempts to define the desired goals should include components of each of these factors (i.e., the client, the task, the environment).	1. Expanding the focus to include client, task, and environmental elements. 2. Treat goal setting as a primary opportunity for collaboration.

STAGE	GENERAL FOCUS	TASKS
Intervention Planning	Identification of strategies that will achieve consultation goals and objectives. While presented here as a separate stage in the consultation process, it must be noted that interventions and intervention planning have been an essential thread in the fabric of entry, problem identification, and goal setting.	1. Provide a multiplicity of strategies 2. Maximize payoffs, minimize costs 3. Mutual agreement 4. Evaluation plan 5. Task assignment
Maintenance	Monitor the efficacy of change strategies and modification of strategies (and outcome objectives) as needed. In light of the preventive goal and the collaborative nature of the relationship, the consultant needs to resist the temptation to jump in and take on more responsibility for intervention implementation. Sharing equally in the process of implementation, as well as its success or failure, is still a goal for this collaborative process.	1. Work with resistance, recognizing that resistance occurs even at this stage. 2. Maintain collaboration throughout implementation. 3. Provide support, and be aware of the possible need to recycle through the process of redefining the problem or goal setting, and generate alternative strategies so that these do not become a blockage encountered in the intervention plan.
Evaluation	This evaluation should target both the degree to which the desired goals were achieved as well as the degree to which the collaborative process was maintained.	1. Establish multiple criteria to assess the success of the outcome and process of the consultation. 2. Employ some measures that will allow the consultant and consultee to recognize the positive impact of the relationship, even if the terminal goals or outcomes were not achieved. 3. Target measures that will help the consultant and the consultee identify the value (to both the consultee's and the consultee's system) of the consultation model. 4. While focusing on the practical utility of the evaluation process, the consultant should consider employing simple, structured designs that would increase the validity of the conclusions drawn from the evaluation.
Termination	While termination of the consultation relationship can occur at any time throughout the process, closure as an anticipated stage occurs at the completion of the entire process of consultation.	Closure when successful: 1. Review original contract 2. Share view of experience 3. Invite consultee disclosure 4. Reinforce the consultee's valuable involvement 5. Help the consultee identify his current needs and the way the consultant might be of continued service 6. Establish availability Closure when unsuccessful: 1. Convey a sense of hopefulness 2. Resist the temptation to simply modify the intervention plan; step back and reconsider the situation, given this new information 3. Recycle (see Figure 13.1)

(client-focused consultation), the consultee (consultee-focused consultation), or the system (system-focused consultation).

Ms. Thomas Meets Jasmine

The Original Referral:

As the counselor for 650 kindergarten through fifth-grade students, our counselor-consultant, Ms. Thomas, received a referral from Dr. Jameson, the music teacher, and the head teacher of the school. The referral requested that the counselor see Jasmine, a fifth grader for whom Dr. Jameson had some serious concerns. The referral read as follows:

> *Please see Jasmine immediately! I am very concerned about her safety. You know I have been working with Jasmine quite a bit (because of her tendency to not participate and be "the mean girl"), and I thought we had a good relationship. I saw her in the hall this morning, and noticed she looked upset. She wouldn't look me in the eye. When I asked her if something was wrong, she looked down said "no" and then stated she wished she was able "to go home, right away!" I know I don't have a lot to go on, just a feeling, and therefore I don't want to do anything official yet, but I heard her say things about "sex" and I think, maybe, she is being abused or something pretty serious. You need to check this out!*

Consultant Reflections:

- I don't know Jasmine, other than seeing her in the hall. This is potentially very serious, so I need to respond quickly and see her.
- It appears that Dr. Jameson anticipates a provisional, direct service approach from the counseling office. That is a bit surprising since he and I previously talked about a collaborative, consultative approach to counseling. I thought he understood and agreed. (Pre-Entry issues.)
- Well, I will need to see Jasmine, but I don't want to reinforce this direct service provisional model expected by Dr. J. This is a good opportunity to reintroduce the collaborative, triadic nature of consultation.

Entry

Before meeting with Dr. Jameson, Ms. Thomas took time to reflect on what it was she was hoping to accomplish and what steps she could take to engage Dr. Jameson in a collaborative relationship, reframing his expectation of provisional service.

(Pre-entry) Consultant Reflections

- I need to reduce the cost of talking with me. Dr. Jameson is always on the move, so rather than formally invite him to the office or schedule to meet with him, I think I'll roam the halls to see if I can spontaneously connect with him.

- If he's expecting direct service, he may feel frustrated or disappointed with me seeing him first. I need to give him some immediate payoff (thank him for his concern and let him know about the meeting I scheduled with Jasmine today) and highlight his "expert power" and value to the process.
- I must remember Dr. Jameson's tendency to want to probe into students' personal issues, and watch for boundaries and confidentiality issues.
- I must remember that the entire school just went through extensive training on the laws and responsibilities governing child abuse reporting. Right now, there is a real, heightened sensitivity regarding professional duties, and anxiety regarding litigation issues. I wonder if that is what is happening here.
- I know Dr. Jameson at a professional level only. He seems to be a concerned educator. I have heard he seems to want to step into the role of a counselor when working with the students. I wonder if he will be challenged working with me?
- Without any other indications (e.g., physical changes, behavioral changes, other teachers' reports), I wonder if Dr. Jameson is overreacting or responding to something else (perhaps lack of information or loss of objectivity).

(Entry) Initial Session with Dr. Jameson

Dr. Jameson: You are going to see Jasmine right away, aren't you?

Ms. Thomas: I know this is very concerning to you, and I will see Jasmine as soon as possible. But I wanted to get your insight on the situation. As we talked about before, it is a lot more productive when I can collaborate with someone who has a lot of experience with the student. In fact, I really would like to see if we can come up with some things that we both can do to help Jasmine. Is that okay?

Dr. Jameson: Sure, I know the consultation thing.

Ms. Thomas: Great. It would help if you could tell me what you have seen with Jasmine. I know we all have been under a lot of stress these past few weeks, so maybe whatever is affecting Jasmine is impacting others. It would be nice to do something now before it gets worse.

Consultant's Reflections

- Dr. Jameson appears somewhat resistant to this approach. I need to keep the costs down and get some immediate payoff for him.
- I know he understands the consultation approach and even the benefits concerning prevention as well as providing intervention, but I'm not sure he's bought into it.
- I've heard he enjoys playing the counselor with the students, and in fact knows a lot about the community and their families. That's the expertise he brings to this consult. I need to point that out while highlighting my own experience working this way.

In the meeting with Dr. J., the consultant agreed to talk with Mrs. Marquette (Jasmine's resource teacher) and to review her records before meeting with her. Dr. Jameson agreed to collect some observations about Jasmine's interaction with others, such as her peers at lunch or other teachers in the hallway. The two decided to meet in three days to discuss these data.

Exploration (Looking at Client, Task, and Environment)

In attempting to explore the depth and breadth of the problem, the consultant begins to collect data on the client, the tasks that appear problematic, and the environment in which the client is functioning. This last component, the environment, includes exploration of the consultee's knowledge, skill, and objectivity as well as the culture, processes, and structures that characterize the school.

Consultant's Reflections

- I know my predecessor used a direct service approach, and that seems to be the expectations of everyone in the school. I need to respect that expectation and start by gathering information about Jasmine. But I need to continue to introduce the idea of expanding our view of the "problem" by including information on the task and environment. Plus, even though Dr. Jameson is used to just sending the students down to my office, I need to keep him involved.

The Client

The consultant, approximating a direct service model, gathered information through review of the cumulative record: the interviews with Dr. Jameson and Mrs. Marquette (the resource room teacher) and even the client, Jasmine. The data collected present the following picture of Jasmine:

Jasmine is a 12-year-old student in fifth grade. She has a full-scale IQ score of 85 (verbal IQ: 87; performance IQ: 76). The school espouses adherence to the values and practice of inclusion (that is, providing all students with the needed education in the least restrictive environment). As such, there are no special education classes within the school, although a resource room is available and some students are programmed into the room for individual assistance, as recommended by their subject teachers. Records show that Jasmine has struggled through school since first grade. Up to this point, her grades have been D's and C's. She has not failed any subjects to this point, and it is expected that she will continue to be promoted each year to the next grade. It has been challenging, however, for her to keep up with the work, and it appears that it is getting harder as she progresses through school.

After a review of her progress this year, she was assigned to work in the Resource Room for mathematics. Jasmine was distraught with that decision and hated being assigned to what she called "the dummy room." However, through discussions with Ms. Marquette and Dr. Jameson, she finally agreed, stating that while it may help her now, she "would get out of it—real quick!"

Jasmine lives with her mother (a waitress), her father (a high school teacher in a neighboring school district) and an older sister (age 15, grade 9). Jasmine and her sister started in this school district at the beginning of this school year, having moved from a neighboring state.

Follow-up Meeting With Dr. Jameson

Dr. J: Well, what did you find?

Ms. Thomas: Well, it is clear how much you care about Jasmine and have worked with her through this Resource Room placement.

Dr. J: That was a real bear. I was battling everyone, even Jasmine.

Ms. Thomas: You know, it is funny you should say that. Maybe some of the reaction you received from Jasmine is a reflection of her unhappiness about being in the Resource Room. I think you said she called it the "dummy room?"

Dr. J. No, it's more than that. That's a proper placement for her. Did you see Jasmine?

Ms. Thomas: She's coming down before lunch today.

Dr. J. Good. You need to talk to her.

Ms. Thomas: But before I do, I really would like to tap your expertise. What did you observe over the past few days?

Consultant Reflections

- Dr. J. seems very sensitive about the Resource Room placement, I wonder if something is blocking his objectivity here.
- It is clear that Dr. J wants me to see Jasmine, so I will, and I will get back to him in hopes that having seen her will be some payoff for him. He didn't want to do anything else until I saw her.

Meeting With Client

Being new to the school herself this year, the counselor/consultant has had only superficial contact (e.g., saying "hello" in the hall) with Jasmine. The initial contact with Jasmine was somewhat strained. She presented as slightly guarded and stated that "everything is fine... except for that dummy class!"

Jasmine stated that school is going okay, except for Resource Room, which she "really hates." She stated that she feels like she is wasting her time in that "dummy room" and is totally embarrassed when she has to go there. In the interview, Jasmine stated that she is "not very popular and has only a few good friends." While she noted that she "would like more friends," she was quick to say that "it isn't really bad, since most of the students in my class seem to be friendly with me."

Jasmine, while appearing guarded in her disclosure, maintained appropriate eye contact and generally demonstrated appropriate social behavior. When asked about home, she was quick to respond that "everything is fine." Jasmine went on to share that she and her parents had recently become members of the church choir, and that she is really excited about singing in the choir and beginning to think that she would like to go to college to become a music teacher. When questioned about her knowledge around sex, Jasmine shared her that sister had been talking to her about it because her sister is dating someone she thinks she's in love with. She shared with the counselor that her mom and dad were going to come in to talk with the principal about moving her out of the Resource Room, and she wanted to know if (the counselor) could help her with that.

Consultant Reflections

- Overall, while being a private person, Jasmine appeared nondefensive about her family, and she appeared healthy, well-cared for, and gave no evidence of abuse.
- Her church involvement appears to be developmentally appropriate and is unsupportive of risky behavior or family abuse.
- I am concerned about the issue of friends. I need to find out more about the extent of her social isolation both in school and perhaps at home to see if that is something with which I could be of assistance.
- I need to get a better feel for the Resource Room and the appropriateness of this placement. This may be the thing I can connect and contract with Jasmine.
- I wonder if the culture here is one that promotes the perception of the Resource Room as a "dummy room." If it does, it will eventually impact other kids negatively.
- I need to try to establish a relationship with Jasmine to help her develop realistic career goals.
- I wonder if Jasmine's reaction to Dr. Jameson had something to do with the Resource Room. Was she angry at him? Maybe she was embarrassed knowing he knows she's in the "dummy class?"
- I need to try to share my observations with Dr. Jameson and get his insights about the Resource Room and how it is perceived.

Feedback to Consultee (Continued Exploration)

Although Dr. Jameson made the referral and was willing to meet with the consultant, he continued to push for direct service. In sharing his observations, the consultant was aware of Dr. J's "disappointment" with the feedback. He assumed a negative physical stance toward the consultant, crossing his arms and appearing to be ready to walk away, not squaring his shoulders. When presented with the counselor's observations, he responded by saying, "Boy, I can tell you're new. She's got you snowed. I know her, and there is something serious going on here!" When informed that Jasmine's parents wanted to come in for a conference, Dr. Jameson appeared to become more agitated, stating, "You don't expect that they are going to come in, do you? They don't care." When asked to explain what he meant, Dr. Jameson simply stated, "I know their type."

The counselor found out that what appears to be an antagonistic or belligerent style by Dr. J. has been experienced by others (e.g., Mrs. Marquette) but seems to be more noticeably directed to the counselors. While he is fair with the kids, he is perceived by students and faculty as not very approachable or personable. Dr. Jameson has more than once expressed a sense of pride in the work he has done with Jasmine, noting "If it weren't for me, she probably wouldn't be doing so well right now." From Jasmine's perspective, Dr. Jameson always treated her fairly, and, while she has no interest in spending time with him, states that she does like him and he did help her. However, she feels that sometimes he gives her "too much attention."

Consultant Reflections

- Dr. Jameson appears to be defensive around the counselors and manifests that defensiveness by becoming abrasive and antagonistic.
- It seems that Dr. Jameson becomes defensive when directly confronted. I will need to continue to build referent and expert power, and use indirect forms of confrontation.
- Dr. Jameson appears to have success with Jasmine both in terms of assisting her with a classroom problem and in developing a personal relationship.
- I wonder if Dr. Jameson has lost some professional objectivity in relationship to Jasmine and is overly involved with being her caretaker? Or perhaps even concerned that if she doesn't need his help, she won't call on him or continue to relate to him?

Exploration (Continued; Exploring the System)

Resource Room (task and environment): Information about the Resource Room was gathered from consultation with Dr. J. and observation of Mrs. Marquette's classroom. The data collected suggest the following.

Jasmine has always had difficulties in mathematics. She barely got D's in her math classes, and although she might be expected to do better in the Resource Room setting, she is struggling just as much. Jasmine is teamed with three other students in the Resource Room. They are doing word problems. The tasks for doing these problems entail (1) converting the written word into mathematical symbols and equations, (2) going to the board with answers, and (3) group work.

Jasmine spends 90 minutes a day in the Resource Room with three other students. The teacher uses a token economy to keep the students on task. While Jasmine can function without this high level of external motivation, she is comfortable with it. The lighting in the room is dim, the room is fairly noisy, and Jasmine sits on the side of the class away from the window. She stated that she is accepted by the others in the class and is in fact somewhat looked up to as one of the smarter kids.

Jasmine's teacher, Mrs. Marquette, is the only Resource Room teacher in the school. Her students like her, but she is sometimes viewed as ineffective by parents and her peers. Most believe that while she is supportive and enthusiastic about the students, she lacks the skills to focus her students on task behavior. The implementation of the token economy came at the suggestion of the principal as a way to assist Mrs. Marquette in keeping the students on task. However, Mrs. Marquette feels that setting up and maintaining the economy has taken more energy than she suspected, and she hasn't been able to attend to teaching the students as much as and in the way that she should. Jasmine is not particularly close to Mrs. Marquette. In fact, she is not very trusting of most of the adults at school.

Mrs. Marquette did state that Jasmine is active in class and is the best student in the Resource Room. In fact, Mrs. Marquette was questioning the value of Jasmine's placement in the Resource Room. She felt that perhaps hooking Jasmine up with a tutor would be a more effective way to help her with mathematics. Mrs. Marquette also noted that she was considering returning Jasmine to her regular math class at the end of the marking period, although Dr. Jameson seems to be resistant to that idea. Mrs. Marquette noted that each time she approached Dr. Jameson with the idea, he would insist that Jasmine needs additional support.

Consultant Reflections

- Jasmine's concerns about the inappropriateness of her placement seem to be supported by Mrs. Marquette.
- Mrs. Marquette's suggestion about returning Jasmine to her regular classroom with the additional support of a tutor appears appropriate.
- To what is Dr. Jameson reacting? Does he know something I am still missing? Is it something going on within him, perhaps interfering with his level of objectivity?
- Does Jasmine know Dr. Jameson has been resisting her return to the regular class? If so, maybe that explains her reaction to him in the hall.
- Why is Mrs. Marquette unable to help Jasmine get placed back into the regular classes? What is her role? Power?

School Culture, Structure, and Organization (Exploration Continued)

The elementary school is in a supportive, white, middle-class, rural community. The school is average size with about five sections of classes for each grade. There is a fairly low teacher to student ratio (1:20). Most students know each other and each other's families. Most of the families whose children are in the school have lived in this community for generations. Further, most of the teachers and staff live in the community, with many having attended this school. The counselor and Dr. Jameson are the only two professional staff members who are not originally from this area.

The consultant is the first and only full-time counselor the school has had. Two teachers also work in the counseling department as 25% of their load. Before hiring the full-time counselor, the counseling was performed by the part-time "teacher-counselors" and Dr. Jameson in his role as head teacher.

While the economy of the community is primarily agricultural, the mission of the school district is to prepare students for postsecondary education. Most of the students go to college and then return to this environment to work and live.

Counselor Reflections

- As an outsider (to this community), I need to go slow and be sensitive to their culture and ways of doing things. Maybe being an outsider may elicit system and community resistance.
- Since I am the first full-time counselor, the faculty and administration are unclear about how the counselor should function. However, it seems they are used to collaborating.

So, a collaborative approach may be acceptable even though Dr. Jameson sent Jasmine for direct service.

- To be effective, I need to develop referent power with Dr. Jameson. Perhaps working on the issues of being "outsiders" and the difficulty of connecting with a closed, somewhat private, community may give us some point of common reference.
- With Dr. Jameson's limited connections within the community at large and within the school community, is it possible he is using his relationship with Jasmine as a way of establishing himself or meeting his own needs for a relationship?
- With the focus on post–high school education, is Jasmine feeling additional pressure, either from herself or her parents, to get out of the Resource Room? Is it possible that the Resource Room is a social stigma, as suggested by Jasmine? If so, that may be an area for future systems-focused consultation.
- I would like to enter at the consultee-focused level of consultation working with Dr. Jameson around possible loss of objectivity, while at the same time assisting him to find a balance between being the disciplinarian and the supportive administrator by demonstrating increased approachability to all students (and staff). I'm not sure if this will be possible.

Goal Setting

Consultant Reflections (Before Meeting With Consultee)

- Working directly with Jasmine on the issue of abuse or promiscuity appears to be unnecessary. But with Dr. J expressing a real concern, I will need to be sensitive in redefining the goal. I will try to reenter with Dr. Jameson around the new issue of Jasmine's Resource Room placement, and her feelings of self-worth and how she views herself as a learner, plus redefine the service to be collaborative working at the level of a client-focused consultation.
- This may be an excellent way to reinforce the collaborative nature of consultation and keep Dr. J. central to the process. Refocusing our efforts on working with Jasmine around the issue of the Resource Room should help since he has been so involved with that and therefore has expert power in that area.
- As we work, we can observe Jasmine's response in the Resource Room, and we can also be gathering more data to test for the possibility of any abuse.
- Further, by working with him around Jasmine's Resource Room concern, I may be able to provide some indirect confrontation (via modeling and parable presentations) to address Dr. Jameson's perceptions of Jasmine as needing to be rescued from a much more significant issue, that being one of safety.

Meeting With Dr. J.

Dr. J: Well, what's our plan?

Ms. Thomas: I've been thinking quite a bit about this. As I mentioned to you, Jasmine is really annoyed about this Resource Room thing.

Dr. J.: Hey, we've been through this. She needs it.

Ms. Thomas: Well, I agree we have been through this, and you certainly are much more the expert when it comes to the Resource Room then I am. But, I was wondering, do you think it would be of any value in building a better relationship with Jasmine and therefore being able to see if anything else is going on in her life if we could establish some measure or criteria for her to move out of the Resource Room?

Dr. J.: I don't understand.

Ms. Thomas: You know how you have experienced Jasmine as somewhat hesitant to speak with you?

Dr. J.: Yeah. That's what initially concerned me.

Ms. Thomas: Well, I thought if we showed that we were working on something that she valued, like setting a plan for her moving from the Resource Room, she would then see us as allies and would once again be more open. This would allow us to see if anything else, like your concerns about possible abuse, is an issue.

Dr. J.: I see. You know, maybe it would be best if I came up with the measure and shared it with Jasmine.

Ms. Thomas: Since Mrs. Marquette has been working with her in the Resource Room, I wonder if it would help to have her on board. Perhaps both of you could come up with criteria that Mrs. Marquette could observe and then share?

Dr. J.: Sure! She sees Jasmine every day. I'll meet with her to formulate some reasonable criteria for Jasmine to meet.

Ms. Thomas: That sounds like a good idea. I wonder, though, if I could join you and Mrs. Marquette when you present this to Jasmine. I'd love to see the smile on her face.

Dr. J.: Oh, yeah. Sure.

Consultant Reflections

- Well, with the goal to set a standard or set of criteria for moving Jasmine out of the Resource Room, I'm hoping she will begin to feel more hopeful. And maybe developing these criteria will help Dr. J to more objectively see for whom and when such resource assignment is needed. (Redefining the task.)
- If Dr. J's judgment is being distorted by a lack of objectivity, working on this standard should not only confront that but serve as a means for preventing it from

influencing his decision about retention in the Resource Room. (Consultee-focused consultation.)

- Involving Mrs. Marquette in the development and monitoring of the criteria for Jasmine will empower her and bring her into a better working relationship with Dr. J. It will certainly help to clarify the role of the Resource Room and its teacher. (System-focused consultation.)

Intervention Planning

Dr. J.:. I'm glad you included Mrs. Marquette in the process. If this is going to work, not just for Jasmine, but for all the students we need to think about the mission and purpose of the Resource Room. In fact, I had to go to Mrs. Marquette for some statement about the purpose of the Resource Room, I couldn't find my copy.

Ms. Thomas: Great idea. If we are going to have a positive effect on all the students using the Resource Room, we will need her on board.

Dr. J. (handing Ms. Thomas a paper): Well, here's what I did.

Ms. Thomas: Great job. Wow! I like how you even created a goal statement for each student in the Resource Room. That certainly gives us the base for creating a measurable outcome. Your goal setting skills are wonderful.

Dr. J.: I guess those skills are useful in many situations.

Ms. Thomas: How about if the three of us meet with Jasmine to tell her the plan?

Dr. J.: Sounds great. What do you think about the idea of asking Mrs. Marquette to use this format to develop objectives and outcome measure for the other students?

Ms. Thomas: That would certainly prevent this type of problem from occurring again! Great idea.

Consultant Reflections

- It appears that Dr. J. felt empowered and valued for his expertise.
- I like the fact that he is using inclusive language, with "us" and "our" plan.
- The fact that he is generalizing the process to include other students is fantastic. It really hits the preventive goal that I was targeting.
- I'll need to reinforce his efforts as well as encourage Mrs. Marquette to continue her collaboration with Dr. J.
- I can't wait until we meet with Jasmine. I know she will want to "get out" immediately, but if we can get her to look at the performance criteria we have set, she will be surprised to find that she can demonstrate these things already, and therefore she will be out soon.

Maintenance

Consultant Reflections

- I've been very impressed with the work that Dr. J. and Mrs. Marquette have been doing to establish specific learning contracts for the students in the Resource Room. I have not only made a special effort to tell them so but have asked that I sit in on some of their meetings to learn from them.
- I have noticed how Dr. J. has been visiting the Resource Room and encouraging the students by asking them if he could see their work. I told him how valuable it was for him to be verbally reinforcing the children for their work. I also told him how his presence and support had energized Mrs. Marquette.
- As I suspected, Jasmine was initially disappointed because she did not immediately get out of the Resource Room. But my follow-up with her seemed to help her see the concrete steps she needs to take and even project a timeline for moving out of the Resource Room. I've encouraged her to share with Dr. J. what she is doing and what she has accomplished, pointing out that this is a great way for her to let him know she's ready to move on.

Termination

Ms. Thomas: Well, we've certainly come a long way in a short three weeks.

Dr. J.: I appreciate what you've done.

Ms. Thomas: What we've done! I know the initial concern was Jasmine, but with you sharing your insights and working with Mrs. Marquette, not only were we able to help Jasmine achieve her goal, but we also reestablished that supportive relationship that you have had with her. But I guess the real surprise for me was that we've developed a new process for Resource Room placement. I think with the learning contracts that you and Mrs. Marquette developed, other students, including some gifted students, may start to be referred.

Dr. J.: If that happens, it would be great. It would be a way to change that image of it being a "dummy room"!

Ms. Thomas: You know, maybe that's something you and I could talk more about. I mean, I wonder what steps we could take to change the culture and perception of the Resource Room around here?

Consultant Reflections

- Well, Dr. J. appears satisfied with the outcome, as does Jasmine.
- I feel really good that we not only addressed the immediate concern with Jasmine but also were able to make some adjustments to the system that should reduce the possibility of similar problems in the future.

- I am really happy that Dr. J. seems enthused about discussing my ideas around changing the culture of the school and the perceptions around the nature and value of the Resource Room. He is truly an opinion leader, and, with his help, we may be able to make some significant system changes. I'll have to set up a meeting to see if we can explore this (Entry).

Case Postscript

The relationship was redefined from one of provisional consultation service to collaboration, and the focus of service was redefined to be one of indirect consultation intervention at the client-focused level. The consultant, in this case, was able to educate the consultee (Dr. Jameson) about the extended focus for the service being one of prevention and intervention and thus focusing on the role played by extrapersonal factors (including Dr. Jameson, the school environment, curriculum, etc.). This redefinition and recontracting required that the consultant to be extremely sensitive to the points of resistance, both within the system and those emanating from Dr. Jameson, and be attentive to developing a reduced cost, immediately gratifying relationship with a balance of referent and expert power. The result was not only a solution for the original presenting concern but also a system modification that should serve an ongoing preventive value.

CHAPTER 14

You as Counselor: A Guided Practice in Employing Consultation as an Integrated Model for School-Based Intervention

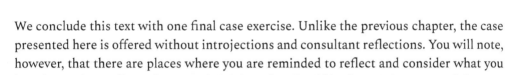

We conclude this text with one final case exercise. Unlike the previous chapter, the case presented here is offered without introjections and consultant reflections. You will note, however, that there are places where you are reminded to reflect and consider what you have learned as well as to begin anticipating what should be done. It is suggested that you utilize the information provided and filter it through your understanding of the consultation process to predict the consultant's next steps.

A Case With Prompts for Reader Reflection and Classroom Discussion

Benny

The current case referral was initiated by Ms. Carolyn Fox, one of three sixth-grade teachers at Westview Middle School. Ms. Fox, who is in her third year of teaching, was seeking some assistance with one of her students, Benny, whom she described as "a very energetic boy." The case proceeds from prereferral considerations through exploration, goal setting, intervention planning, and implementation. While the stages of the consultation process are once again presented as almost linear, it will become apparent that the process cycles back and forth across these stages.

As you read the case data, you are reminded to practice "thinking like a consultant." The reflections presented will help you pause and focus on the issues that may need to be addressed. It may be helpful to discuss your response at these points of reflection with a colleague or supervisor to benefit from their perspectives.

As you read through the case, consider each of the following guiding questions:

1. What are the expectations regarding the consultant role and job definition? Do the expectations, the job contract, place limits on the things the consultant is free to do?
2. What factors unique to this system must be considered as a means of reducing resistance in this system?

3. What unique consultee variables or factors must be considered to reduce consultee resistance to a collaborative consultation? What special relationship considerations should the consultant be aware of to develop and maintain a collaborative consultee relationship?
4. From an ecological perspective, how might understanding of the ecological systems (i.e., microsystem, mesosystem, exosystem, macrosystem, chronosystem) contribute to the counselor-consultant's understanding of the problem and development of strategies with both intervention and prevention value?
5. What type or level of consultation intervention should be employed (i.e., client focused, consultee focused, system focused)?
6. What is the specific focus for consultation intervention (i.e., goals)?
7. What intervention techniques or strategies appear appropriate and possible for this problem?
8. Are there any special needs of the client (ability or disability, English learner, e.g.) that need to be considered in approaching this case? If so, what and how would that information give shape to the intervention and prevention strategies?
9. What modification to intervention strategies would be needed to expand the impact to include tertiary, secondary, and primary prevention?
10. How will you know that the consultation was successful, both in outcomes and in process, and how could you demonstrate that success to the consultee or others?

Pre-entry

Mr. Dobbins, the school counselor, has done an excellent job over the course of her six years at Westwood Middle introducing the faculty to a consultation mode of service delivery. He has developed a healthy, collaborative working relationship with all the teachers and has established the expectation that teachers are referring themselves for assistance when initiating a referral to the counselor. This expectation of collaboration is reinforced by his request that teachers complete the following form when making a referral.

Working Together

To help us in our working together, please jot down a few notes regarding the following:
- Please provide a brief description of your concern.
- What are some of the student's strengths, successes?
- Please describe a time when the student performed or achieved at the desired level.
- Assuming that we are successful, what would be different as a result of our working together?

      Teacher: _____ Grade: _____ Date: _____

Entry

Ms. Carolyn Fox, the consultee in this case, has spent the past seven years teaching sixth grade at this relatively affluent, suburban school comprising 583 students enrolled in grades six through eight. Teaching between 23 and 26 students in each period of her social studies classes, Ms. Fox employs a student-centered approach to teaching, emphasizing student creativity, self-directed learning, and cooperative group activities. Her classes are usually boisterous, alive, and energetic with students actively engaged in projects. Ms. Fox is known among her peers for displaying strong encouragement, nurturance, and patience with her students. But as of late, she has been exasperated by the hostile and aggressive behavior displayed by Benny, and she sent the following request for assistance.

Working Together

To help us in our working together, please jot down a few notes regarding the following:

- Please provide a brief description of your concern:

> *Peter, I really could use your assistance. Benny, while only 11 years old, has already established a long history of bullying his peers. As you are aware, he has used aggression to meet his needs and maintain power over the other children starting with first grade. Hitting, pushing, threatening, and verbally abusing others have characterized his peer interactions. It is getting to the point where I am afraid of having him work in the learning teams, and it is really upsetting.*

- What are some of the student's strengths, successes?

> *Benny has a keen intelligence and exceptional talent for drawing. These qualities have helped him be successful academically.*

- Please describe a time when the student performed or achieved at the desired level:

> *We engaged in a "Classroom Buddy" activity with the students in the life skills class. Benny was spectacular working with these students, helping them draw and even helping his peers with the other students. He took on a very caring, leadership role.*

- Assuming that we are successful, what would be different as a result of our working together?

> *Hopefully, we can help him develop a more positive relationship with his classmates and use more verbal, assertive behavior when he is feeling frustrated.*

> Teacher: Carolyn Fox   Grade: 6A   Date: Nov. 15

> *Your reflections as counselor-consultant? (Developing a working relationship: How might Carolyn's history and her image among her peers interact with her involvement in this current referral?)*

When they met, Carolyn stated that Dr. Hanson assigned Benny to her section precisely because of her style of engaging the students positively. She continued, "The hope was that being in a class with that type of climate would encourage him to be less aggressive and more civil. But, to be honest with you, I've been less than successful. We are now into November, and he is well into his old, aggressive ways. This is affecting me. I can't believe I haven't helped him and that he is now starting to get under my skin. I am hoping you have the magic answers.

> *Your reflections as counselor-consultant? (Entry concerns: Issues of confidentiality; role clarification; building collaboration, etc.)*

Exploration

It is clear that Ms. Fox has given it her best and is currently frustrated and disappointed in her failure to resolve the issue.

> *Your reflections as counselor-consultant? (Helping skills: How would you engage your "helping" skills during this early interaction? What cautions do you need to take as you are developing a working relationship?)*

As Ms. Fox shares her story, Peter, our counselor-consultant, listens for any indication of previous success as well as any consultee resources that can be employed. Specifically, the consultant asks the consultee to elaborate on Benny's experience with the Classroom Buddy project with the students in the life skills class.

As the consultee discussed that project, she continued to express her dismay about being unable to generalize Benny's positive behavior in that situation to her classroom. With each self-downing comment, the counselor-consultant reframed the pronouncements of failure, disappointment, and frustration as patient, diligent, and even creative efforts to help a very challenging student to succeed. The consultant was quick to note how many of the strategies employed would have been things he would have considered.

> *Your reflections as counselor-consultant? (Collaboration: What steps were taken to develop a mutual and nonhierarchical relationship? Are other steps needed?).*

As they continued discussing Benny, they both began to realize just how much Benny liked Ms. Fox and looked forward to getting her nurturing attention. Unfortunately, as noted by the consultee, much of the attention he receives has been directed to correcting his misbehavior. The consultee, somewhat apologetically, reported that she had found herself using critical, negative comments when correcting Bennie, a response style that she has found upsetting, noting "I don't like the way I am becoming."

> *Your reflections as counselor-consultant? (Consultee focus: Given consultee's valuing of a positive approach, how do we understand the current pattern of engaging in negative comments and punishment? Is it a function of consultee knowledge, skill, or objectivity limitations?)*

In providing examples of Benny's behavior, the consultee would often put herself down by making comments such as "I really screwed up" or "Maybe it's time for me to get out." She would even give behavioral indications of her emotional upset (e.g., watering eyes and shaking voice). The consultant was very sensitive about affirming Carolyn's feelings while refocusing the conversation on her strengths and successes. The consultant identified and emphasized even the smallest evidence of her success with Benny as well as other students.

Your reflections as counselor-consultant? (Consultation, not counseling: Remembering that consultation is focused on work-related issues, how would you respond to her expressions of negative feelings about herself and her professional ability?)

Goal Setting

The consultee is frustrated with her inability to remedy the situation. The consultant allowed her to vent her frustration and provided her with supportive attention and active listening.

Your reflections as counselor-consultant? (Relationship: How might the consultant's attendance to the consultee's frustration serve to strengthen the relationship? Think exchange theory! Consider rewards and costs of the consultation and proposed strategies.)

As the discussion continued, the consultee was asked to describe her goals for the client, Benny. In response, she stated that she would like Benny to "get along with his peers and follow classroom norms of civility and cooperation."

While her goals of developing Benny's level of civility, cooperation, and compliance are appropriate, these need to be more concretely defined. It was important to describe these goals as behaviors (and their associated thoughts) that Benny will be doing. The consultant asked the consultee, "What will Benny be doing when he is civil and cooperative? What behaviors has he already exhibited in your class or at any other time that are civil and cooperative?"

Your reflections as counselor-consultant? (Goals to objective: How would this question facilitate the creation of intervention and assist in evaluation?)

As Ms. Fox and the consultant continued to identify even the smallest increments of behavioral change that would be desired (i.e., objectives), the counselor-consultant posed the following: "Carolyn, if Benny were completely civil and cooperative, what would that look like? How would he be behaving?" After gaining that description, the consultant asked the consultee to consider the following: "If this very best behavior was represented by 10 on a scale, and his very worst behavior a 1 on that scale, where you would score his current behavior (i.e., baseline)?" To this, the consultee responded "4."

As the discussion continued, they developed a scale describing how Benny may function at various points along this 10-point scale.

Worse 1 Bullies others	2	3	Current 4 Helps others in art	5	6	7	8	9	Best 10 Shares
Throws tantrums			Lines up for lunch						Complies with teacher requests
Ignores teacher requests			Plays the game UNO with Tim						Smiles when interacting with his classmates
Bangs on desk			Kindly asks and answers questions						Works in a group cooperatively with peers
Pushing his peers			Volunteers to help in class distributing worksheets						Uses "I feel" statements to express feelings

With more clarity about the desired changes in Benny's behavior, the consultant turned the discussion to things that Ms. Fox will need to do to support Benny's movement up the scale.

> *Your reflections as counselor-consultant? (Extrapersonal factors: What is the preventive value of this new focus?)*
>
> *Your reflections as counselor-consultant? (Resistance: What sources of resistance may occur in attempting to shift focus from Benny to Ms. Fox?)*

Intervention Strategies

As the consultant helped Ms. Fox consider her behavior in relationship to Benny's functioning, they began to identify the importance of reengaging her typical positive and nurturing approach. In discussing the value of her attention, it was decided that perhaps her attending to his negative behavior was, in fact, strengthening that behavior, and that it would be better for her to direct her nurturing attention to Benny's appropriate behavior rather than attending simply to his inappropriate behavior.

The consultee felt that if she focused on his natural strengths and ability to help others, she could begin to delegate more responsibilities and opportunities to Benny. This would help him develop more positive ways to interact with his peers and gain appropriate status. Further, she hoped that this would provide her with much more energy and time to devote to other students. This would help her to feel once again more competent and satisfied with her teaching.

> *Your reflections as counselor-consultant? (Beyond intervention: How might this shift reflect the consultant's focus on intervention and prevention?)*

To more concretely identify intervention steps, the consultant invited Ms. Fox to describe what she might do to help Benny move up the scale from 4 to 5. Ms. Fox proposed the following goals for Benny at level 5 and the things she would do to support his movement up the scale. She decided that she would have Benny help her create a bulletin board on the Westward Movement, with drawings and maps of his creation, and for his help, she will give him time to play UNO with Tim. As they continued to discuss her reactions to Benny, she noted that she would attempt to ignore minor disruptions and, when needed, give Benny a soft (private) reprimand while redirecting him to the task at hand. Should this fail, she would have him go to a seat away from the group for a "break time" until he was ready to rejoin the class.

> *Your reflections as counselor-consultant? (System: What system elements may need to be considered in the employing of "break time"? Is there a role for the consultant at this point?)*

Maintenance

The intervention to reinforce positive, prosocial behavior and either ignoring or employing timeout in response to disruptive behavior appeared to fit well within the consultee's values and skill set. As is true for any focus of change, challenges to continued progress may occur. As such, the counselor invited the consultee to meet and discuss her experience, and together they would address any issues that may be hindering future gains.

> *Your reflections as counselor-consultant? (Maintenance: What do you anticipate may occur to challenge continued progress?)*

A focus in each of these sessions was to reinforce the consultee's sense of a positive trajectory and its consultee-centered locus of control. For example, the consultant was highly supportive and reinforcing each time Ms. Fox reported situations where Benny was participating in class (e.g., a time when she and Benny drew a map of the Oregon Trail) or giving evidence of being more polite and accepting of his peers (e.g., when she actually "caught him" standing patiently in line at the water fountain, letting classmates go first.)

Termination

In one of the meetings, Ms. Fox expressed her feelings that the attainment of level 10 was not required to define success. She felt that she had currently attained the level of success (8 on her scale), for which she was satisfied. Thus, the current consultation contract was terminated.

Before terminating, the consultant reviewed with the consultee the various steps and activities in which they had engaged. The consultant highlighted the specific steps the consultee had taken, the behaviors she employed that helped Bennie move up the scale. The consultant thanked the consultee for the opportunity to work together and reiterated his availability should the consultee seek assistance in the future.

> *Your reflections as counselor-consultant? (Termination: As you reflect on the success of this consult, and as a result the appropriateness of termination, is there any value, any need, to move beyond level 8 as the criteria of success?")*

Postscript (Reentry and Mediation)

Upon completion of the case, the consultant reflected on his experience in hopes of identifying ways to improve his consultative skills. He also began to consider the idea of providing a school-wide in-service on the issue of "catching them at being good," a point he felt may have some prevention value. *(Reentry: Following the termination of this case, what targets for a mediational mode of consultation can you identify?)*

A Concluding Thought

Not an End, but a Beginning!

Throughout this text, various methods and strategies for diagnosing problems, establishing goals, engaging in consultation relationships, and implementing intervention strategies have been discussed. It must be emphasized, however, that as with other forms of helping, it is the quality of the person—or in this case, the school counselor-as-consultant—that is far more important than any skill or strategy. As a skilled, effective counselor-consultant, it is essential that one be first and foremost an authentic, ethical, and caring helper.

While this is the end of this text, it is only the beginning of an ongoing and continuing process of becoming a skilled, effective, and ethical consultant. We hope this was a good beginning, and we wish you well as you continue your development.

KD/RP

2018

About the Authors

Karen L. Dickinson, PhD, is an associate professor in the Department of Counselor Education at West Chester University of Pennsylvania and coordinator of the School Counseling Certification program. Dr. Dickinson has over 10 years of experience teaching at the university level in counseling preparation programs and has spent over three decades in the K–12 educational system supporting students as a general education and special education teacher, and school counselor.

Dr. Dickinson is co-author of *A Student's Guide to Handling Stress* (Cognella, Inc.) and *Ethical Practice: Beyond Knowing Ethics to Being Ethical* (SAGE Publications); contributing author for *Working with Students with Disabilities*, a text for school counselors; and ancillary author for *Field Experience: Transitioning from Student to Professional*, both published by SAGE Publications. She has presented nationally and internationally on the topic of bullying and students with disabilities. Other presentations and research focus on the school counselor as advocate and leader, and training the 21st-century school counselor to support diverse student populations.

Richard D. Parsons, PhD[1], is a full professor in the Counselor Education Department at West Chester University. Dr. Parsons has over 40 years of university teaching in counselor preparation programs. Prior to his university teaching, Dr. Parsons spent nine years as a school counselor in an inner-city high school. Dr. Parsons has had a private clinical practice for over 30 years and serves as a consultant to educational institutions and mental health service organizations throughout the tri-state area of Pennsylvania, New Jersey, and Delaware. He is the recipient of many awards and honors, including the Pennsylvania Counselor of Year award.

Dr. Parsons has authored or co-authored over 80 professional articles and books, including *The School Counselor as Consultant: An Integrative Model for School-Based Consultation* (Brooks/Cole). His most recent books include the series of four training texts for school counselors, *Transforming Theory into Practice* (Corwin Press); and individual texts including *Becoming a Skilled Counselor, Field Experience: Transitioning from Student to Professional* and *Counseling Theory: Guiding Reflective Practice* (SAGE Publications), and *Counseling Strategies That Work! Evidenced-based for School Counselors* (Allyn & Bacon).

---

1 Source: https://us.sagepub.com/en-us/nam/author/richard-parsons

Index

CPSIA information can be obtained
at www.ICGtesting.com
Printed in the USA
LVHW012350020621
689199LV00009B/290